Irony in the Mind's Life

Robert Coles

Irony
in the Mind's
Life

Essays on Novels by James Agee,

Elizabeth Bowen,

and George Eliot

A NEW DIRECTIONS BOOK

Manufactured in the United States of America
First published clothbound by the University Press of Virginia in 1974 as the Page-Barbour Lectures for 1973 and brought out as New Directions Paperbook 459 in 1978. Published simultaneously in Canada by McClelland & Stewart, Ltd.

Library of Congress Cataloging in Publication Data

Coles, Robert.
    Irony in the mind's life.
    (A New Directions Book)
    Includes index.
    1. English fiction—History and criticism—Addresses, essays, lectures. 2. Agee, James, 1909–1955. A death in the family. 3. Bowen, Elizabeth, 1899–1973. The death of the heart. 4. Eliot, George, pseud., i.e. Marian Evans, afterwards Cross, 1819–1880. I. Title.
PR823.c58   1978   823'.03   78–6651
ISBN 0–8112–0689–0 pbk.

New Directions Books are published for James Laughlin
by New Directions Publishing Corporation,
333 Sixth Avenue, New York 10014

To the memory of
Perry Miller
William Carlos Williams

Preface

THE OCCASION FOR this effort to pull together some long-standing theological and literary concerns has been the annual Page-Barbour Lectures sponsored by the University of Virginia. It was a moving and important experience for me, being in Charlottesville in late April of 1973. My brother, William A. Coles, had taught English literature there at a time when I was trying to find my bearings in the most metaphysical of medical specialties (I was then so full of psychiatric thinking!), and I received from him on the occasion of many visits a good number of lectures about "provinciality," not the kind George Eliot had directly in mind for her "study"— though with her one can't exclude any intention. It was a privilege to be invited back to that campus and asked to tie together at least a few strands of a particular life.

Finally, I acknowledge my wife's counsel, as well as the practical help she gave to the manuscript. We worked together on this while living in Albuquerque, New Mexico, where I was trying to gain some sense of how Indian and Chicano children grow and come to terms with the world. Once I came home and told my wife that a young Indian boy had asked whether I ever try to "look beyond, look over the mesa and far off, as far as your eyes can carry you." Then his mother, hearing the question, added: "It's too bad that most of the time we only want to look at what is right in front of us; we are the slaves of our timid eyes." My wife thereupon suggested that for the lectures I try to write on what is to follow rather than on certain aspects of my ongoing work "out in the field." This is not the first time I have to say thank you.

Contents

Irony in the Mind's Life

*Essays on Novels by James Agee,
Elizabeth Bowen, and George Eliot*

Every limit is a beginning as well as an ending. Who can quit young lives after being long in company with them, and not desire to know what befell them in their after-years? For the fragment of a life, however typical, is not the sample of an even web: promises may not be kept, and an ardent outset may be followed by declension; latent powers may find their long-waited opportunity; a past error may urge a grand retrieval.

George Eliot, *Middlemarch*

Introduction

Wᴴᴇɴ Sɪɢᴍᴜɴᴅ Fʀᴇᴜᴅ began listening with unprecedented care
to a group of Viennese men and women other doctors had stopped
seeing, he had already given up one career. He came to psychiatry
from neurology and experimental neurophysiology. He had been
interested in the effect of cocaine on the central nervous system.
Though he was a well-educated man, steeped in the classics, he had
no great interest in philosophy, certainly not in theology. Nor was
he especially interested in the philosophical novel, the novel of
ideas. Though he once raised his arms in respectful surrender
before Dostoevski's genius, his mind was really excited by drama-
tists: the Greek tragedians, to whom he owed so much, and
Shakespeare, whose various plays he returned to again and again in
his writing. He himself had a dramatic turn of mind. He fitted the
"psychopathology of everyday life" into a stark and compelling
mythological language. In an uncharacteristic moment he abandoned all modesty and called himself a conquistador.

He was also a man able to stand alone for a long time. Scorned
by his medical colleagues, ignored by the powers and principalities
in Vienna's academic world, bitterly attacked, when mentioned at
all, in professional journals, he struggled on: proud, stubborn,
enormously diligent—and, not least, ambitious. He wanted to
understand nothing less than the whole range of man's mental
activity: what our thoughts amount to when we sleep as well as
during the day; the unwitting as well as the intentional; the hidden
as well as the all too apparent. To do so he was willing to isolate
himself from most others; his letters to his friend Wilhelm Fliess
reveal not only a brilliant man working his way toward important
discoveries but a man very much turned in on himself. His dreams
were his tools; through them he glimpsed others—first, the patients
who were so vexing and puzzling, with their bizarre and sometimes
showy symptoms and their nagging insistence that someone, anyone, comprehend them; and, finally, the rest of us, who were going

to be told by this doctor that the distance between any two human beings, however different in temperament and background, is not all that great.

Freud's professional and intellectual isolation enabled him to know himself and a few patients rather well. To go from what he learned thereby to a more general description of the mind's structure and function required not only a high order of intelligence but considerable nerve. By 1900, when *The Interpretation of Dreams* was published, Freud had spent about five years examining closely what others took for granted (dreams, reveries, the various trains of thought we all experience); and yet, as a nineteenth-century scientist, deeply influenced by the prevailing mechanistic physiology of his time, he must have felt both in possession of important secrets and in possession of virtually nothing. How dare a *scientist* come forth with a book about dream-symbols, followed by another full of anecdotes, parables, and peasant stories, given the kind of analysis literary critics or philosophers might find genial? No fool at any point in his life, Freud expected the reaction he got. He feared he was *so* ahead of his time that there would be no other kind of reaction.

Ironically, however, he implicitly acknowledged that what he was formulating in a particular way and attempting to put in the service of doctors and patients, others had all along known and summoned for their quite different purposes: to teach people or entertain them, or help them find a place for themselves in the universe. He connected the conflicts he had found significant in his own life and in the lives of those he was treating to experiences undergone by heroes of the ancient Greek theater. Oedipus and Electra were now said to be alive and everywhere. And, very important, it isn't only that we possess the same desires and fears those two did but that we, like they, spend a lifetime coming to terms with those desires and fears and do so in relatively similar ways. We deny what is obvious to others. We fancy ourselves "free," yet we are driven, if not upon occasion hounded. We behave one way but feel in ourselves quite contrary moods. We seek after people, engage upon projects, though often enough we ourselves recognize that there is more to our pursuits than we can perceive. Passions are concealed. Rages mask love. A sense of weakness prompts a burst of anger. Envies turn into acts of generosity. What is wanted is abruptly dismissed as worthless. It is a topsy-turvy world Freud portrayed, a world in which no one can be quite sure of anything without taking a good long look—perhaps with the help of another who has had some experience in taking a special sort of long look.

When a man like Freud is doing just that in lonely isolation, looking for self-knowledge in places others have walked casually or hurriedly by, he has all he can do to keep his wits about him and try to make a successful journey. The more he starts dwelling on what others have seen in the course of their various journeys, the less ground of his own will be covered. In 1895 or 1900 Freud, the man exploring and making discoveries, was not the one, even had he been so inclined by past interests, to look back a few years at what George Eliot had come to know about the human mind, or Kierkegaard. Nor was he then the one to stop and consider what various theologians or political philosophers have made of human nature. Later on, secure in his own achievements, he would indeed turn to others, take note of what a Leonardo or a Dostoevski or a Diderot had seen before him and in connection with interests and inquiries quite unlike his. Such comparisons were modest and were tactfully done, though not always with great success. Freud was nothing if not introspective and candid about his own feelings: he knew better than to turn the work of other people into putty for his particular mental constructions. He could be a bit truculent when he wrote of Dostoevski: after he has psychoanalysis "lay down its arms" before what he chose to call "the problem of the creative artist," he immediately goes on to say: "The moralist in Dostoievsky is the most readily assailable." Later, Theodor Reik would obtain from him in a letter the frank admission that "in spite of all my admiration for Dostoievsky's intensity and pre-eminence, I do not really like him." Still, there was respect and, even more valuable, a certain discretion.

Unfortunately a master cannot transfer everything to his disciples. Psychoanalysis as a clinical discipline has weathered much opposition from without and dissension from within and emerged the stronger. One man's ideas have become an impressive body of knowledge, a useful means of psychological treatment, a very special instrument of research, a theory of human nature that has its limits but is to this day suggestive—all of which is given institutional expression and consolidation in an international association and member organizations that reach across the globe.

However, when analysts and those influenced by them have left their clinical work to apply their thinking to other fields, the results have been less worthy of mention. Especially in the field of literary criticism, psychoanalytically oriented writers have all too often (continuing right to the present time) transferred with reckless abandon concepts meant to explain certain psychological developments observed in a clinical situation to novelists and the characters they create. Sometimes such efforts have betrayed not only literary ignorance but narrowness, and even spite or malice. Not every essayist determined to fasten words like *oedipal, pre-oedipal, oral, anal, genital* on a man or woman who has written a novel and peopled it out of his or her imagination is going to come forth with Freud's honest self-scrutiny and admit his prejudices or, maybe even more to the point, his envy.

I have no wish to discuss here the limits of the various psycho-analytic efforts to "explain" novelists and their novels, not to mention believers and their faith or political leaders or philosophers and their deeds or ideas. I deny that intention, not in order to slip out of a difficult and controversial issue unbruised, but rather because quite frankly this book has no part in the tradition that has generated the controversy. In a sense, then, the first thing I have to say about what follows is decidedly negative. I have no interest in figuring out what ailed some of the religious or political philosophers I refer to throughout the book, and especially in the first chapter. I suppose one like me can with a good deal of justification analyze the Rousseaus of this world and, as well, a man like Kierkegaard. Such individuals have made no secret of the pain they have gone through, the psychological disorders and early sorrow. Nor is there any reason to think that the mind at work constructing a story is removed from the need to express symbolically the desires and fears others who don't sit down to write nevertheless find ways of putting into words or living out. After a while, however, what strikes a certain kind of critic as interesting impresses others as banal. If everyone has oedipal conflicts, oral promptings, obsessions, and compulsions, then what have we learned when we discover so-and-so, finally, to be a human being, driven like other human beings, even tormented upon occasion? It is one thing to be endlessly fascinated with patients, however similar their difficulties are at some conceptual level. They come, after all, for help; and to a doctor that is a challenge enough. But writers seek to entertain, to obtain a variety of emotional responses, to instruct, to cause their readers to stop and think about various things; and their characters are meant to serve those ends. To tell us that a writer is also a human being (possessed of a certain kind of psychological makeup) and that his characters also have the sound of, the feel of, human beings (urges and preoccupations that the rest of us have) may not be to tell us very much.

In any event, I fear it will be easier for me to say what I am *not* up to than to spell out exactly what this book is about. Its history, I am sure, begins with the dissatisfaction I felt while in psychiatric training; I grew tired of hearing people typed and classified—often enough called thinly disguised names, all in the name of science. At that time I was given a suggestion by one of my supervisors at the Massachusetts General Hospital, a woman psychoanalyst much interested in art history. Dr. Elizabeth Zetzel suggested I read novels and learn from them a more intricate, a more subtle kind of, psychology. Another psychoanalytic teacher, Paul Howard, permitted, indeed encouraged, me to take part in a seminar on systematic theology Paul Tillich gave at Harvard in the late 1950s. In that seminar I was again brought face to face with Saint Augustine, Pascal, Kierkegaard, not to mention the Bible. I say "again" because at college I had covered much the same ground in courses I took with Perry Miller—a professor of English who might well have been called a historian, a moral philosopher, a man all taken up with theological interests, as opposed to convictions.

In Paul Tillich's seminar we often discussed the distinction between the pastoral and the prophetic modes of existence. Georges Bernanos, in *Diary of a Country Priest*, has set down once and for all the obligations and dangers that accompany a life devoted to caring for others, attending their wants and healing their wounds, all within the limits of what is possible. In novels like the three discussed here one meets up with individuals and families similarly struggling to make do, to find themselves, to obtain some satisfying and fulfilling continuity in the brief time allotted them or any of us. Always around, however, are those who with grace or confusion or, occasionally, malice, want to comment on things, take the lead in bringing about a new way of thinking or acting. One does not have to be a political or religious leader to have a prophetic relationship to others. Uncle Ralph in Agee's novel, St. Quentin in Elizabeth Bowen's, Dr. Lydgate or, in his own way, Bulstrode in

Middlemarch—these are the prophetic voices, maybe at times the voices a given author wants to emphasize in order to exorcise.

From Dr. William Carlos Williams, as from Perry Miller, I had earlier heard the same distinction made. We want to live out our lives, but some get curious about the future or won't rest easy until they take stock of the present. Dr. Williams spent hours taking care of patients, helping them (and himself) live out a life, much as the priest does in Bernanos's novel. But he also wrote poems, stories, essays. Perry Miller taught in classrooms, received visits in his Widener Library study from dozens and dozens of students. But he also wrote books that gave new point to the Puritan divines. Every theologian, philosopher, novelist, or poet somehow has to struggle with a similar tension in his or her thinking and writing; when the tension disappears, banality or megalomania sets in, depending on which element that provides for the tension is missing. When Adam and Eve showed themselves not content to live out an exceedingly comfortable and eternal life but, rather, hopelessly susceptible to, if not inclined to the blandishments of, curiosity (a desire to know more, to discover, to test and try), they were demonstrating a capacity for just such tension. Eden was pastoral; but those two implicitly asked for the right to look any place, to defy rules in the interests of broader experience, a larger (prophetic) assumption of initiative. The result has been man's history.

For me that line of thinking about human beings and their problems has made more sense than the strictly psychoanalytic viewpoint I acquired and still very much call upon as I do my professional work. The work itself, perhaps anyone's work, is best described by George Eliot at the end of *Middlemarch*, when she apologizes with a bit of irony for Dorothea's failure to become a Saint Theresa, the full-fledged prophet (who also had her daily and unheralded tasks to perform): "for the growing good of the world is partly dependent on unhistoric acts; and that things are not so ill with you and me as they might have been, is half owing to the number who have lived faithfully a hidden life, and rest in unvisited tombs."

In retrospect I realize that the "unhistoric acts" I was hearing about from my patients as I was learning, I hope, to do them some good deserved a kind of recognition they were not getting. What kind, though? Agee's, Bowen's, George Eliot's kind? Pascal's or

Kierkegaard's? Rousseau's? The kind William Carlos William brought to bear on the people of Paterson, New Jersey, or Perry Miller on the likes of Cotton Mather? Well, one could do worse, and often we do just that in those offices and clinics; and in our professional writing. We imprison people with phrases. We deny people the subtlety of thought, the complexity of feeling that is theirs as much as any conquistador's, be he or she of a literary, philosophical, or psychological species. We want absolutes, and if they are not available (God having been declared dead, and a number of substitutes not having worked out so well), we want things made crystal clear. What drives one man to highlight and thereby simplify can make others rush for simplifications. The prophet wants to see sharply, and, alas, the rest of us, harrassed by day-to-day perplexities and confusions, settle for any markers we can spot. All well and good—except that these days some of the prophets are ill suited to that calling; anyway, they have more than enough pastoral obligations, given the psychological stresses we hear so much about. And, ironically, perhaps things would go better in those offices and clinics if "nervous" people were given the benefit of a few doubts. (A nostalgic and imprecise word like *nervous* has its advantages: a maximum of suggestiveness, a minimum of exactitude. No wonder it has given way to one elaborate pretentious psychiatric nosology after another.)

I have wanted in this book to call upon a number of thinkers and writers who have insisted upon asking the broadest questions about man's nature. They provide an example for the rest of us, not because they have always been proved right, but because they have taken pains to admit how tempted they themselves have been to remove prophecy (in its broadest sense) from what Tillich would call the "ground-being" of everyday life. I begin with Christian and secular thinkers who have not been afraid to criticize themselves, contradict themselves, throw up their hands in amazement, bewilderment, awe, or wonder—even as, undaunted, they have pushed along with more ideas, more speculations, more efforts to penetrate mystery or define it with ever increasing emphasis (for such and such reasons) as impenetrable. I then move on to three writers and to particular novels they have given us. I try to examine those novels, react to them—give them a reading, it might be said. It so happens that the novels lend themselves to a chronological sequence—childhood, youth, the grown-up years that I suppose I have to call "maturity," though I distrust the word as it is used so often these days. It also so happens that certain tenets of my profession, child psychiatry, require life to be treated that way; all too arbitrarily they urge doctors to fit human beings 'into various "age-groups." Yet each of these novels rather delightfully transcends the artificialities and rigidities such distinctions can and do make for. Rufus is not singled out as a six year old, who thinks *this* way, has *that* set of problems; nor Portia, ten years older and similarly transfixed. As for George Eliot, she can move across barriers of age, sex, and class with a grace and ease that at the very least is remarkable. Critics from earlier ages would no doubt call such an ability edifying, a word that implies something both inspiring and instructive—and such a mixture these days is not always readily available.

I hope that the apparent correspondence between the subject matter of three novels and my own professional inclinations will turn out to be the least of the ironies this book underscores. Its title derives from a thread of irony that runs through the words of all the writers taken up, including the anonymous one (or ones) who wrote Genesis. What seems to be is for such writers only a beginning in an uncertain voyage from one sort of appearance to another; and what is most obvious may be of less consequence then what is only implicit and sometimes thoroughly covert. As for the rest of us, a particular philosophical position or viewpoint, however ambitious and wordy, may come across as contradictory, limiting, or simply inadequate in the presence of certain paradoxes. Beyond that, some issues elude or defy (depending upon one's attitude) all social science terminology—in which case resort to a story, with attendant use of metaphors or of a webbed collection of symbols, becomes not simply a matter of preference for a particular (artistic) medium (in contrast to a scientific approach) but a matter of conscientiousness as opposed to a pretentious reliance on what George Eliot calls the "theoretic," which is buttressed by a resort to fact only when convenience dictates.

In Genesis we are given, at the very least, a metaphor that is also a riddle. Human nature made itself felt in Eden; yet why it did, prompted by what circumstances (the psychology of Adam and Eve, the sociology implicit in the serpent as an agent) we are not told. God was betrayed; yet God had a hand in his own betrayal, having put the serpent there and made man and woman susceptible. From then on human nature has been a subject of inquiry (both dogmatic and skeptical) for man, who clearly has a vested interest in finding out how (under whose auspices, through what chain of events) he came to be the creature he now is. In this regard the dogmatists (in a nonpejorative sense of the word) have not always been inflexible, any more than non-Christian philosophers like Rousseau, Hobbes, or Locke have consistently been open-minded to the various ironies and paradoxes that inevitably confront a social thinker. Believers like Pascal or Kierkegaard can appreciate, even elevate to a point of principle, life's ambiguities. Avowed skeptics or men basically indifferent to religion can come up with formulations that render enigmas of the past or the present all too transparently solved. If such an inclination is to be found in *any* theorist (such as Hobbes, Locke, and Rousseau were) then the problem becomes the humdrum one of man's vulnerability, his sense of precariousness: a bereaved Knoxville family looking here and there for various kinds of explanations; a still growing young English lady doing the same; and, finally, the people in a nineteenth-century provincial setting wanting to know more and willing rather often to settle for almost anything in the name of that "more."

If there is any theme in this book it is the persistence of irony. One finds irony in the various faiths we uphold, in the political and social and psychological ideas we have had handed down to us, as well as in the lives we live in the Knoxvilles, Londons, and Middlemarches of this world. If the direction of this book goes against positions taken up by certain contemporary thinkers (or novelists, who also can tailor things rather too finely in order to fit their own purposes), then I will have to let the matter drop there, or, at best, let it be mentioned in a footnote. I may have begun the path that is continued through this book out of a certain annoyance if not outright despair; but I hope these pages indicate how much there is of value to read and think about, and in that spirit I have tried to write for the sake of making connections, stressing certain themes, certain modes of analysis and reflection, rather than arguing or taking up an assertive, if not polemical, position of my own. In doing so I draw upon initiatives long ago stirred in me as a student of Perry Miller's and in a way (by letter and conversation) of William Carlos Williams's, about whose work I once wrote a thesis before my own work in medicine, inspired so very much by his example, became entangled in abstractions that,

I suspect, he wanted to spend time examining only through the medium of his poetry. I dedicate this book to Professor Miller and Doctor Williams; they each spent a lifetime resisting those who like to pigeonhold and classify, and they each knew when to laugh, not the least at their own efforts to think and write about man's nature and his personal or social predicament as the self-conscious one in the universe. It has been twenty years since I felt the influence of those two men; I am glad to be able to say thank you now, and yes, glad the spirit of each of them won't let loose its grip on some of us who were lucky enough to be captivated.

I   Human Nature in Christian
and Secular Thought

ONCE CHILDREN BEGIN to fathom the meaning of time, they salute, across all those centuries, God's Adam and Eve. In Genesis 2 man's inclination to name things, to classify at almost infinite length, is given explicit recognition—and, rather interestingly, tied to a specific state of mind: "It is not good that the man should be alone; I will make him an help meet for him." Alone if not lonely, Adam was the recipient of a gift. God made "every beast of the field, and every fowl of the air"; then we are told that he brought them all to Adam and stood by, "to see what he would call them." Nor would the Lord be disappointed. Something in man enabled him to "call" each and every animal and bird created, though Adam still lacked "an help meet." We can only speculate whether he simply noted that persisting absence or felt it as an aching kind of loneliness. Nevertheless, soon he was deeply asleep and, upon awakening, recognized "bone of my bones, and flesh of my flesh"; knew, in other words, that in the future woman would be man's companion: "therefore shall a man leave his father and his mother, and shall cleave unto his wife: and they shall be one flesh."

Immediately afterwards and, significantly, before the all-important third chapter of Genesis, with its Garden of Eden scene, we are reminded that the two (Adam and Woman; Eve had yet to get *her* name) were naked, were man and wife, were not ashamed. A distinct possibility or potentiality has been indicated in an almost casual way—a contrast indeed with the more ominous and sad narrative that follows in the rest of Genesis. The two are not only able to recognize one another, but a sense of the future and its necessities comes on them—the merest hint, perhaps, of what is ahead: they cling together. Of course, earlier on God had taken care to warn Adam about "the tree of the knowledge of good and evil" and upon that occasion had made clear what would happen: take a bit of this particular fruit and death is the consequence. Still, it is one thing to be told in no uncertain terms to stay away from something, lest a disaster appear whose characteristics can only be appreciated when and if it does happen, and quite another to gain a sense of time, an awareness of what is around the corner in the form of tomorrow and the next day and the one after that. In the former instance there is an awful vision suggested, but its arrival need never occur; in the latter, one is made aware of time as something that takes place—and so requires the everyday kind of commitment implied in the realization Man and Woman had (Adam and the particular Woman he recognized), that they shared a destiny of sorts together, meaning a future ahead of them, with all the implication of years and years to be spent, hence kept in mind as theirs.

In the second year of life children certainly do not all of a sudden come by Adam's vast taxonomic skill, but they do demonstrate an urgent need to point at various objects and give them names; and I have found that principle to hold in my work with American children from various regions and backgrounds. I remember a migrant farm worker, at sixteen the mother of a toddler of seventeen months, complaining to me that the child woke her up every morning, so incessantly did she stand in the room and shout out the name of things, *her* things. No doubt the extreme poverty of that unstable and transient household (if such it could be considered) contributed a certain desperation to the little girl's efforts, but small children from far more affluent homes can and do match her zeal all the time. This particular migrant child simply exaggerated (and, maybe, caricatured) what the rest of us learn in the very first year of life: the sun comes up; the sun sets; so there is a beginning of light, an end to it—and the same holds for darkness. Furthermore, people often enough come and go with that rhythm, and with them a hello, food and a change of clothes, or a goodbye followed by a silence that persists for a considerable number of hours.

Even as the psychologically disturbed can often present to an observer exaggerated fears and anxieties which, on a much reduced scale, we all share and struggle with, an extremely impoverished family in Appalachia or the Mississippi Delta or the hill country of northern New Mexico can, perhaps, bring us (even in twentieth-century America) a little further back toward Adam's time, yet in so doing illuminate how much human beings (in this case, infants and young children) have in common, regardless of when or where they were born. In some rural homes I have visited electricity is still absent, and candles or oil lamps used rather sparingly. The families have little to offer their children in the way of material goods or possessions (toys are unheard of). Again and again I have had to get used to a day that ends at sunset (at which point the family has eaten and is ready to retire) and begins at the very first sign of light, usually signaled by the birds, who have their own reasons to celebrate that moment publicly.

In those early morning or late afternoon hours I have heard children just learning to use words refer to "my morning" or "our day" or "the evening we have." They have been told by their mothers that there are *some* things even they can, and most assuredly will, possess. In contrast I have to mention a five-year-old boy, of well-to-do New England suburban background, whom I treated for some months when I worked in the child psychiatry service of the Children's Hospital in Boston. The diagnosis of childhood schizophrenia had been put on the patient, and he was described as badly "regressed," meaning he often spoke incoherently and chose not to exercise the controls over his body's functions that he himself had gained several years earlier. "Animal-like" was one phrase to be found on his psychiatric record. Every time I talked with the child I had questions put to me like these, often asked one after the other, without letup, and without (it seemed) any real interest on the child's part for my reply: "Who owns the sun? Does someone call it away, and then it gets dark? Will I be here tomorrow, or someplace else, where I won't know anyone? Can you find a button that will make the night go away, then bring it back? It would belong to you then, wouldn't it?"

Absurd questions for a child of his age to be preoccupied with, yet questions that once rather naturally entered his mind, even as they do the minds of so many other children in the second and third years of life. Now the way parents respond to those questions tells us a good deal; the schizophrenic child was told by his exhausted, confused mother that "there are some things no one owns, and the sun is one of them." I recall a morning when I heard that mother asked with special urgency whether the moon (if not the sun) might be purchased—this, before man landed on the moon, thereby providing a touch of what psychiatrists call "reality" to what then was a completely bizarre train of thinking. The answer: "There are some things you can't have, you can't even go near. If you came to the moon, you'd be cold and you wouldn't have enough air to breathe, so you'd die."

As for Adam and Eve, they were told that there were limits on them, too. Adam had within him at creation the ability to survey the world and sort it out, so to speak. With Eve's arrival he had been given the assurance that his existence would not be solitary but rather would have the kind of continuity and *thereness* the presence of another person provides. All they both had to do was heed God's warning with respect to "the fruit of the tree when in the midst of the garden." Needless to say, Adam and Eve did not willfully and on their own accord become transgressors. The serpent, we are told, was subtle; the point was to reassure Eve, remind her of God's generosity (the beautiful world he had created and set before these two creatures), and appeal to her incredulity first, her natural curiosity and exuberance next. "Ye shall not surely die," Eve was told, and then reminded that a bite of that particular tree's fruit would open up her eyes and even make her like a god, "knowing good and evil."

The rest can, again, be called history, and it has been a history that without letup has intrigued and puzzled philosophers and theologians. It is safe to say that short of Judgment Day itself, the riddle of man's nature will go unsolved. From the time of Genesis on, human beings have shown themselves to be, at the very least, finite and limited; they have only so long to live, and their virtues have never been all that overwhelming. Karl Barth has emphasized how repetitive history has been since the downfall of Adam and Eve, and it is hard to disagree, even if one has the right to be absorbed in the struggles of one's own era, however repetitive and unsurprising they turn out to be.[1] Of course, not everyone today finds Adam (or, indeed, Christ) as interesting as Barth does. Once the concept of original sin, as it emerges in Genesis, at least accounted for the endless recurrences, the arrivals and departures, rises and falls, thrusts and counterthrusts, that may enthrall a historian interested in recurring patterns but drive a theologian to

---

[1]See his *Christ and Adam: Man and Humanity in Romans 5* (New York, 1957). I have found Barth's book enormously suggestive. Also of great help is Henri Rondet's *Original Sin: The Patristic and Theological Background* (New York, 1972); and one must be grateful to Reinhold Niebuhr for a major twentieth-century reconsideration of man as sinner and original sin in *The Nature and Destiny of Man* (New York, 1949).

that sad and not inappropriate word *boring*. And since each of us is Adam's descendant, our personal lives have been as monotonously predictable as those larger cycles that the Toynbees of this world have portrayed. None of us is spared the limitations theologians have consistently remarked upon—and traced back to the Garden of Eden.

Today it is obviously not the Bible and its various doctrines that the educated upper middle class of this country calls upon to explain history or human nature. We are likely to point out how significantly our protoplasm or our genes limit us; somehow they carry within them a plan for us, a biological destiny, in which everyone would include old age and death, and many would include a variety of instincts, drives, "imperatives"—to the point that our daily capacity to be mean, greedy, and possessive about one another or about our individual property as well as our nation's territory, all are seen as handed down as birthrights to the flesh from parents to children. In contrast, there are those who emphasize the wrongs that social, cultural, and political institutions perpetrate. Children are molded by those institutions, those environmental forces from the very beginning, and it is a tribute to our plasticity, our near godlike ability and willingness to accommodate ourselves to the particular world we grow up to join, that we are all so different—Americans or Chinese, burghers at home with technology, natives of the Amazon or inhabitants of those Pacific islands that anthropologists have been so inclined to study and tell us about. Social scientists certainly don't find our lives boring. They know how much work there is to do, and often they have dreams: a certain kind of world will bring about a hitherto unknown condition characterized by widespread peace, prosperity, contentment, and on and on.

No sociologist or anthropologist can deny that up to now the sorrow mentioned in Genesis 3 has persisted over the generations and throughout the world; the issue is transmission. Are we the way we are because it is given that we become so—by God's decree or nature's (biological) insistence? Might we be different beyond our wildest hopes (or fears) were we to be brought up in some way yet to prevail in history? Even natural scientists, supposedly less likely to indulge in farfetched conjecture, have speculated in the same vein—and when they do so, it can be on the grandest of scales. Need we even age? Or, as we continue to unlock genetic combinations and devise ways of transplanting organs (someday the brain itself?), can we learn to live, if not forever, then certainly for a longer span than we now dare dream?

Those questions are not asked as a consequence of several centuries of scientific enlightenment. Long before Comte started using the word *sociology*, or "field work" was ever done among "natives," or nuclear physics and molecular chemistry combined with modern medicine and surgery to enable some more-than-fatuous basis for speculation about our longevity, philosophers wondered what we *once* were, what we *might* become—if; and the nature of the ifs, of course, had varied over the centuries and from continent to continent. Within the Christian tradition one senses the same kind of qualified hopefulness: if only faith became everyone's possession, man's destiny would at last be free of the shadow of that event in Eden.

Saint Paul and Saint Augustine, not to mention Pascal and Kierkegaard, and in our time Niebuhr and Barth have wondered how it could be that, to draw upon the famous fifth chapter of Romans, "by one man sin entered into the world and death by sin, and so death passed upon all men for that all have sinned." They have had to fall back not so much on an explanation as an Old Testament promise that became something else: a moment in historical actuality, wherein a particular life came to mean so very much to so many, but also an extraordinary event—the Incarnation itself, the union of divinity with humanity in Jesus Christ. For the fact is that all along, well before Christ's arrival, he was anticipated—as if many of those who believed the account offered in Genesis had to question the finality of the Lord's decision, hence by indirection keep certain possibilities open to all of us as mere mortals. In Saint Paul's concise and haunting words, powerful and suggestive enough to keep dozens of exegetical scholars busy for centuries: "For as by one man's disobedience many were made sinners, so by the obedience of one shall many be made righteous." And for Paul, righteousness is but a prelude, a foretaste of something much more, "eternal life." At one point as he mentions "Adam's transgressions," Paul even insists (as if to vex us no end) that the very first man, whose fall set the stage for our kind of existence, "is the figure of him that was to come," meaning Jesus Christ. In Corinthians (1.15) we are asked to accept this parallel: "The first man Adam was made a living soul; the last Adam was made a quickening spirit." For those who struggle successfully for faith, the Garden of Eden really does become what it has always been for secular agnostics, a thing of the past, a moment in an old out-of-date history.

Paul lived nearer to Christ's time, so perhaps had a more immediate view of the problem: the Savior had at last arrived, and what the world needed was conversions, more and more of them—until, in a sense, the Garden of Eden was restored, this time without that one ominous source of temptation. By the time Augustine wrestled with the question of original sin, three centuries had elapsed, and the empire Paul had vainly tried to convert had in fact been won over but was in the process of falling apart. No wonder Augustine, Bishop of Hippo and Roman citizen, fought so hard against the pelagian heresy. His contemporary, Johannes Cassianus, had the nerve to believe that man's efforts, in and of themselves, could somehow, some day, lead him to salvation. Yes, God's Grace was acknowledged, but the stress was on man's initiative and the ultimate redemptive value of his moral efforts.[2]

In the monastery of Saint Victor, located near Marseilles, all the way across the Mediterranean from Augustine's Roman Africa, Cassianus and his fellow monks cultivated the ascetic life, not as an act of penance, not in the hope that as a result God's mercy would be obtained, not with the fervent expectation that faith professed and cultivated would be faith rewarded, but out of quite another conviction. They believed that the ability to develop and sustain a certain kind of life on this earth was its own reward, because thereby man demonstrates his sufficiency—as one at last able to organize himself in such a way that he is not a sinner, but through his own willfulness destined for salvation. It was the self-confidence, the unexamined zealousness, the utter hopefulness of such monks that offended Augustine. Pelagius himself would even go further, insist upon man's goodness, his freedom to exercise his will constructively with almost unlimited success. His motives were the highest, of course; he was appalled by the smugness, laziness, and spiritual indifference or fatalism he saw everywhere, all justified in the name of God's Grace: what he would decide, he would decide, and

---

[2]Of real help is J. H. Figgis's *The Political Aspects of St. Augustine's City of God* (London, 1921). The reader learns not only about the saint but his adversaries. The most readable translation of *The City of God* is, I believe, Marcus Dodd's (New York, 1950).

when his decisions were revealed, that would be that, so there was little use taking much initiative of any kind in the brief spell allotted us here on this earth.

In contrast, Augustine had no such faith in the value of anyone's moral struggle, however persevering and exemplary. He had gone through his own extended trial but was not about to turn his *Confessions* into a sly piece of self-enhancement, through which (an additional bonus for his ego) others are called to account and rebuked: see what I did; see what it is possible for man to do, given the will God has graciously provided. In *The City of God* all of us as the descendants of Adam are characterized as quite literally hopeless unless rescued through baptism; only through the acquisition of faith are we saved. Saved from what? From our nature as sinners—because the very "will" the Pelagians wanted corrupt Romans to exercise more resolutely was the "will" Adam and Eve fatefully indulged, to everyone's ruin. Augustine saw men and women as reduced to beasts as a consequence of that moment in the Garden of Eden. Depraved, lustful, acquisitive, we fool ourselves into thinking we are refined and sensitive, when in fact, left to our own devices, we step by step die spiritually, even as death waits to claim our bodies. Even the man of faith cannot be saved on this earth, restored to Adam's original state as the good and innocent person who would live forever, so long as he agreed to keep within certain foreordained limits. Death was meant to be punishment for Adam and Eve; but death is also the one way for the soul to escape the bondage of the flesh. No baptism, no passionately upheld faith, no loyalty to the church, can free us here and now from the web of sin and evil and death that surrounds us. Deliverance is a postmortem event; it is then that the just man or woman rises in a spiritual state—at last perfect—to a heaven where pain, suffering, and malice are unknown.

Augustine was quite literal minded about the manner in which original sin gets transmitted over the centuries. Corrupt men and women lust after each other, and in so doing beget children, who at the very moment of conception are stained. His so-called traducianism even shunts aside God Himself from the inexorable progression of sins committed, sins handed down, sins carried on. The individual human soul is not miraculously created by God at birth but rather is passed on from parents to children, and with it the corrupting influence of sin. We are linked directly and intimately with Adam and Eve, and, in a sense, God is absolved of a particular concern with each of us. Once things happened as they did in the Garden, our fate, nature, and destiny on this earth were irrevocably set—though men will differ radically in the proportion of good and evil they possess. Cain, for instance, belonged without question to the City of Man; whereas Abel was headed for the City of God. So even though every one of us is finite and susceptible to all sorts of hurtful or greedy passions, there is a division among us between those to be saved and those to be damned. Nor does Augustine see God as somewhat detached from the apparently endless chain of *human* events that link all men and women to Adam and Eve. The story of the deluge and Noah's ark are tied to God's anger, which is not to be confused with our kind of bitterness, resentment, or outright hatred. God is mindful of man and is upon occasion a teacher; if many immoral people were lost as a result of the flood, Noah (a man in the tradition of Abel) was saved, and what happened to him can happen to all of us, insofar as we become convinced members of the church Christ established.

Who was Cain? Adam's son, of course—and his fratricidal action was the result of his immense and continuing self-love. Augustine sees that Biblical moment as endlessly repeated; he mentions the parallel of Romulus and Remus. Wary, suspicious, a bishop at a time when vandals everywhere seemed on the verge of triumph, Augustine had good reason to avoid being as clear-cut as he may have wanted to be. In *The City of God* he insists that appearances can deceive. Those who pay visible and even fervent respect to the church can betray Christ, and even the most wicked of people have a place in God's scheme of things. They may be struggling harder than anyone knows for God's Grace (as Augustine himself did!), or their very malice may serve to toughen and inspire the true Christian, though the fact that evil has such power for good among the saved indicates that it is a constant source of temptation, an utter given, so long as the day of Armageddon remains far off. Happiness in *The City of Man* comes off as an illusion. Even in an ostensibly happy home, never mind the world of commerce or politics, misery and nastiness and grief abound. And even above this life, in the highest reality of the universe (as Augustine visualized it) conflict exists. There are bad angels, and there is Satan, one of whose "expressions," some would have it, was the serpent in the Garden of Eden.

He who wants to enter the City of God cannot be reminded often enough how deceptive things are. Satan can take the guise of an angel of light. In a world where God himself formed both light and darkness, made weal and created woe, man is hard put to find answers for himself, and indeed can only rely upon the Holy Church, to which, accordingly, Augustine would grant unlimited power so far as worship goes. How can men be allowed freedom of worship when they are sinners and, even if repentant, always tempted? According to the book of Revelation even the risen Christ, upon his return to earth, after which he will reign eternally, must contend with Satan by binding him with a great chain for a thousand years. No wonder the rest of us feel and ought to feel confused as well as tempted—and one temptation we experience is the rage that goes with our inability to fathom life's ironies and ambiguities. We see the sun and rain nourishing weeds as well as corn or wheat. We watch a Christian people fall before the onslaught of pagans. The thief escapes and his victim dies. What has God in mind? But with the asking of that question we reveal what is in our minds—pride, presumptuousness, a distinct lack of faith. There comes a point where inquiry turns into blasphemy; so, again, the bishop of Hippo had to make it quite clear what his prerogatives ought be. The man of dissent, the man bent on following his own will here, there, and everywhere is no mere individual opponent but part of a much larger and more dangerous army. And the more ingenious the argument, the more original and even impressive the willed act, the more serious the countermeasures required of those one day to live in the City of God.

One might imagine that Augustine's view of man's predicament might have little appeal for an ironist and tempted skeptic like Blaise Pascal. He was not a product of the Enlightenment, but he was a man of great scientific education and curiosity, a contemporary of Newton, with Kepler, Galileo, Descartes, Huygens, Torricelli, Harvey, and Bacon as predecessors. If science and religion had yet to clash openly, the secular humanism generated by the Renaissance was certainly a force in Pascal's seventeenth-century France. Montaigne was another predecessor, after all; and his cleverly stated man-centeredness would have come as no surprise to Augustine—one more reminder how treacherous the intellect is. For Montaigne, and for many of Pascal's contemporaries, the mind deserved close and respectful attention—and not because it was inherently mischievous or sinful but for precisely the opposite reason: whatever happiness we are to have on this earth depends upon how much control we gain over ourselves, and that development, in turn, has to do with the way we regard ourselves, and those important "others" we spend much of our time with, our family and friends and neighbors. Whether one emphasized the Stoic side of Montaigne or his skeptical Epicurean side, he comes out unquestionably an egoist, a word that has to be used in this case without prejudice. Augustine's *Confessions* are full of retrospective examples of self-absorption, all meant to show how variously pride can clothe itself. Montaigne's *Essays* revel unashamedly in self-analysis, and not for the sake of any scrupulous avowal of past wrongdoing. The reader is encouraged to look closer at himself, and maybe make that kind of effort a way of life, a means of discovery. If there is any City of God to be found, the mind will harbor it.

Pascal would have none of all that, though—such a man-centered effort at rationality and analytical philosophy covered with the thinnest possible self-protective veneer of professed religious faith.[3] A worldly, sophisticated man, beautifully educated, not only in languages and theology but science, he managed to anticipate and take on the whole Enlightenment before it really unfolded; it can even be argued that he is one of two Christian psychologists who can more than hold their own with the agnostic kind this century has quite naturally produced, the other being Kierkegaard. The *Pensées*, elements in an intended *Apology for the Christian Religion* that was cut short by his death in 1662 at the age of thirty-nine, lacks Augustine's powerfully narrated sense of man's instinctual life but possesses what is for us in this age a far more convincing analysis of the mind's complexity.

[3]There are some fine biographies of Pascal (with explication of his philosophy of religion). H. W. Stewart's *The Secret of Pascal* (Cambridge, 1941) is especially interesting. Also Morris Bishop's *Pascal: The Life of Genius* (London, 1937). No one writing in English has ever, maybe will ever, approach Sainte-Beuve's *Port-Royal* (Paris, 1878) for sheer devotion and appreciation; but a relatively recent two-volume study of Pascal and Kierkegaard very much speaks to the modern (existentialist) reader; it is scholarly yet readable: Denzil Patrick, *Pascal and Kierkegaard: A Study in the Strategy of Evangelism* (London, 1947). Patrick stresses the aversion Pascal felt for the growing optimism of his scientific predecessors and colleagues. In certain respects Reinhold Niebuhr has similarly embraced the valuable contributions of Marxist political theory and Freudian psychology without succumbing for a moment to the messianic promise they are made to offer in the hands of secular enthusiasts.

After all, as Freud (in his own way recapitulating centuries of Christian history) rapidly discovered, that "seething cauldron" called the Id could only explain so much about mental life. The Victorians, and his first patients among them, spent a lot of time denying the presence of various psychological appetites, not to mention their continuing influence on our daily life. Because he wanted to understand those patients (not judge them, not play miracle man or witch doctor to them, not win them over as uncritical followers), he let himself listen and be educated, and then had the courage to set before the public what he had discovered about others, but also about himself, whom he dared proclaim a human being not unlike the most disturbed of neurotics in important respects. Soon he had to move back a bit, though. It had been all-important that he not exempt himself (and by implication, the rest of us) from the urges and fantasies he heard given expression and went on to comprehend so brilliantly. Yet whatever he shared with his patients, whatever unites all of us—the lusts Augustine unforgettably mentions and documents in all the subtlety of their operation—cannot obscure the fact that Sigmund Freud bore little resemblance to the Rat man or Irma or any of the other patients he saw over the years. Augustine and the Freud who wrote *Interpretation of Dreams* and *Psychopathology of Everyday Life* knew how devious and mischievous we all are at any given moment; and the Freud who wrote *The Ego and the Id* or *Civilization and Its Discontents* had come to realize what Pascal as a determined apologist for a particular religious faith could never let himself forget—the mind's capacity for coherence and good judgment despite all the demons, the pressures and counterpressures that assault anyone all the time.

At the end of his life Freud stood in awe of what he had seen and heard; there were still more psychological mysteries to explore, and his theories, he was frank to say, were a beginning and not much more. Similarly, Pascal had in mind a formidable opponent indeed as he wrote the *Pensées*—perhaps someone like himself, possessing a complicated and resourceful temperament that, finally, eludes every effort at definition except the broadest, the least begrudging. Paul, that most ambitious and energetic of apostles, dared say "I am made of all things to all men, that I might by all means save some." That was at once a modest aim, a shrewd acknowledgment of the enormity of a task and an unashamed assertion of self-confidence—all believed to be inspired by the Lord, though, rather than obtained through conscientious attempts at self-perfection. Pascal had no less an inclination to take seriously his adversaries, whom he hoped to win over as companions. Nor did he feel himself inadequate to the objective he had in mind. Like Freud, who also faced stubborn and wily patients day in, day out, and who was anxious for his own reasons to win them over but never sure which ones would yield, and for how long, Pascal had an uncanny ability to put himself in another's place, be at least many things to a certain number of readers, whose thoughts are given respectful attention in the *Pensées*, even as they are also challenged or refuted.

Put differently, Augustine was a moral and philosophical evangelist; Pascal was a psychological observer of skeptical, self-centered contemporary man. Though Pascal had his own evangelism to accomplish, its unrelenting persuasiveness is a function of a sensibility Augustine might well have found incomprehensible if not abhorrent—all that effort to meet more than halfway the devilish doubters who call themselves intellectuals. Especially interesting in this regard is Pascal's attempt to come to terms with the doctrine of original sin. He clearly knows that no other aspect of Christian doctrine comes so close to setting limits on mankind. He is not content to reiterate what others have said, and demand acceptance as a measure of faith. The particular kind of pagan he is addressing is no wavering Roman or aggressive but susceptible vandal. In seventeenth-century France, as in twentieth-century America, lip service to Christian pieties was not rare; and one suspects that if Pascal had had his choice, he would have preferred out-and-out agnostics or atheists, maybe even a few belligerent vandals, to those who put in their time at church and went on to the next order of business. Most frustrating, no doubt, were the intellectuals who shared his lifetime; they knew enough not to challenge the church openly—and Pascal knew how artful and cunning (and, eventually, penetrating) a mind can get when compelled to slide around things, resort to indirection and guile. His response was to breathe new life into the Bible; without apologizing in any way for its view of man he baldly acknowledged certain hard-core mysteries going right back to Genesis 3—and made them the anchors of his argument rather than articles of faith or dubious propositions best put aside as relics of another age.

He was a Jansenist and would never apologize for the inexplica-able division of man into the elect and the damned. A just God shocks us by doing precisely that in the case of an uncountable number of believers—not that any of them will ever, while on this earth, know themselves to be so singled out. Central to that distinction, central to the Christian view of man's nature, Pascal realized, is the vexing and (to his fellow intellectuals, let alone to us three hundred and fifty years later) thoroughly improbable doctrine of original sin. "Certainly nothing shocks us more rudely than this doctrine," he admitted, and then went on in a near agitated tone to indicate how he finds such a doctrine indispensable: "And yet! Without this mystery, the most incomprehensible of all, we are incomprehensible to ourselves. The knot of our condition takes its twists and turns in this abyss; so that man is more inconceivable without this mystery than this mystery is inconceivable to man."

How to explain elements of the doctrine of original sin? There was Adam's innocence, yet his comprehension of so much; there was his ongoing happiness, yet his need for Eve; there was their satisfaction in each other, yet together they fell; and, most difficult to comprehend, there are the hereditary stains that curse each of us every minute. One can feel Pascal's difficulty in accepting that way of looking at man's daily behavior. He repeatedly emphasizes the ambiguities that in the minds of others then and now make the Biblical view of man inconsistent; even absurd. We are capable of greatness; we are mean spirited. Good men are bad at critical points in their lives; bad men can demonstrate gifts of heart and mind that puzzle us. These "astounding contrarieties," he insists, only go to show that no explanation of man can ever be rational and convincing unless it acknowledges how hopelessly irrational we all are, if logic and the judgment of the intellect are to be our guides. Faced with a similar riddle in the twentieth century, Freud developed what he himself described as a "mythological theory of instincts," one element of which, as a matter of fact, tries to account for the same universality of death whose origin Genesis 3 aims to describe.[4] Freud meant his "death instinct" to be taken

---

[4]Freud candidly refers to his theories as mythological in his exchange with Albert Einstein: "Why war?" Both men (it was the 1930s) were guarded indeed about man's future. See *Complete Psychological Works of Sigmund Freud*, standard ed. (London, 1957) vol. 22.

both literally and figuratively, both as a specific description of our progress "down hill all the way" to the grave and as a broader way of doing justice to the destructive impulses (the sinfulness) we continue to demonstrate toward each other, not all of it taking the form of anger, but rather the coldness, the lack of concern, for which self-absorption—call it narcissism or the sin of sins, pride—can be responsible.

Pascal emphasizes the hidden God (*Deus absconditus*) whom Isaiah addresses: "Truly Thou art a God that hidest Thyself." He keeps referring to that quotation, but he does not let the matter rest there. He dares talk like a pragmatist: "If there were no light, man would not hope for a remedy. Thus it is not only just, but useful for us, that God is partly hidden, and partly disclosed, since it is equally dangerous for man to know God without knowing his misery, and to know his misery without knowing God." Rather, a spectrum of ideas and feelings is included in such a description; we are certainly a long way from Montaigne's or Descartes's world, so intact and clearly visualized and homogenous psychologically. No effort is made to resolve ambiguities or mysteries. Man's contradictions are not only stressed, they are insisted upon and declared ineradicable—not because Pascal was antiintellectual or stupidly, perversely, against reason, but because he saw the mind's limits, the heart's province: "And that is why those to whom God has given religion by feeling of the heart are very happy and very legitimately persuaded. But to those who have it not (in this way) we cannot give it except by reasoning, while waiting for God to give it them by feeling of the heart, without which faith is only human, and useless for salvation."

Pascal's "heart" is given voice in Psalm 119, his favorite. He was not pursuing the mystical. He was not out to set madness against both common sense and good sense. He saw the mind as more than an agency for analysis and more analysis. He saw the logic of emotions. Were he alive he might today smile tolerantly at our desire to convey that logic with words. Deeply respectful of science, he nevertheless saw its limits well before they became all too apparent. He wanted to evoke or suggest, rather than define, a way of approaching the world—in contrast, say, with the Cartesian method, where first principles are arbitrary hypotheses and where another kind of reality is postulated than the one Pascal was groping to apprehend.

Pascal's preoccupations would two centuries later receive Kierkegaard's undivided attention, to the point that despite the obvious
differences in the way the two men wrote and the differences in
background and character, one feels in the presence of spiritual
twins when their respective lines of argument are set side by side.
Both men were fascinated by the doctrine of original sin, and
Kierkegaard's *The Concept of Dread* is subtitled "A simple psychological deliberation oriented in the direction of the dogmatic
problem of original sin." It is a far from simple analysis his Vigilius
Haufniensis (The Watchman of Copenhagen) offers. We are brought
right back to the Garden of Eden and asked to think about Adam.
What was he like before he sinned? What prompted the Fall? Were
Adam and Eve thereafter really any different psychologically and,
if so, in precisely which respect? Like Pascal, he knows better than
to satisfy his readers with explanations that only beg the question.
He has no interest in Adam's various thought processes, his rationalizations, or in Eve's; and as for the serpent, he has no interest in
his role, either. Let others ask whether God might have set the
stage for man's Fall by placing the serpent in the Garden—or for
that matter endowed man with *concupiscence*, which only needed
arousal to become sin. At some point in all these theological and
philosophical arguments one is confronted with that moment when
Adam and Eve in fact did something, whereupon they changed,
their life became different. The "dread" his book aims to describe
has its roots in the psychological and physical growth each of us
experiences. When Adam was told not to do something, he was by
implication told he *could* do that very thing—he might, if he so
wished or decided. Hence a certain "vertigo of freedom," which is
at one point described as "the anguishing possibility of *being able*."
    Kierkegaard saw all of us facing Adam's predicament as we grow
up. Today's psychologists and psychiatrists would, if they were so
inclined, describe his view of human nature as developmental. He
connected Adam to each growing child's life—that is, Adam was
not outside history by virtue of being first, and for a while, without sin. As infants we are without sin, he points out. Not that he
intends to explain sin, list its causes. Sin is inexplicable; but it is
not something that *is*, he reminds us, but something that *happens*,
and therefore one can only describe its preconditions, so to speak.
"In the state of innocence Adam's spirit was a 'dreaming spirit,' "
he emphasizes, and so it is with us. One moves from the baby's

dreamy innocence to the grown-up spiritual struggles of decent or wicked men and women, the critical transition being the Fall: "Sinfulness is not sensuality, not at all; but without sin, no sexuality, and without sexuality no history." Were we not "able," were there no possibilities before us, by virtue of our bodies and minds having become developed, having become capable of wanting, capable of sensing their ability to go, to go get, to go get and keep, then we would be helpless to act, and indeed unaware that actions of various kinds (freedom seized, tested, tried, given actuality) are within our realm.

In *The Concept of Dread* the Fall is not regarded as a tragedy in the lives of two particular but inseparable individuals, Adam and Eve, but rather as an utterly necessary basis for their emergence as human beings. It is foolish, Kierkegaard says, to ask "What if Adam had not sinned?" Once one feels able to ask such questions, let alone write books like *The Concept of Dread*, one's fate is already similar to Adam's. Adam's self-consciousness, the first moment in history, followed an event. Being did not simply unfold. Doing set the stage for being. To ask a question about Adam the sinner is to show oneself a sinner. (Not that Kierkegaard had any doubts on that score.) True, there might have been another way for Adam; but had Adam pursued it, he would have been the last as well as the first man—and unlike every single one of us, utterly beyond our imagining psychologically. Faith is the real opposite of sin. If Adam could only have rested easy and believed, if he could only have placed himself in a real position of trust, continuing and inviolable, with respect to God and his universe, then he would have shunned that fatal exercise of will. Is it ever possible for us, being the way we are, to have that kind of faith, to suspend our willfulness? No. But Kierkegaard sees dread, the anguished awareness of life's possibilities as they become for each of us concrete and inviting, "as a means of salvation" when joined to an effort at faith. In *Fear and Trembling* Abraham's willingness to sacrifice Isaac is held up as an example of just such spiritual development; but Abraham was an old man and, no doubt like the rest of us, an inveterate sinner. Perhaps, to turn Kierkegaard on himself, it is not foolish but, rather, tempting to ask what the world would be like had Adam not sinned; because sin is always tempting, and one sin is the mind's devious inclination to do on the sly what it knows full well to be impossible.

Mostly, though, Kierkegaard was not given to fatuous speculation. He dwelt on Adam out of an intense interest in his fellow burghers of Copenhagen: "As Adam lost innocence by guilt, so does every man lose it. If it was not by guilt he lost it, neither was it innocence he lost, and if he was not innocent before he became guilty, he never became guilty." The Fall of man, Kierkegaard's *Sundenfall*, has to do with all of us, since sin goes on—another way of saying that man persists. In contrast to Augustine, who wanted to analyze each sin, each personal flaw or social misdeed, he could only smile at "the momentum of sin" we each of us add to, world without end, by the very fact of our existence. (We soon enough lose the infant's faith, and few of us gain it back in extreme old age, as Abraham did.) He was uninterested in moralistic condemnation or self-laceration. Like Pascal, he had an exceedingly long view of things and tended to smile rather than pull his hair and scream. On the other hand he was by no stretch of the imagination an optimist, nor was Pascal. They both suffered a good deal toward the end of their lives and died young. Pascal resigned himself to more mystery than either scientists or theologians (he was both) would ever permit themselves to acknowledge, let alone seem to rejoice in. Kierkegaard resigned himself to the possibility of resignation, the most elusive and demanding kind of faith, Abraham's kind, wherein there is a "teleological suspension of the ethical": one accepts the fact that anything might happen, because God's wishes are the determinants, not man's. Even our sense of good and evil, he felt, are mere by-products of the freedom we by nature possess.

Kant saw that freedom as enabling us to be almost infinitely perfectible: we more and more act, and in so doing learn the difference between good and evil; thereby we become by the exercise of freedom better men and women, more angelic, if never angels. For Kierkegaard freedom is objectively tied to sin—and subjectively to a vexing and humiliating sense of guilt which (if we are half-alive to our condition) only makes us feel less and less worthwhile, a state of mind that often prompts self-deception. We do not wish to know how we really feel, even as we try to dodge any confrontation with the Bible's lessons. Better to whistle in the dark—often done in church. Better to exult in yet another self-enhancing moment. Kierkegaard was a "depth psychologist"; he respected the mind's ingenuity.

Nothing can be done about the presence of sin or its consequences; all the prayer in the world will not make one whole and good. Pascal emphasized the dual inheritance of mankind: we must expect to be doomed, even if by a miracle some of us escape that fate. Kierkegaard was less hopeful: into everyone's soul sin will continue, and with it our thoroughly appropriate sense of anguish and sorrow or, of course, our indifference. But he did insist that each of us need not turn an occasion for regret into yet another occasion for sin. That is, we can become Stoic, stand up and acknowledge the difficult time we have to go through, and thereby show how self-sufficient we have learned to be, turning our cheeks, bowing with a certain subdued cockiness before the great unknown, which some gather together as Him, the Unknown.

To that much-tormented Dane such an approach must have been all too familiar: he had never been beyond self-pity, even had a few reasons for it, and so could spot the dread necessity of it anywhere. On the other hand, always self-critical, he turned on his own gloomy outlook—evidence of his lack of faith. Salvation, he admitted, can indeed come—from the outside, with the consoling assurance that one's guilt is forgiven by God, who alone can forgive it, even as one's sins and their consequences remain. He saw Christianity as "the splendour without equal," the faith which, when obtained, enabled a kind of release he himself, apparently, never would feel. He even went so far as to give numerical expressions to his personal sense of despair, or radical sinfulness: only ten or so people in a whole generation really experience what Christ meant when he said to the paralytic, "Thy sins are forgiven thee." (Speaking of extremist Jansenism!) In the clutch Kierkegaard was a theologian, a *Christian* psychologist less interested in (hopeful about) the possibilities of "therapy" than determined to face down the almost impossible odds he saw everyone struggling against. Pascal saw those same odds—and so did Freud, whose method of awareness, psychoanalysis, was never (by him, at least) held out as a means of eliminating life's everyday psychological ordeals and their consequences. All three men tried to go back to the beginning, the psychological beginning of each of us, the historical beginning of all of us, as conveyed in Scripture. In so doing each reluctantly had to settle for "discoveries" or "explanations" the rest of us, especially in this century, find unsettling and so are best watered down: original sin or the concept of dread or the death instinct, each declared absolutely unavoidable and always there—who can live a comfortable, quiet, self-assured life with those notions lying too close to life's surface?

The Christian view of man's nature—full of stern judgment but generous with redemptive possibilities—has had a strong influence on secular philosophers of one kind or another. Political theorists, educational critics, social and psychological observers—all of them have had to come to terms with Genesis either as believers, by pursuing its implications, or as dissenters who have wanted to put their incredulity and scorn into words. Augustine could not refrain from "applying" his faith—describing the kind of society a Christian church requires so that it be in a position to do justice to its mission. Pascal and Kierkegaard were for the most part detached, interested in theological speculation rather than social commentary; but they were saddened by various trends they could not help observing and upon occasion would burst out in scorn at those whom they believed at fault: in Pascal's case, prominent intellectuals; in Kierkegaard's, the somewhat smug and apparently untroubled bourgeoisie he quite correctly saw all around him in Copenhagen. Pascal sensed early on the rising secular currents that his church, all churches, would soon have to recognize as a challenge. He shared a century with Hobbes and Locke and died just fifty years before Jean-Jacques Rousseau was born. None of those three men had any interest in winning souls for Christ, yet none of them could shake off the Old or the New Testament and, most especially, the estimate the Bible makes of our nature—as it was once (in Eden) set or determined, as it has continued to assert itself, and, if one is to call oneself a believer, as it will always be, at least until some final apocalyptic resolution of history itself comes upon the world.

Thomas Hobbes came first; he was born thirty-five years before Pascal but outlived him by almost twenty years. He lived in France for eleven years while Pascal was growing up and learning to become what he also distrusted, a pragmatic scientist and wide-ranging thinker. *Leviathan* is still read for its political philosophy, which is based on an especially trenchant and unsentimental analysis of human psychology, but substantial portions of the book are given over to a discussion of Scripture, including the meaning of Adam's transgression, for him and the rest of us. Hobbes had a historical mind; he wanted to trace the behavior he witnessed in his fellow Englishmen back in time so that what he saw to be effects could be linked up with causes. He was much influenced by Galileo, and he was convinced that the mind could be as easily tamed by the scientific rules a keen observer like him could come up with as any other of nature's phenomena. He denounced the Papacy, but he refused to do so in the name of any religious belief. He shunned Christian imagery, but he was interested in the Bible for what it told about man's continuing struggle to come to terms with himself. He avoids the term *original sin.* Like the psychologists who centuries later would follow him in greater numbers, he declines to judge human behavior, insists only on describing it and fitting it into a theoretical point of view that he believes to be both useful and suggestive. The man who is so often quoted as characterizing man's life in nature as "solitary, poor, nasty, brutish and short" was, in fact, the very same man who would abstain quite insistently from moral judgments: "the desires and other passions of man are in themselves no sin. No more are the actions that proceed from these passions, till they know a law that forbids them."

Hobbes is well known for his "state of nature," his theory of "natural right" and "natural law," his belief that in some distant past a "social contract" was entered into, thereby committing each and every one of us, as descendants of the signatories, to certain rules of conduct under the sovereign authority of a government. Much of what he described as right and proper depends upon his reconstruction of human history. If he would not use Biblical imagery, he could not dispense with the curiosity which, at the very least, has prompted recourse to that imagery for thousands of years. What was it like, east of Eden, long ago? Hobbes's state of nature can rather obviously never be validated by any historian; nor will cross-cultural anthropological research tell us all that much, either; because what we learn from studying primitive people (Hobbes at one point calls the Indians "the Savage people of America") is that everything and anything can be found among them, depending on who they are, where they live, what traditions they have inherited or circumstances they are compelled to deal with. Referring to his "state of nature," Hobbes remarks: "It may be thought, there was never such a time, nor conditions of war as this; and I believe it was never generally so, but there are many places where they live so now." Still, he certainly did believe that his psychological view of man's inclinations and possibilities warranted the large-scale generalization he made—even if he doesn't come up with any firsthand contemporary descriptions but merely declares his theory to be valid, perhaps on the basis of things he had heard about those "Savages" in America and elsewhere. He is after an analytic device, a means of regarding man's social psychology. He had already decided what our individual psychology is all about: we are told that men are by nature competitive, suspicious, wary of one another (he uses the word *diffidence* to suggest that tendency), and hungry for glory. The result, long ago in that state of nature, was a "war of every man against every man." The result also was the rule of "force and fraud."

Not for Hobbes the gregariousness Aristotle posited as man's birthright. Nor would he accept Aristotle's hierarchical view of human nature. True, some men are born smarter or stronger than others. But extremely weak and not very bright men can kill the most gifted and able of neighbors; so we must believe that as Adam's descendants multiplied they lived desperately uncertain lives. When Hobbes talks about the "state of war" that ensued, he once more is speaking allusively: there was a climate of fear and alarm, because everyone wanted things, some of them belonging to others, and no one could trust anyone's intentions. If Hobbes had little interest in Adam before Eve, or both of them before the serpent, he had not forgotten what happened between Cain and Abel; nor could he forget what Isaiah and Jeremiah witnessed and condemned so stridently, a measure perhaps of some heretical voice in them that must have made them wonder more than once (since even prophets can be doubters and sin) why the Lord should have any kindly interest at all in these, his blasphemous and self-aggrandizing subjects.

As a matter of fact it can be argued that Hobbes, who carefully refrains from judging us as depraved or sinful by inheritance, finds man's nature more gloomy to contemplate than, say, Augustine—and I mean apart from the redemptive hope the author of the *Confessions* found outside of himself, in God's Grace. (Likewise, even Kierkegaard, ever doubtful about himself and others, emerges in comparison as basically an optimist.) Reason was never so frail in Augustine's life, however assaulted by passions, as it is in Hobbes's man. Having dispensed with Aristotle's "political man," outgoing and disposed toward some kind of sensible affiliation with others,

Hobbes makes short shrift of the Platonic tradition. We didn't think through our predicament and come up with sensible answers to it; natural man, rather, went through one difficult and dismaying experience after another, until, finally, his instinct for survival, and nothing more, compelled a drastic compromise, both with himself and his fellow man: "The Passions that incline men to Peace, are Feare of Death; Desire of such things as are necessary to commodious living; and a Hope by their Industry to obtain them."

Only then does reason enter, as an instrument, really, of those passions—to suggest "convenient Articles of Peace, upon which men may be drawn to agreement." Freud, especially the early Freud, would not disagree very much. The fear of death, he knew, can cause the mind to mask its acknowledgment of what is coming—dreaded extinction. But when we conceal something, we show its power over us. As for the desire Hobbes mentions, it might easily be tucked away in that broader, more forceful concept of Libido. Freud did have the faith of a doctor, of a writer—and Hobbes, too, was a writer—that reason somehow can give us greater leverage over ourselves. But his primitive man (in *Totem and Taboo*, where he also speculated about the distant and unknowable past) was not unlike the one Hobbes portrayed: both fearful and ambitious, subdued yet ready in an instant to kill, the product, he believed, of a prior uneasy peace, in which the ruler lorded over the ruled, only to be supplanted by a guilty coalition of self-protective murderers.

Hobbes's younger colleague of sorts, John Locke, was similarly preoccupied with the state of nature. In his *Two Treatises on Government*, published (1690) just before the massive *An Essay Concerning Human Understanding*, Locke takes pains to refute Sir Robert Filmer's notion that kings rule by a divine right ultimately inherited from Adam.[5] He saw Adam as no patriarch, certainly no

---

[5] Good discussions of this and related issues are to be found in C. B. Macpherson's *The Politics of Possessive Individualism* (Oxford, 1967); also, *History of Political Philosophy*, ed. Leo Strauss and Joseph Cropsey, (Chicago, 1963). A lucid and sensible account of Locke's influence on the West's democracies can be found in J. W. Gough's *John Locke's Political Philosophy* (Oxford, 1950). As for Adam, he keeps appearing—and not only in theological texts. The anthropologist Edmund Leach writes (*Claude Lévi-Strauss*, New York, 1970): "Adam and Eve were created as ignorant savages in Paradise in a world in which animals talked and were helpmates to man; it was through sin that they gained knowledge and became human, and different, and superior to the animals." Whether, in fact, we are superior is another question. Lévi-Strauss is by no means sure, given the destructiveness of modern man.

one to hand down sovereignty to anyone. Rather than dwell on the mysteries of the Garden of Eden—he makes it clear that they are really beyond anyone's ken—Locke follows Hobbes; we are given a working hypothesis, a speculative description of how natural man once lived. He and his neighbors are portrayed as having " a state of perfect freedom to order their actions and dispose of their possessions and persons as they think fit, within the bounds of the law of nature, without asking leave or depending upon the will of any other man." The "law of nature" is, of course, spelled out; it obliged everyone not to "harm another in his life, health, liberty or possessions," and it also obliged everyone to take care of himself. Locke insists that "self-preservation" is at the core of our being; it is "the first and strongest desire God planted in men, and wrought into the very principles of their nature." One can wonder why Adam and Eve failed so miserably to preserve themselves—eternity was theirs, and lost—but again, Locke has no interest in that part of Christian doctrine. Like Hobbes, he took the liberty of constructing his own garden, and to a degree he went along with Hobbes: man wants to live and at all costs tries to watch out for his various interests.

On the other hand, Locke's natural man is far more rational and ethical than the one Hobbes summoned for his readers. Hobbes dreaded the instability, and worse, that is to be found when individuals and collections of individuals are uncontrolled by a powerful sovereign. Without the political constancy and firmness a kingdom or empire provides, there is only the chaos of warring gangs or tribes, not to mention the avarice and thoughtlessness of countless frightened individuals who, deprived of law and order, survive as best they can, and in so doing show their worst side. Locke allowed for the transgressor and explicitly acknowledges that "every man hath a right to punish the offender, and be executioner of the law of nature." He also acknowledged something else: "I doubt not but it will be objected that it is unreasonable for men to be judges in their own cases, that self-love will make men partial to themselves and their friends." That is one of those "inconveniences of the state of nature," and so the need for men to "make themselves members of some politic society." In a sense, then, Locke's state of nature presents us with riddles, even as the Garden of Eden does. At one point we are told that "peace, good will, mutual assistance and preservation" characterize that state; at another point those "inconveniences" mount up, to the point that one is reminded of Hobbes's description.

Locke, too, feared anarchy; certainly he feared despotism as well. He would probably not in the least be bothered by the inconsistencies one finds in his psychological analysis of man; he dreaded tightly knit, well-formulated abstractions and devoted much space in his study of "human understanding" to an attack on them.[6] He celebrated direct observation, personal experience, discursive inquiry, and demonstration tied to concrete situations or experiments. He considered the best kind of awareness to be intuitive: "This part of knowledge is irresistible and, like bright sunshine, forces itself immediately to be perceived, as soon as ever the mind turns its view that way; and leaves no room for hesitation, doubt or examination." There are other "parts" of knowledge, he knew, and he also knew that the mind had to exercise judgment, seek out logically grounded (insofar as it is possible) probabilities. His heart, though, held intuition dear; and for all his judiciousness, his painstaking effort to be reasonable and analytical, one senses in him qualities that Rousseau and Kierkegaard, so much more emotional and congenial to many of us in this century, would recognize with satisfaction. He wanted the best for his fellowman— to the point of imagining him to be a most decent fellow who wanted only to mind his own business; if allowed that leeway, he would almost as a matter of reflex show a large streak of idealism. True, things can be badly organized, so that men turn on one another; but when they do so, one senses the shock he himself would feel were he there as a witness. And I suppose it can be said that he *was* there, at least to a degree; seventeenth-century England was going through much disorder, and political intrigue had generated serious social unrest, in turn prompting untold anxiety (how does one ever quantify such developments?) in thousands and thousands of men, women, and children.

Hobbes, whose life spanned four-fifths of that seventeenth century, could only shrug his shoulders and say, in effect, that is

[6]Chapter IX, on "The Imperfection of Words," is as important today as it ever was, maybe more so, given the new terminologies that keep cropping up—out of nowhere, it seems. A recent book which re-creates the world Hobbes and Locke lived in and influenced in their different ways is Christopher Hill's *The World Turned Upside Down* (New York, 1972). The chapter "Sin and Hell" is an especially useful and subtle psychological analysis of a Christian view of man very much in process of modification by the seventeenth century.

the way things work out: we are by nature self-centered, indifferent
to the fate of others, all too willing to take advantage of anyone or
everyone; given a sensible authority over us, we change, become
law-abiding and responsible, and, not unimportant, *predictable*,
since our lives on a personal basis reflect the larger (social and
political) life that goes on about us. In contrast, Locke expected
more of man and believed he had good reason to do so. In the
Essay he wavers for a while, seems on the verge of denying us free
will, making us subject to various passions, not all of which we are
apt to know at any given moment, and some of which we never
fully give their due as forces at work upon us. But by the second
edition of the *Essay* he has us able to "suspend the execution and
satisfaction" of those various desires; we are, therefore, buffeted
but not without a will of considerable force and influence. As he
looked around he saw decent burghers set upon constructing for
themselves a tidy, well-regulated life. They were not yet capitalists
but they were businesslike and ambitious, and they belonged to a
nation that was even then a force to be reckoned with. Such people
deserve an enabling environment, not to coerce them into acting
like better human beings, but because they are precisely that,
decent and kindly human beings, hence worthy of such circumstances.

As his century's kind of psychologist, he wondered how it
happens that we become the basically honorable people he proposes
us to be, given a sustaining civil or political order. Like Freud and
others who would follow him, he was sure the study of man's
behavior could turn into a science, one as certain as mathematics,
he baldly insisted. Yet he could not live up to that promise. What
he could try was to be exact about a whole range of psychological
words—and it would do none of us any harm to take note of the
ease with which he understood the unconscious and tried to clarify
terms we of this era have learned to be so possessive about, like
identity and *personal identity*. As with any first-rate thinker, the
point at which he stumbles can be as instructive and valuable as the
long discursive stretches he so clearly takes in stride. Locke's
natural man is certainly not the fallen Adam and his descendants
whom various Christian theologians (as various as Augustine, Pascal,
and Kierkegaard) have given us. Locke's natural man ought have
the authority of his passions, because on the whole, when not
threatened, they seem constructive enough. Yet, if so, why are we

given outright hedonism? In his words: "That we call *good* which is apt to cause or increase pleasure or diminish pain in us." And then we are told this: "*Moral* good and evil is only the conformity or disagreement of our voluntary actions to some law, whereby good or evil is drawn on us from the will and power of the law-maker." Ultimately we are back to "God's will," which Locke without apology called "the true ground of morality," thereby letting us know that nature's man and nature's laws simply couldn't suffice for him.

A man thoroughly suspicious of ecclesiastical fanatics and their demands upon increasingly secular societies, he was at the same time a convinced Anglican of what used to be called broad religious sensibility. The divisions among England's Protestants pained him. He sympathized with Dissenters, had strong misgivings about those who in the name of any government set out to harass this or that kind of believer, and, needless to say, had a strong man-centered ethical bias to his thinking, which, coupled with his rational turn of mind, make him sound like a Unitarian, or what were then called deists. But he could leap, to use Kierkegaard's verb; and he did so often enough to distinguish him from those who most emphatically refused to do so.

In the *Reasonableness of Christianity* he writes shrewdly about Saint Paul's letters and makes quite clear his conclusion, articulated toward the end of his life, that human reason is simply not enough; revelation is needed, for without the experience of God "through His Spirit," all religion is empty and meaningless. One has to accept Christ as God's Messiah if one is a Christian, and Locke believed himself to be that. It was only so far, after all, that Locke could permit natural man, or the rest of us, who are willing members of various societies, to go on his own, or on our own. Hobbes never even thought to worry about the problem; men are the way they are, by inclination not very attractive toward each other in many respects; therefore let us arrange things to subdue the destructive and enhance what constructive passions there are. Locke saw much that is fine about his fellow citizens and, indeed their ancestors, but in the end, like Hobbes, he could not trust wholeheartedly the momentum of what he saw—without, that is, calling upon divine help. Still, he did not do so as Augustine and Pascal had before him, or as Kierkegaard would after him—in such a way that God and his Grace become central aspects of man's psychological situation, not to mention his ultimate fate. One can read much of Locke with the mind of an agnostic, academic psychologist or an English philosopher of the late nineteenth or early twentieth century—that is, in no way be troubled by bothersome religious suppositions, even though, it has to be emphasized, they did crop up at critical moments in the *Essay* and elsewhere.

Though Locke is primarily known to us as a political theorist whose ideas strongly influenced our Constitution, he observed human beings out of a wide-ranging curiosity that extended not only into the intricacies of mental function but the social and educational needs of children. In 1683 he had left England some-what fearfully for Holland; a royalist reaction against the Whigs had begun under Charles II. While he was in Amsterdam, his friend Edward Clark of Chipley, Somerset, had written him for advice about the proper way to bring up children. The result was (in 1683) *Some Thoughts Concerning Education*, meant to help an English squire bring up his son, but full of a good deal of implicit moral philosophy. Young children were too often severely re-strained, Locke believed. They ought be given loose rein, at times full rein. As they grow older their character has to be molded, and that development must take precedence over the acquisition of factual knowledge. Children need useful knowledge—and don't need too many languages, too many abstractions. They also need exer-cise, fun, rest. (Locke the physician emerges most clearly in this essay.) Most important, parents should involve themselves intimately in the education of their children, a recommendation not simply pietistic in nature. It was in the seventeenth century that well-to-do parents like Locke's friend Edward Clark became noticeably more concerned with the upbringing of their children, to the point of real self-consciousness: what should be said and done was dis-cussed passionately and argued vehemently.

Philippe Aries has given us an extraordinary account of that development in his social history of family life in Western Europe, beginning with the tenth century, when children were in many respects looked upon as adults, able to mingle in a community which certainly was larger than the small one we today call "the family."[7] At eight or nine, boys and girls had for some time

---

[7]Ariès's book, *Centuries of Childhood: A Social History of Family Life* (New York , 1962), is one of the most original and stimulating books of a recent genre: the child as a

become part of a village or town, "sharing in the work and play of their companions, old and young alike." Privacy was unheard of, for rich and poor alike. True, the family existed—through it life persisted and property was handed down, not to mention one's name. But children were apprenticed at about the age of seven, and even rich children were taught in the company of both others their age and grown-ups—and by experience rather than in a classroom setting, where principles of various kinds are held up for scrutiny and memorization. Nor was the medieval church all that attentive to the needs of the young. Monasteries flourished. The church's energies were harnessed to the future, to that kingdom where, presumably, age disappears and all of us live (or suffer) eternally. The church's energies were also given over to worldly matters, but these had to do with political intrigue and military conquest. So children went on a crusade, but it is we who find that remarkable. They quite naturally went on a crusade; for that matter, many of those men who went on various crusades might be considered by us "children," "mere youths," or "just growing up."

In the fifteenth century to a small degree, in the sixteenth century more, but with great momentum in the seventeenth century, family life began to change, among other reasons because

concept of sorts, a product of certain developments in the West. Other important additions to that genre: the vast and authoritative *Children and Youth in America: A Documentary History,* ed. Robert Bremner, 3 vols. (Cambridge, Mass. 1971) and the span of time is from 1600 to 1932, with more to come, one suspects. For the United States, two well thought-out and written books are Joseph Hawes's *Children in Urban Society: Juvenile Delinquency in Nineteenth-Century America* (New York, 1971) and Bernard Wishy's *The Child and the Republic: The Dawn of Modern American Child Nurture* (Philadelphia, 1968). For England: Ivy Pinchbeck and Margaret Hewitt, *Children in English Society* (London, 1969), the first volume being concerned with life as it went "from Tudor Times to the Eighteenth Century." The authors promise to take us eventually up to this century. Also of considerable interest and worth are Oscar and Mary Handlin's *Facing Life: Youth and the Family in American History* (Boston, 1971) and S. N. Eisenstadt's *From Generation to Generation* (New York, 1956). These two books combine to give a broad historical and sociological view of family life (in America, all over the world) that is less specifically focused on children. Finally, another way to approach the changing situation of children over the generations is through an examination of what is written for them, what they are given to read. An excellent study has been done by Cornelia Meigs and others: *A Critical History of Children's Literature* (New York, 1953).

the church itself was going through a profound crisis of self-scrutiny. Prodded perhaps by the various Protestant sects, which had from the beginning resented the indifference bishops and those below them so often accorded the everyday lives of people, the Catholic church had begun to take its pastoral mission more seriously. And anyway, with each century eschatology became harder to sustain with the kind of immediacy, drive, and sense of urgency that were so natural to Paul or even Augustine. Pascal's sister, Jacqueline, who eventually became the nun Sister Euphemia and who died when Locke was twenty-nine years old, could write this: "Looking after children is so important that we are bound to prefer that duty to all others when obedience imposes it on us, and what is more, to our personal pleasures, even if these are of a spiritual nature." Once that last qualifying phrase could be added without embarrassment, a new sense of responsibility had been felt by the clergy. At the same time the middle class was expanding, was anxious to set itself apart from the masses and to make sure that its distinctive position be perpetuated in the only way it can be, through the lives of children and grandchildren, who now had a secular destiny that had to be treasured and made as solid and secure as possible.

No longer were children simply children, or infants until seven, then apprentices, workers, part of the great crowd of humanity God for his own reasons continued to place on this earth. Now Jacqueline Pascal's pupils were "little ones" and "big ones." Now a whole pedagogic literature began to develop, to which Locke's *Thoughts* belongs. For centuries children had been taught to read and write at home, or in the course of their daily activities as workers, helpers, friends of this or that priest or gentleman. When they began to stand out as a special class of sorts, a group of people who by virtue of their age and vulnerability and promise required a whole new world of attention, parents began to seek after advice (what to do, when, and how) and the pillars of the community (clergy, doctors, lawyers, scholars) were hard put for answers.

Locke was not the only one asked to extend his interest in human understanding to children. The Jansenists, inclined to be sparing about holy communion, held children back later and later from their first communion; in a sense Jacqueline Pascal "applied" a theological doctrine to the young by noting how mischievous and unruly they can be and therefore in need of a certain kind of education as a prelude to that especially sacred and mysterious rite. Like Locke, she saw both sides of children: their openness, their susceptibility to (and need of) guidance, their innocence; and on the other hand, their capacity for wrongdoing and even malice. She considered discipline and constant attention the answer to the latter; and the effort to provide them was for her a sacred calling, because so much is at stake—a recognition that, again, implicitly affirmed a belief in the complexity of a child's spirit.

It is hard to indicate for today's reader how revolutionary all this was in the context of the times—seventeenth-century France and England. Our century is the century of the child; if we know anything (maybe even *believe* anything) it is the virtual sanctity of infancy and childhood. We take for granted our baby doctors, nurseries, schools, toys, children's clothing and furniture. We of the middle-class Western world have removed our children for increasly longer periods of time from the market place; we see in a boy or girl not only our own selves extended and strengthened but to some extent the incarnation of everything important in life, even a means of uncovering mysteries otherwise denied us. Our work is "for the children." The futility we may feel about so much is bearable, "so long as the children are doing well." As for my own profession, its reliance upon childhood will surely one day in the future be the subject of a social historian's scrutiny. That successor of Ariès no doubt will marvel at what took place in three centuries—from the obscurity of membership in the human species, children became by steps an object of curiosity, of special attention, of fiercely possessive and ambitious cultivation, and, finally, of a passionate devotion that has at the very least religious overtones.

Any of history's intellectual figures has his or her roots: immediate as well as distant predecessors, friends, and colleagues who help nurture ideas and by their presence give sanction to an original and suggestive line of reasoning. Yet sometimes an essay, a book, a theory, or even a series of apparently idle speculations will suddenly appear as if out of nowhere with an extraordinary kind of contagious persuasiveness: people are not affected, but converted, and such an influence persists for generations to follow. Jean-Jacques Rousseau, it seems, aroused that kind of reaction in seventeenth-century France; and, one gathers, at the very least, in eighteenth-century Germany and nineteenth-

century Russia. His *Discourse on the Arts and Sciences* won the
academy at Divan's prize (1750). Before that he had met and
impressed Diderot and been invited to write articles for the
Encyclopedia. With the award of the prize he became famous and
the object of a cult. Salons rushed to embrace him. His operas,
heretofore neglected, were presented at court, and he received a
royal pension. The aristocracy, from Marie Antoinette down,
regarded him as a man of the greatest wisdom, even if he was under
forty. Though in a matter of years the French court and many of
his intellectual friends—offended by his ideas or by his provocative
behavior—would desert him, the world at large listened more and
more closely as the novels, essays, and autobiographical recollections poured out, many of them written in exile. Some called him
the spiritual father of the French Revolution, which began eleven
years after his death, and some to this day see him as another kind
of spiritual father: the first philosopher who really looked closely
at children for nonideological reasons, grasped what their lives are
like, observed the rhythms of growth and development, and, most
important, tried to build a theory of education based only on such
observation—uninfluenced, that is, by the prevailing religious and
cultural orthodoxies of the day.

Rousseau was born and brought up in Geneva, and he knew his
Calvin, maybe in his bones as much as his head. He was not the
skeptic Voltaire was, but he was no conventional churchgoer, let
alone believer. Still, he loved the moral and spiritual force of
Christianity, and the Christian view of man was the one he started
out with and used to begin building his own, eventually idiosyncratic, psychological constructions. In fact, without becoming too
strained analytically, one can fit Rousseau's first, polemical discourses (*On the Arts and Sciences* and *On Equality*) into the
Old Testament account of man's social and psychological origins.
The natural man (*l'homme de la nature*) he posits and contrasts
with us (be we of the seventeenth or the twentieth century, we
have to be considered conventional men, society's people, *l'homme
de l'homme*) is no one Rousseau ever saw, for all the long walks he
took in the woods near Saint-Germain. ("Deep in the heart of the
forest I sought and found the vision of those primeval ages whose
history I bravely sketched. I denied myself all the easy deceits to
which men are prone, I dared to unveil human nature and to look
upon it in its nakedness, to trace the course of times and events
which have disfigured human nature.")

Without the greatest show of humility he confesses that it was an abstraction he managed to comprehend: human nature. Perhaps the nakedness he saw, the bare bones of man's past, is not unlike another nakedness: "And they were both naked, the man and his wife, and were not ashamed." Perhaps Rousseau wanted to emphasize what Genesis 2 tells us preceded the development described in Genesis 3. I have no idea how long Adam and Eve were unashamedly naked, but I believe Rousseau imagined them going through an unmeasurable but definite stretch of time before they "took of the fruit." Moreover, if one wants to give the Fall of man a history (see what happened in the Garden and immediately thereafter, eastward of Eden, as taking place over a span of time), then much of Rousseau's description comes, almost literally, from Genesis— rather an irony, in view of the reputation he has had among people not especially interested in a fundamentalist kind of Christianity or, indeed, any kind at all.

Even Calvinist doctrine grants man a moment of genuine, untarnished goodness, during which he seemed naturally rustic, able to regard nature with satisfaction and comprehend it, able also to live at peace with the world, at one point sleeping long and hard, at another point finding and enjoying the company of woman, and being of comfort to her. Again, the Bible does not tell us how many hours or days or weeks elapsed between the time spent that way by Adam and Eve and the "incident" described in the next chapter of Genesis—though, significantly, Genesis 1 is quite explicitly time-conscious. We are told that Adam lived to be a very old man (930 years, if we are to accept the account in Genesis 5), and among his sons were Abel, a keeper of sheep, and Cain, a tiller of the ground, in many respects rather unequal men, soon enough mortal enemies. Similarly, Rousseau has his prepolitical and presocial man living a rustic life, close to nature, under conditions of virtue, simpleness, innocence. He also enumerates stages in man's development as he leaves the state of nature and becomes civilized, meaning, for Rousseau, first corruptible, then corrupted.

In the beginning there are gatherers, people of various (and unequal) endowment but knowledgeable and disposed to be kind and decent. Later on, men and women settle down; they hunt and fish and domesticate animals and learn the properties of plants. They also learn how to live with one another and do so communally, in peace and harmony. Still, somewhere, somehow, sometime—Rousseau, like the rest of us, is in the dark as to when and exactly how and for what specific reason of the mind—men became covetous. It is interesting that such a moment did *not* come upon civilized, urban people. There they all were, those fine human beings, living side by side on a thoroughly moral and exemplary basis—yet suddenly one of them (or some of them, or all of them) begin to change: "The first man who, having enclosed a piece of ground, bethought himself of saying 'This is mine,' and found people simple enough to believe him, was the real founder of civil society."

From then on things went from bad to worse; but despite his concern to spell out the consequences in the career of natural man, we are never told why the change occurred. What prompted that first man to leave his idyllic rural community and stake out land for himself? We are back to the riddle of man's Fall—always it seems to happen without prior warning, without the narrator's explanation, or at least without any causal connection that appeals to rational men, a subspecies of Rousseau's *l'homme de l'homme*. Once again the chronicle of Genesis turns out to resemble Rousseau's story: wickedness there was, but with the flood and Noah a new spell of decency and good feeling came upon man, who seemed almost regenerated, surrounded as the old man of 600 years was by beasts and fowl, not to mention his wife and sons and daughters-in-law. God even entered into a covenant with those survivors; there would be no return to the Garden, but no interference, either, of the dreadful kind just visited on the earth for forty days and forty nights. Men and women and beasts multiplied and were replenished, and for a while everyone was united and part of a worldwide community. ("Behold, the people is one, and they have all one language.") God having said that, however, he apparently had some other fate in store for "them," for us. He actively intervened one more time, not in defiance of his covenant—no more rain—but in a less dramatic and fearful way that would, in fact, set the stage for what we (and certainly Rousseau) would call civilization: many tongues, with all the self-consciousness and pride and mutual distrust involved; a once united people scattered; and, not least, the determination of some to build the city called Babel.

For Locke there was no question that such a scattering, followed by so much building and a new sense of proprietorship (as against others, who live there, not here, and talk in another way, not our way) generated tensions, hence the need for individuals (and groups of individuals) to change their notion of what freedom is all about. Rousseau could only agree—but sadly, believing the development a disaster, the basis of theft, exploitation, and social injustice. Still, he came to see that there was no turning back on history. It can be argued that God himself concluded the very same thing when he intervened as his people were struggling to build a tower, a city, a monument to their own ambitions, dreams, and capacities. "And now nothing will be restrained from them, which they have imagined to do"; when God so thought, he saw, perhaps one can say, the hope in that worldwide community of men, the yearning for a return to the status quo ante, and, it can be added, if one can dare guess his reasons, the pride demonstrated, hence the need yet again for a divine descent. ("Go to, let us go down, and there confound their language.")

In his appendix to his *Discourse on Origins of Inequality* Rousseau boldly and surprisingly challenges the critics he knew he would have: "What then is to be done? Must societies be abolished? Must we again return to the forests and live among bears? This is a dedication in the manner of my adversaries, which I would as soon anticipate as let them have the shame of drawing." The point is to go on, aware of what once was or, put more cautiously, what might have been; and thereby aware of what was lost—and might be, at least to some extent, regained. The point is to construct a social and political theory that does justice to man's complicated history, the background against which his complicated psychology has developed. And this Rousseau did in *The Social Contract*, which only seems to contradict some of his earlier ideas. Unquestionably modern society is not savagely attacked as it was in the two earlier discourses; rather, having gone back in time and speculated about what once happened, Rousseau now is very much preoccupied with the present and is completely realistic about man's limitations, whether God-inspired or attributable to the psychological consolidations that have taken place over the generations, since our kind of world, our kind of society, became all there is to be found on this earth.

Given God's repeated interventions, or, to switch to a secular interpretation, given man's obvious present-day behavior, as it has demonstrated itself throughout recorded history, one can only find

truly moral men in a certain kind of society, to which they pay
allegiance, because the alternative no longer is natural man but the
immoral man of Genesis 11 (so God saw him) or the similarly
immoral man Rousseau was canny enough to recognize in all of us.
The men and women Genesis 11 tells us were scattered "upon the
face of all the earth" are the alienated men and women of *The
Social Contract,* the individuals in a state of amoral isolation who
ought be made moral participants in the affairs of a strong and
ongoing community.

As did Plato in his *Republic,* Rousseau had in mind for *The
Social Contract* nothing less than a grand design for a civil and
political society. He had to justify such a design—that is, explain
why he would even want (in theory, needless to say) to take his
beloved natural man and place him ever so irrevocably in a highly
organized world, regulated in dozens of ways by a "sovereignty,"
the executor of the general will. No question, he goes back on
himself. Not only does he emphasize what his kind of government
does for the individuals who would be lucky enough to be under
its authority; he cannot resist at one point referring to "a stupid
and unimaginative animal"—those who lived without a "social
contract." No one will ever resolve Rousseau's various inconsistencies; he was a tormented, emotional, utterly compelling moralist
who experienced violent swings of mood, only to extract from
them what he could, all of which he made sure he shared with his
countrymen. One can simply try to learn from his imaginative leaps
and to respect the ambiguities he so obviously could not master,
only take the risk of emphasizing in his highly personal, original,
and urgent style of presentation.

When portraying natural man, he was passionately at his side,
finding the best in him. When portraying the ideal small democratic
state that he dreamed for communities all over the world, each of
them bound by devotion and need to a social contract, he was
again passionate, now intensely taken up with the future rather
than the past; and he was (one says so without prejudice) a polemical propagandist, who wrote to stir people, to remove them from
smug and complacent habits of mind. I do not want to reconcile an
"early" Rousseau with a "later" Rousseau—it is useless even to
set up such categories, because his nationalist novel *La Nouvelle
Héloise* and his *Émile,* a long treatise on education, both devoted
to the virtues of natural man, were published within a year of

The Social Contract—but rather indicate that his struggles, his contradictory suppositions and inclinations, have been so enormously influential and revealing because they bring before us once again (and in a manner that secular, "enlightened" men can appreciate) enigmas as old, at the very least, as man's effort from Genesis on to write about them.

The mark of Rousseau's genius was his breadth of vision, his refusal to be trapped by any theory, even one of his own making. He could never raise inconsistency to a virtue among intellectuals—one of many reasons he scorned them—but he could at least throw himself both shrewdly and fervently into a dilemma and end up flagrantly on both of its horns, with the result that generations after him, also made up of men who know how to dream nostalgically and yearn desperately, would find in his writing a believable affirmation of their own situation. One moment he reads like Hobbes—sharp, cynical, brooding, anxious to make clear how dangerous human beings can be to one another under certain circumstances. In another place he would satisfy Locke, as he goes about dreaming up carefully arranged and balanced social and political structures. Further along he can match Augustine with his own eighteenth-century *Confessions*—full of recriminations, doubts, frankly self-pitying apologies, and proud reflections upon a hectic and controversial life. He never could be as detached as Pascal was, nor did he come close to seeing the mind in all its tangle and muddle the way Kierkegaard did; but he shared with them a tenacious kind of ethical concern that perhaps can be considered the unifying thread that gives to all his writings a real coherence.

Rousseau's influence on Kant has been soundly documented, and their respective personalities and modes of living contrasted. Kant especially admired *Émile*, and it is something to ponder, the stern, thoroughly disciplined German philosopher, so logical and precise and weighty in his thoughts, becoming captivated with the moods (and some would say the large and foolhardy excesses) of a French educational theorist whose fictitious pupil is made to go through years of unusual training in order to illustrate abstract propositions that occasionally give one another momentum but just as often collide, leaving the reader stimulated but confused—though, one has to add, driven to read yet more of Rousseau. Cassirer emphasizes the intensity and commitment of Rousseau's

moral self as especially attractive to Kant.[8] (*Émile* is on many
occasions a far sterner, an even Calvinist book than many of its
other admirers, who abound to this day, are likely to admit.) "We
can never know absolute good or evil—everything in this life is
mixed." We are told that in a rather hopeful and buoyant section
on boyhood, when the whole world seems to be opening up for
Émile, even if he is declared not old enough to reason. "The felicity
of man here below is therefore a negative state, to be measured by
the fewness of his ills"—this from a man so commonly regarded as
an incurable romantic, the father of an educational revolution
destined to last even longer than the political one that started in
1789.

Kant taught what he called anthropology; he wanted to appraise
man and his works systematically. Words like those in *Émile* must
have struck home for him the way Hobbes's words sometimes do
for us—or Freud's. And a point of view that emphasizes man's more
emotional, potentially wild and nasty side is especially necessary
for an idealist, a man insistent upon man's capacity and obligation
to use his freedom for a very particular kind of self-enhancement,
the perfection of the mind's ethical sense (its ideas about what is
good or bad, what matters or is of no consequence whatsoever).
Very important, too, Rousseau never lost sight of the individual, to
whose increasing perfection Kant was so devoted. Even in *The
Social Contract* or in his *Thoughts about the Polish Government*,
published posthumously (1782) and written toward the end of his
life, when he was at his most morose, vain, and accusatory, the
whole purpose of the social institutions he recommends is made
clear to be the progressive enoblement of each person's dignity—
and with it, responsibility to act on behalf of others. A member of
the Polish nobility (Count Wielhorski) had asked how his country's
institutions might be reformed and Rousseau plunged into his

---

[8]Ernest Cassirer's *Rousseau, Kant, Goethe* (1945; rpt. Princeton, 1970) is enormously
helpful, not only about Rousseau and his influence on Kant, among others, but about
matters novelists like James Agee and Elizabeth Bowen take up: "Can the heart,"
Cassirer asks, "really show us the way to that single and original natural religion that
Rousseau is seeking and trying to teach? Is the heart not rather itself the most multi-
farious, changeable, and variegated thing in the world? If we follow the heart alone, are
we not at the mercy of every breath of air? Does not every new impression we submit to
create a new self and with it a new God?" This tension between intellect and emotion
runs through the novels discussed here only slightly less explicitly than through
Rousseau's writings.

answers with such zeal that he seems to have forgotten all the future Émiles—who presumably would need protection as children even from Rousseau's version of Poland. How could he, as he does, recommend that Polish children be trained very specifically as future citizens, from whom the state will need to (has a right to) ask much? He, who had railed against nation-states, deplored the corruptions that society places upon children, urged the child's isolation from wicked political and economic forces that he was sensitive enough to see as intimately connected with the child's upbringing; he, who scandalized all sorts of "powers and principalities," ecclesiastical and governmental, with his disdain for them and all they stood for, was now virtually designing a program for the systematic indoctrination of a nation's children. Likewise in *The Social Contract* he could become obsessed by that general will of his, to the point that each of us is asked to serve its purposes—and, a critic might say, none of us is left with a shred of individuality.

Again, I doubt anyone can fashion out of such irreconcilables a consistent and well-argued critique, such as those Kant produced. But it can be said that Rousseau, sometimes scattering himself (in microcosm) like a true descendent of Noah, demonstrated what Kant tried to propound logically in the *Critique of Pure Reason*—that the categorical imperative, or moral law ("act as if the maxim from which you act were to become through your will a universal law"), may be grounded in the freedom we have to act and, before that, the freedom we have to think about why and for what reason we are to act; yet, even so it is an imperative which has limited influence upon us, because by nature man belongs to two worlds, the emotional as well as the intellectual, or rational. We are not, therefore, thoroughly informed or moved by that imperative; it stands outside us, at times affected, if not weakened, by our moods and appetites. What is objectively desirable is subjectively contingent.

Perhaps Kant saw Rousseau's struggle as an honest and feverish effort one lived out, not formulated—to recognize and affirm such a duality in man; and to do so required, Rousseau knew by intuition, Kant by reasoning, not sacrificing either the mind or the heart. Kant may have lived an exceedingly controlled and sober life, but he felt what he wrote of—the power of subjectivity; and in Rousseau he felt that power not to have run amok, but to have been up

against an equally forceful intellect. I suppose today we can easily
consider Kant's admiration to have been nothing more than envy,
even as Rousseau's inconsistencies can become, finally, an expression of ambivalence if not outright schizophrenia. Put aside in the
course of that approach are ideas fought for, and often enough
maintained and given integrity against all sorts of opposition, both
rational and irrational.

Whatever Rousseau's failures in consistency, at any given moment
in his writing career he was an exceptionally conscientious and
dedicated worker who took great pains to win over his readers to
the particular cause he was at the moment espousing. In the case
of *Émile* that cause was the dignity of childhood, its momentum,
its rhythms, its life history. To his great credit, he had watched
children very carefully, and whatever his ideological vested interests
(and it can be argued that no writer is without them, even those
who deny such in their own articles or books), there is ample
evidence that the children Rousseau observed more than survive,
in his writing, the abstract bent of his mind. He must have wanted
that to be the outcome; he had little use for theory-minded
intellectuals, precise encyclopedists, and clever skeptics who could
undo everything and come up with nothing believable, never mind
sacred.

It would have been especially ironic and sad, therefore, had he
turned his observations of children into a lifeless, overwrought
treatise, full of generalizations attractive to the "best minds."
Instead we are given what child psychoanalysts like Anna Freud
would call direct observation: year by year and stage by stage the
actual activities of children are described, starting with the infant
and going right through to the young man or woman about to
marry. He misses very little; perhaps never before had a philosopher
spent so much time taking note of what children require as they
move along in years. And it is all done from the child's, even the
infant's, viewpoint—how it must feel to wear this, be fed in that
way, to be taught one or another subject at such-and-such an age.
The form of the book is bent to the purpose of the reader's
education: fact gets mixed with fiction, detailed descriptions are
followed by careful analysis of the evidence presented. No wonder
the young Tolstoy would find Rousseau's writing so irresistible;
War and Peace itself, on a much grander scale, would defy categorization, thereby fulfilling the author's intent: character portrayal,

narrative history, and philosophical speculation are mixed in such a way that the book is sui generis. *Émile* and its companion, *La Nouvelle Héloise*, belong to a relatively lean and idiosyncratic tradition.[9]

Rousseau, Swiss born, also anticipates a countryman, Jean Piaget. He noticed in the eighteenth century what Piaget would spend a lifetime documenting in our century—the sequence of intellectual growth and development and the implications of that sequence for parents and other educators. Parents are *the* educators, Rousseau insisted, and ought never surrender that prerogative to others, because in doing so they agree to deprive the child of more than attention and affection, but the continuing instructional use to which their example and influence can be put. Uncannily he sensed what Ariès documented, what we today know all too well—how intimidated and self-conscious parents can become by virtue of their desire to give their children everything: for the best of reasons others are called upon and regarded as virtual gods—from those who run nursery schools or elementary schools to those who teach hobbies or sports or practice children's medicine, let alone dispense "guidance." They all should be called upon, of course; and Rousseau was one of their most significant ancestors.

But he wanted to strengthen the hands of parents, not cause in them feelings of inadequacy, bewilderment, and impotence. To do so required paying attention to what they must go through, day in and day out, as the growing child presents them with obstacles, opportunities, moments of confusion, times of real pleasure that sometimes can even turn to awe—that so very much can happen, and often so quickly, so *accidentally*, it seems, meaning with little if any preparation or encouragement. It can be said that *Émile* was written to dispel just that notion of childhood as a series of innocent or merely fortuitous events. As Piaget would later prove to us with his experiments, there is a pattern to the child's physiological and psychological development: certain abilities or faculties of mind come into their own before others; certain modes of thinking and reflecting upon the nature of things depend upon X kind of stimulation or Y kind of circumstances or, for that matter, on a certain studied indifference on our part, because nature is not without its own initiatives.

[9] Rousseau's strong influence on Tolstoy has been carefully analyzed by Boris Eikhenbaum in *The Young Tolstoi* (Ann Arbor, 1972).

All in all, Rousseau's view of childhood is more subtle than some of his propagandists would want to allow and less vulnerable to criticism than some of his critics might hope. He does indeed get himself on weak or loose branches; he can take after man's institutions indiscriminately, and he can worship nature with a kind of hypnotic abandon that can only become exhausting and render the reader incredulous.[10] Human beings are to blame for all disasters, we are told—to the point that we wish that the person who watched children so meticulously had kept an eye out for what went on in those forests he loved so very much. Man, who "perverts and disfigures everything" is, after all, part of a world always plagued by disasters, not only hurricanes and tornadoes and floods, but a built-in hierarchy of dominance and submission, of those who devour and those who are devoured, of construction and destruction, that cannot be ignored, even if one may choose to appreciate such facts of nature without moral judgment: the law of the jungle. Nature erodes nature, animals prey upon animals, and, true, men can be especially awful to other men. There is every reason to emphasize that last point and, more, indicate how man's institutional life can become murderously aggrandizing and stifling: worst of all, it can simply persist as if beyond the power of anyone's judgment. On the other hand, Rousseau knew that if this world's Émiles are destined to be "fettered by Social institutions," they are also born finite and in the best of worlds will grow old, tired, and, inevitably, at the prospect of death, apprehensively self-protective, often at the expense of others. All of that, too, takes time; all of that has a sequence, is built into life's progress, makes for (on the part of each of us) a far from perfect "adjust-

[10]But the reader wants more. Rousseau is inviting, provocative, entertaining, even when impossible to go along with. Several books that take up his ideas in whole or in part have also managed to capture his imaginative spirit. I strongly recommend Marshall Berman's *The Politics of Authenticity* (New York, 1970) for its treatment of both Montesquieu and Rousseau from the vantage point of modern psychological theory. From quite another direction, one calls upon Irving Babbitt's *Rousseau and Romanticism* (New York, 1919). A valuable exegetical book is William Boyd's *Educational Theories of Jean Jacques Rousseau* (New York, 1963). And Claude Lévi-Strauss has been considerably drawn to Rousseau. In *Totemism* (Boston, 1962) one is told: "It is only because man originally felt himself identical to those like him (among which, as Rousseau explicitly says, we must include animals) that he came to acquire the capacity to distinguish *himself* as he distinguishes *them*, i.e. to use the diversity of species as conceptual support for social differentiation." Rousseau also figures significantly in *Tristes Tropiques* (New York, 1961).

ment," to draw upon a word which, in its present usage among so many of us, Rousseau would have scorned.

Émile deserved more than he was likely to get; Rousseau wrote his book because he knew how much might be done for such a child but likely wouldn't be. In a way, though, he obtained something for many future Émiles. He made it hard for generations of sensitive parents and teachers to fit children, willy-nilly, into various schemes and programs that have nothing to do with the pace of their emotional and intellectual growth. He became what the grown up Émile, now a father, asks him to become: "the teacher of the young teachers." If he failed, it was in finding a balance for his ideas about children: his essays and treatises occasionally fail to do justice to the complexities of the relationship between anyone's life, however well-nourished and protected and cultivated it was from the moment of birth on, and the inevitable society that stands there, waiting for all of us, and more a part of us than Émile's protective counselor ever acknowledges.

Ultimately, of course, the riddle Rousseau was contending against confronts the author with himself, something Tolstoy realized full well. One can embrace any cause, yet still carry within oneself all that has been so forthrightly and insistently rejected. One can write *War and Peace*, know full well the many sides any life has, yet get almost absurdly caught up in single-minded messianic ideologies that deny others what they clearly ought have, their own right not only to live otherwise but to be respected for doing so—and appreciated, even admired, when such is their due. One can teach Émile for years with great care, and indeed keep him free of a great deal of the world's cant, hypocrisy, stupidity. But who is to teach the teachers, even the best of them, in such a way that now and then the blind do not lead the blind?

Émile's teacher gets no analysis whatsoever, not in this book, at least. Elsewhere, yes—in passages where citizens are recognized for what they are: even the best of them in need of the authority any complicated society can do without only at the risk of complete disintegration. It would have helped to come across reveries in *Émile* of the kind Tolstoy was such a master of presenting in *War and Peace:* reveries during which the teacher, in the style of the *Confessions,* talks about his own hopes and fears, his failures (or does he never have any?) to live up to his expectations, his knowledge (might he not have it?) that whatever he does see, there is still blindness to be overcome, hence ruts and crevices in his primrose path and, alas, quite literally a dead end for each of us. The road at various points has to get muddy or bumpy for the teacher or parent: the child is there not only waiting for help but susceptible to the consequences of those moods one must grant even to the best of us. And to complicate matters even more, that child is not *only* susceptible; at birth we may more or less be that tabula rasa Rousseau presents, but there is only so far any world, however encouraging or oppressive, can take the child, as Rousseau's own childhood, so grim and even tragic, demonstrates. Yes, he was never to shake off the neglect and pain of those early years; but he would become the man Rousseau: an observer and writer who could take children seriously as perhaps no one before had ever done, at least in a way the rest of the world could attend to and learn from. (One does have to acknowledge, however, that what he could preach he may well have been unable to practice. He was capable of abandoning his children—even denying them legitimacy.)

One wants in Émile some of life's constant tension between awareness and action, appreciation and implementation. One wants sympathy not only for children, who so often, as Rousseau will not let us forget, bear the brunt of our failures, but for us, who are as we are, having gone through what we have gone through, so much of which Rousseau wants badly to spare every Emile who will ever live. If not sympathy for us, at least a practical kind of concern; after all, Rousseau had good reason to risk the irony and say in *Émile*, "I hate books." No such words from him or anyone else will substitute for the everyday obligation parents have to experience childhood with children—books of advice or no books—and in doing so, be found again and again wanting, even as their children will inevitably stumble and occasionally fall flat on their faces—indeed will need to do so.

It is at that moment, the moment when an adult recognizes that he or she has fallen short, been found wanting, that a reverie or two from Émile's teacher would have been so valuable—and served to transform a book from an important educational tract into a work of art. But Rousseau never provides the moment, let alone the subsequent reverie. And if it can be said that tracts are more useful than ambiguity-filled novels, then one has to answer: not useful enough. Still, Tolstoy had his reasons for insisting so strenuously that *War and Peace* was not a novel. If the child does not want to be fettered, neither does the novelist, and insofar as he is successful, he accomplishes that most difficult of tasks—a mixture of the analytic and exhortative that is grounded in the very concreteness and particularity Rousseau knew children crave, whether at play or in a classroom. Not for them abstractions; and as for us, we ought have a limited tolerance of them, too. Over all, Rousseau recognized his own biases and corrected for them. But book by book he slipped, especially in *Émile* and *La Nouvelle Héloise;* and for that we have to be surprised as well as regretful. Both books were essentially novels (of sorts, at least), and the novel is a form especially suited to the needs Rousseau had as an analyst of human nature, an observer of children and young people and their older teachers. (He wrote strenuously uphill; the novels were finished in the face of a deteriorating psychological condition.)

Perhaps he did enough, though; surely he succeeded in alerting all of us to the special experience that childhood is. It is an easy step from him to Freud and, even more, to Erik H. Erikson and Anna Freud; the childhood he respected enough to cherish and throw in the teeth of a society he believed almost infinitely corrupting (see what all of you have done, do every day, show every sign of wanting to continue to do!) is the same childhood our psychoanalysts have also respected, believing as they do that none of us really forgets and that all of us, of whatever age, harken back in various ways every day to habits, practices, or states of mind we long ago picked up and gradually learned to feel compelling beyond our daily comprehension. If one turns from Rousseau to other novelists, though not to the Tolstoy who admired him so extravagantly and shared some of his obsessions and contradictions, it has to be done with the full knowledge that several novels will be needed—three upon this occasion, and each one a good one—to give amplitude to, and correct for, all that a book like *Émile* so ambitiously presents.

II Childhood: James Agee's
A Death in the Family

JAMES AGEE'S *A Death in the Family* in certain important respects is an unpromising companion for, or antidote to, *Émile*, or any of Rousseau's other books. Agee has been called a romantic, as was Rousseau, but he had little interest in preaching to others and less interest in isolating himself or anyone else from the surrounding society. His *Let Us Now Praise Famous Men* is a moral document, one of lasting merit; yet it is, if anything, self-lacerating. No one is going to read it and know what is the right thing to do; if anything, the reader becomes overwhelmed by the complexities of character and situation documented. We learn in that book and in the author's substantial body of journalism how useful, even inspiring, a particular corrupt situation can be. Here I go along firmly with Agee's friend Robert Fitzgerald, who has no patience with the desire various social critics have to attack *Time Incorporated:* Agee was an exploited fool, or a defenseless victim of all those blandishments—money, influence, seductively pleasant working conditions.[1] Agee himself may have blasted the New York literary world, but he also loved it, lived near it or in its midst all his writing life, and was no eccentric, anarchic Rousseau, with a number of scores to settle, both personal and philosophical, and with the energy, the will to settle them at any cost, including condemnation, exile, and poverty.

At one point in *Let Us Now Praise Famous Men* Agee writes much like Rousseau in *Émile*; it is the section called "Education," and Alabama's rural schools do not come off very well. Even then, however, scorn is mixed with sadness and pity; and most important, we are not given an alternative, any kind of blueprint.

---

[1] Fitzgerald's introduction to the *Collected Short Prose of James Agee* (Boston, 1969) offers a personal evocation of the man and writer that is at once affectionate and unsentimental. W. M. Frohock, in his essay "James Agee—The Question of Wasted Talent," in *The Novel of Violence in America* (Dallas, 1950), presents a contrasting view: Agee is seen as profligate indeed with his energy and capacity as a writer.

We are asked to look at the self-defeating and narrowing habits that beleaguered and poorly paid teachers inflict upon children from extremely marginal homes. Agee draws from school texts and regulations in order to indicate the distance of mood and attitude between a self-consciously proper and conformist educational system, tied ever so closely to the powers-that-be, and the children who go to those schools—and in them became bored, annoyed, disgusted, frightened, or merely amused in their own way. He wants a better life for the families he has come to know, a better education for their children; but he is not about to offer us a social contract or an educational program of his own as substitutes for what he has seen in that stretch of farm country between Montgomery and Birmingham, Alabama.

He sets down every nuance of the child's relationship to an unusually forsaken section of America; and when he finishes telling us what he sees, we are also made to see—if there is any decency left in us. But even as we are brought along by a writer who can drastically shake up his readers, tear them from their own world and bring them to another, which they are enabled to visualize through prose of stunning richness and power, we are also let down, sometimes dropped in the midst of nowhere. Agee can enumerate his many heroes (too many, some might feel) at the end of *Let Us Now Praise Famous Men*, but they are a small consolation to any social activist or reformer who wants to go *do* something—say, about those awful schools in the South, among other places in this country. But how dare the outsider interfere? How dare James Agee and Walker Evans interfere? Dozens of times those questions are implicitly or explicitly asked by James Agee. (Walker Evans is blissfully, enviably spared the need for words or apologetic explanations. He has obviously arranged things, born down hard and lean on his subject, and presents it—them, rather—to us; through his photography we will never know whether he has any second thoughts, misgivings, or self-recriminating obsessions.)

One can imagine Rousseau's admiration for those two extraordinary social observers—and his impatience with them. For Kant their effort would be quite enough. They went. They saw. They were moved. They tried to tell others. They showed their intense moral anguish, their struggle to know and comprehend the world. But for Rousseau they had only begun with the ending of that long book of theirs. What about the children of those three families so tenderly and respectfully portrayed? Surely there must be some advice their parents and other parents like them might profit from hearing. And we, the influential ones who read books—there must be all sorts of things we can be told to do. Suffering is criminal, and suffering is unnecessary, or so Rousseau believed. One is obligated to come up with ideas, suggestions, programs, and not out of despair or guilt. Things are bad, but once they were better, and someday they might again be better.

Needless to say, no Christian theologian doubts that things will be better; but not because any of us will have washed the world clean. Augustine, Pascal, and Kierkegaard could not restrain themselves from social criticism, but always they left it rather quickly for another kind of discussion and argument. It is interesting, in view of Agee's obvious religious sensibility, how little we are told about the religious beliefs and practices of those three Alabama families. I can presume to imagine, on the basis of my own work in rural Alabama, what devout believers those men and women were; in the 1960s, three decades after Agee and Evans had gone south, I saw on Sundays what a church could do to the countryside of mid-central Alabama. In the words of one political organizer I knew—and he was both resentful and envious as well as begrudgingly factual: "They strip the whole town and all the farms nearby clean, that's what those churches do; they draw them like a magnet, the poor beaten-down people, hungry for anything they can get—and a sermon is free, you know."

Augustine and Pascal might have been offended, but one can imagine Kierkegaard smiling broadly. He would begin where that black civil rights worker left off—think of the astonishing encounters that may well have taken place under such circumstances; worn, thin, tired, grieving people, so near being without hope, so desperate for something, anything, so humbled by the world's injustice, yet still so determined to go and listen and look and sing and pray and be told and be reminded and be promised. Surely sometimes they must, paradoxically, get exactly what they are looking for; and indeed, as their would-be political spokesman said, it must be free—God's Grace freely bestowed upon those least expecting it, those most resigned to their circumstances.

For a time Agee conceived of *Let Us Now Praise Famous Men* as a work of many volumes; he wanted to document "human actuality," and he knew how much of it he had seen, even in a short summer's time.[2] Perhaps he eventually would have become more programmatic, though I doubt it. Those Alabama families drove him neither to theology nor philosophy, let alone social or psychological theory; they drove him to dedicated, excited, and at times rather apologetic description. Through others so different he came to know himself a little better; but such self-knowledge did not lead him to envision and map out a City of God, or a Social Contract, or an educational program for Southern tenant farmers.

We know from his correspondence with Father Flye how both interested and uninterested he would continue to be in religious matters. Drawn to a Christian view of man, he was wary of institutionalized religion; his keen eye for the phony and the pretentious never went bad. We also know from occasional passages in *Let Us Now Praise Famous Men* how averse he was to generalizations. He shirked at offering an agenda to anyone. That long, baffling, impressive, absurd list of names he tacked on to the end of *Let Us Now Praise Famous Men* is nothing if not a solemn and hilarious blast at ideologues—so many people, and no thread connecting them but one man's sensibility. His object was to see, then put in words—envision and encompass and convey. To do so he would resort to improvisation, poetic flights, straightforward narrative, sly provocations, wordiness, exuberant (never really mean) assaults upon assorted enemies, calculated disorderliness of presentation, rudeness to the reader every now and then, quickly made up for—more than made up for when an exquisite kind of decency and gentleness of spirit open up on the page and soon infectiously take hold of all of us, annoyed and enthralled, who have remained with the author.

I have taken a bit to say that Agee was a writer, a poet and novelist who wrote more than his fair share of essays, reviews, movie scripts, but never turned to sustained moral argument or psychological analysis; only indirectly, as befitted his needs and moods in constructing a poem, a short story, or a novel, would he urge things on people or try to show what he knew about the mind's various inclinations or struggles. With respect to the latter,

[2] I have tried to describe the influence this book had on some of my own generation in "James Agee's *Famous Men* Seen Again," *Harvard Advocate*, February 1972.

he knew a lot, of course, as does any good novelist. But the very nature of the novel requires that such knowledge be rendered indirectly, refracted through the particular characters constructed for a particular story. There can be asides, long ones even; the whole enterprise falls apart, however, if theory and speculation reduce characters and a plot to mere literary devices for a thinly disguised effort at the exposition of or, more strongly, the pronouncement of a point of view. Not that there usually isn't one; in Agee's case, in the case of Elizabeth Bowen, and most especially George Eliot, there most certainly are points of view to be found. These are, however, tied to concrete situations summoned and fashioned by the novelist's imagination. The given point of view is necessarily dispersed, its various parts or segments brought to life through incidents or situations or through the interior life of one or several individuals whom the author, to some extent, uses—how successfully, tactfully, or intrusively and gratuitously, depends upon his skill, needless to say, rather than his good judgment as a psychologist or sociologist or his wisdom as a moralist.

I would not, however, be paying this kind of attention to three particular novels by James Agee, Elizabeth Bowen, and George Eliot if I did not think that in the hands of a certain kind of novelist a methodological breakthrough (to call upon a heaviness of expression none of those three writers would find congenial) takes place. The novelist does indeed have a clear-cut and well-developed point of view and even can be found working at its presentation as conscientiously as at the novel's conventional or formal requirements, though again, not to their neglect or detriment; and precisely *because* that latter possibility has not occurred— that is, the novel is a success in its own terms—the given point of view has not only value and interest but a special kind of truthfulness, a reality all its own or, better, the kind of actuality Agee wanted for his portrayal of the three tenant families he came to know in July 1936.

To give a point of view to such an order of existence, to render ideas in such a way that they have not only the concreteness a novel by definition provides but the living breathing sound and feel of life itself is no mean feat, even if novelists aren't often regarded as the high priests other thinkers are—from theologians, philosophers, and political philosophers in the past to our own social scientists. Moreover, if he has a point of view to develop on the side, the aesthetic requirements the novelist feels can become especially demanding. The preacher may well have to be curbed. The idealist ought not forget incidents, accidents, the sweep of events. The moralist likely will confront stubborn natures, willful presences, instances and sets of circumstances that won't yield to his wishes, even if they are of his own making! The believer meets up with the skeptics he has created. The theorist offers cases which run against his theories and which at the very least require of him language both tentative and frankly speculative, lest rigidities and provincialities be exposed for what they are. And it is an astonishing tribute to the human mind that all of that, so contrapuntal in nature, can take place in one mind as it works on a problem—the telling of a story. One day, perhaps, scientists of all persuasions will give deserving recognition to *that* "integrative process," *that* "synthesizing procedure," *that* "research method."

Right off, then, I have to insist that *A Death in the Family* is not about childhood, or the way boys and girls grow up, or learn to cope with tragedies like the loss of a parent. Yet the novel does touch upon all of that; in fact, Agee unquestionably has a consistent vision of the child's special kind of human situation, and he wants to unfold the vision before us unobtrusively but as fully as the Follet family and their fortunes (or moment of awful misfortune) will permit him. It is not hard to summarize the plot of this novel; its title is pure description. The Follets live in Knoxville, Tennessee, in the second decade of this century. They are plain people, not poor, but not well-to-do or of high education. The father, Jay Follet, is in his middle thirties, had once worked in a post office way off in the Panama Canal Zone, had tried to teach himself law, had for a time been a heavy drinker and not the best breadwinner, but now seems to be coming into his own; he is a big strong man, of sturdy and long-lived mountain people.

The Appalachians are not far from Knoxville, and though Knoxville 1973 is not Knoxville 1915, the essential drama and contrast Agee incorporates in the marriage of Jay and his wife, Mary, are still to be found, because the hill people are not yet vanquished; they tenaciously cling to their ancestral land, even if some of them, like Jay, get lost to the city—and to a marriage with a woman like Mary Lynch. She is of a middle-class city family, not all that high up socially, economically, or educationally; certainly, it is a family whose people are not from the working class, which

(for low wages, indeed) has so long supplied Southern factories
with obliging and grateful men and women. Dispossessed themselves from farms not unlike the one Jay Follet came from, those
factory workers have come to cities like Knoxville in desperate
hopes of a better life, only to exchange one form of misery for
another. There are a paycheck, less hunger and malnutrition, some
amenities, at last, to life, but there is also a deep sense of sadness
and loss that can amount, in my experience, to nothing less than
a kind of bereavement: so much is gone, a whole way of life, really;
and one never wanted that to happen—wanted simply to find work
and avoid virtual starvation.

At the start of the novel, as the six-year-old Rufus prepares to
go with his father to a Charlie Chaplin movie, the tension between
his mother's background and his father's comes across loud and
clear. What the father enjoys, the mother calls nasty and vulgar.
The mother is Anglo-Catholic, deeply pious, somewhat reserved,
most definitely a lady, a proper lady. Her father likes Thomas
Hardy novels, reads the *New Republic*, is an agnostic. Her father's
sister, Aunt Hannah, is intellectual, shrewd, and, more than that,
wise; her religious faith is less mystical than Mary's, less personal,
one wants to say, though these days there is the temptation to
summon words like *emotional* or even *hysterical*. The maiden aunt
has long since learned to remove herself in significant measure
from the faith she puts in God. Life is beyond anyone's comprehension, she realizes, but God is not to be turned on or denied on
that account—simply believed. She does not fight her brother's
disbelief, but she does seem made uncomfortable by her niece's
outbursts of proclaimed piety. Pride works in many ways; devotion
can conceal a self-centered, demanding streak of possessiveness:
I will give you my all, but hear it, see it, take notice of it—me, me,
me.

I carry Mary Follet too far, extrapolate the quality of her
religious faith to the point of caricature; but so does the author,
in his gentle but occasionally impatient way. Soon, all too soon,
that faith will be tested as never before: Jay Follet will be killed
in an automobile accident, and his wife left to bring up their son,
Rufus, and his four-year-old sister, Catherine. How such a woman
handles that test of God, how her son, especially, tries to comprehend what he sees and senses and overhears or is directly told
about the event, how a family comes to terms with itself—all of

that is the plot, meager enough, static perhaps, therefore a real challenge to a novelist. The tension that moves things along is obviously the anticipation: was Jay killed, how badly was he injured, did he come through it fine, his wife and parents and wife's aunt wonder through the hours of the night while the children sleep. But the larger tension is announced at the very beginning of the novel and persists (in the mind of the boy, Rufus) right through to the end: between the high-minded mother who is wont to use the word vulgar and the father who likes his liquor, has an openly sensual and earthy quality, and, we quickly learn, feels lonely and moody, even as he deeply loves his wife and children.

That tension suffuses the initial scene. The father and son have escaped together. They are at the movie, then they walk, then they enter a "market bar," then again walk. Later on they sit together on a rock in a dark vacant lot, watching the night, scanning the city's lights, noticing the stillness of the evening, broken occasionally by various sounds. Finally they approach home in silence, feeling so very close to each other. Yet also removed from each other; the boy can already feel his father gone, enveloped in the darkness, and that does not happen, one feels, because the author wants to come up with some hints or deal in overworked symbolism.

Agee knows that a disaster brings to focus and heightens the importance of what has preceded it, tragically, unexpectedly, the natural ups and downs of a person's life, a family's life, have to be tested and found either wanting or sufficient; and such a test can be as unfair and hard in its own way as the awful precipitating crisis. Agee had to begin somewhere, and it was not all that clever of him to give us a father and son intimately together for what turns out to be the last time. The psychological elements he chooses to emphasize before the phone rings, bringing Ralph's voice to his brother, Jay, with news of the grave illness of their father—Jay would go, find the news exaggerated, and die on his way home—are quite another matter: they are elements not every writer, however good, would choose to present so clearly and immediately, and they are also elements, I would argue, that in a few pages establish Agee's view of human nature. It is a view familiar to us of the twentieth century: the enormous influence of childhood is rather obviously stressed. It is also a view that theologians and philosophers from this or other centuries might

find altogether more satisfying than various experts in child development. What we now call a trauma is an occasion not for
psychological collapse or for growth in response to a crisis but
rather for the unfolding of grace in both old and young. A family
is enabled to regard itself rather closely and feel blessed as well as
stricken badly.

The Follet home is not a disturbed one. It is a home about to
be singled out for a premature disaster, but one has to be a rather
determined psychopathologist (who can, of course, always notice
something anywhere) to turn a basically sound marriage—indeed,
one glowing in the presence of two fine children—into a tangle of
disorder and disturbance. *A Death in the Family* is not an account
of Jay Follet's "long day's journey into night" as it is briefly
witnessed at the end by a six-year-old boy, then absorbed into his
own consciousness. Jay loves his wife and she loves him; and both
of them love their children. Still, there has been, and there continues to be, tension. The father no longer drinks as his brother,
Ralph, the undertaker, does, but as they walk after the movie he
tells Rufus, "Reckon I'll hoist me a couple," and worries that his
wife will find out.

The boy has to keep a secret, which the boy is glad to keep
because thereby he moves closer to his father. He *is* close, but he
also has felt "estranged." The author hastens to add, before we
make too much of it, "that there was really no division, no estrangement, or none so strong, anyhow, that it could mean much,
by comparison with the unity that was so firm and assured here."
As the two sit on the rock and take in the night's quiet and special
kind of light, they experience "a particular kind of contentment."
And yet, a few sentences on, we do learn (through the boy's sense
of things) that Jay is "more lonely than the contentment of this
family love could help." That love, which the boy sees and does
not have any reason to question, nevertheless "even increased his
father's loneliness, or made it hard for him not to be lonely."

What are we to make of all that? I doubt the psychiatric word
ambivalence will do. Not even *mixed feelings*, an older, less ominous way, maybe a more subtle way of putting things—mixtures
permit more leeway than valences—quite does justice to what Agee
seems to have in mind. He was writing at a time (the 1940s and
early 1950s) when a word like *estranged* was bound to be noticed;
it carries the reader into the heart of this midcentury's existentialist

thinking. But the word is overused, and used ironically; this is not *Nausea* or *The Stranger* or their antecedents, *The Trial* or *The Castle*. We are in Knoxville, and a man and his son are unmistakably enjoying each other's company in the evening after a good movie and a stop in a bar. No air of mystery or intrigue hovers over them. Nor is there any breast-beating or extended self-analysis. It is the child whose sensibility carries us along; we see what he senses, admittedly, in this scene, put into descriptive words by the author. Most of what the boy feels has to do with pleasure: his father is paying him loving attention, and he is glowing in response. For a second, though, it occurs to him that he feels different, because often his father was away, or preoccupied, but now he is here, unmistakably near and attentive.

Estrangement amounts, finally, to a child's awareness of a certain change in life's rhythm: one that is ordinary and unremarkable, not meant to be analyzed by a clinician or turned into a microcosm of man's alienation from himself. If anything, the scene is pastoral, and the novel's arrival in postwar America was something of an anachronism. At that time J. D. Salinger was writing about slightly older boys and youths, and *they* knew what estrangement was. Their acute and sophisticated religious and philosophical ordeals, accompanied by dramatic and complicated psychological seizures, often set in motion by the most innocuous of incidents, can only be contrasted with the brief time Rufus and his father had together, and, for that matter, the air of relative imperturbability the stricken Follet household conveys throughout the story, for all the grief expressed directly or indirectly.

A good deal is made of Agee's visual preoccupations; sections of this novel do indeed stimulate the reader to picture scenes in his mind—Knoxville, the hills, the sky, the houses and the care they receive.[3] And there is that Chaplin movie at the very beginning, a source of disagreement, then of sustained pleasure; in any case, not something casually attended. Agee the film critic has a fine time giving us an actor and his audience caught up with one another. I wonder, though, whether it is Agee's well-known camera-eye that is being indulged or whether this long-standing poet and short story writer, with a keen interest in life's complexities and

---

[3]For example, Kenneth Seib in *James Agee: Promise and Fulfillment* (Pittsburg, 1968) refers to "Agee's cinematic technique in the novel."

ironies that precedes his career as a movie critic or script writer, wasn't anxious to place us as firmly and subtly as he possibly could in a particular place and time.

We are constantly kept to a story; there is no larger theme, no lesson subtly or not so subtly worked in. In so doing Agee was no doubt immediately denying his readers much they may expect and feel themselves entitled to have: prompt speculation about the meaning of death; the beginning of a discussion of the way children grow up and come to terms with certain overwhelming and unexpected assaults; and maybe a remedy or two, or an example of what ought be said and done in this sophisticated, emotionally self-aware century. Nor are such gestures or obsessions so much to ask of a novelist; Thomas Mann outlived Agee, and before both of them there is a splendid tradition of avowedly philosophical and psychological novels that might have served to inspire a writer like Agee, who knew quite clearly who to live up to and what to gain sanction from.[4]

But he resisted; this is not a novel that concentrates its energies on states of mind, what they are like and how they are changed. Nor ought we say an author was nearly consumed by his many concerns, hence unable to give this novel of his the kind of sustained analytic attention its subject matter might otherwise have obtained. Agee was certainly a discursive writer, and a man rather easily distracted. Yet this is a tightly written novel. He intentionally refrains from using his characters to illustrate the unconscious at work in children or the torment an overworked conscience can bring to a bereaved wife. Even the lyric moments are kept under careful control, for Agee a considerable achievement. It is as if late in what was to be an all too short life he had found a demanding task that required a delicate balance of soft music and hardheaded storytelling; without the latter we would have one more psychiatric tract or a sentimental piece of writing about children, their special loveliness and sensitivity, their uncorrupted beauty, all of it destined to disappear when what psychologists call socialization has been completed. And a part of Agee may well have held to that notion until his last day on earth. I think we all do at moments,

---

[4]If *Let Us Now Praise Famous Men* is a thoroughly idiosyncratic work, it is full of references to writers, artists, literary struggles, artistic dilemmas, contemporary trends and tastes.

particularly when we look at a smiling, open child, and talk with
or hold him or her. Nostalgia carries us back. The need to find
some island of decency and attractiveness, some reliable source of
grace and perfection, gives the nostalgia an added boost. Much has
been made of that element in *A Death in the Family*, but only a
few sections, mostly the italicized ones placed by Agee's editors
at the ends of Parts I and II along with the section called "Knoxville: Summer 1915," written in 1938, contain much nostalgia,
and it is a highly qualified kind. In fact, some of the most fearful
and unnerving moments in the book accompany that nostalgia:
the father's brooding, incomprehensible silences, as recalled by an
older Rufus; the terror night can bring to a child; the nightmares
that give such terror unforgettable psychological substance; the
ominous family squabbles as they filter down to the child's mind.

Not that we aren't made to appreciate the appeal American life
of yesterday had; it was not just simpler then, but far less threatening. Neighbors were known and friendly. The country wasn't far
off, even if one lived in a city, let alone a small town, and many
cities were what we would now look upon as small towns. The
world didn't seem ready to end any minute or possibly in a year or
two. Water was pure. Air was clean. True, there was (there always
is) another side to be set down; even Knoxville must have had
some tenements, some areas that may not have been like Chicago's
west side or New York City's lower east side of that period but
were not like the neighborhood the Follets lived in, either, But the
author isn't claiming to speak on behalf of all families everywhere
in pre–World War I America. This is a modest novel, not a family
saga, not a book of social criticism made to fit the demands of
fiction.

Did Agee have *any* larger purposes in mind, one might reasonably
wonder—apart from telling a story that he knew well out of his
own life? I think he did, but it is a purpose that may be easier to
describe with negatives, because it is a purpose so at variance with
our expectations and our experience as readers and members of a
specific social and cultural tradition. Rufus Follet is no wise, un-
spoiled child of nature. He doesn't see miraculous things that
others, grown up and "fallen," miss. He is not troubled and therefore privy to secrets that escape the rest of us, who are normal
but complacent and all too well-adjusted. He is not a genius. He is
not a strange idiot with steaks of intuition or goodness that put

others to shame. He, is not an abused or hurt child whose suffering
has ennobled him. No social or political disaster has given him
knowledge beyond his years. When a psychological stress befalls
him he neither falls apart nor emerges remarkably intelligent and
discerning. He lacks animal cunning and even upon occasion that
guile children are famous for having.

Moreover, he and his sister can be ignored, found to be difficult,
bothersome, wrongheaded, obtuse—and rather than use such an
occasion to show how malicious, thoughtless, or uncaring older
people are, the narrator substantiates the rightness of their feelings
toward Rufus or Catherine. The children squabble, become petu-
lant, make life miserable for one another. But that, too, is not
given any special attention. They make up. They are devoted to
each other, too. In a similar vein, their father wants to be away
from them, is all taken up with his own thoughts and memories;
yet he still loves them dearly; and their mother can find them
annoying and troublesome without turning into a witch in their
eyes or a mixed-up monster in her own. Indeed, for a novel that is
not long and has been praised but called incomplete or unfinished,
A Death in the Family possesses a leisurely quality that can be
puzzling, even unnerving.

Eleanor Steber, who sang the music Samuel Barber composed
as a response of sorts to "Knoxville: Summer 1915," has recalled
how a cultured German friend of hers felt about Agee's prose:
"To her, it could all have been simplified into a matter-of-fact
sentence or two."[5] No doubt any novel can be, including *Budden-
brooks*. But Agee could write short lean sentences when he wished;
and he certainly, as a poet and short story writer, could condense
his thoughts and give them tightly drawn metaphysical expression.
Nor was he a stranger to action, movement. The very quality in
him of the script writer and movie critic must have driven him to
wonder whether one incident, a death that is first held possible,
then found to be actual, could properly sustain a full-length novel.
That German lady, had she gone through all of *A Death in the
Family*, might have become even more bored and confused: no
drama; no real events (even the death is reported secondhand, and

[5]So we are told on the record jacket of Samuel Barber's *Knoxville: Summer of 1915*.
Formerly available on Columbia Records, MS5843, it is now to be found on Odyssey
Records, 32160230.

by the time we get the news we are exhausted, as are the characters themselves, by the long vigil, the accompanying talk and more talk, much of it seeming to lead the characters and us nowhere in particular).

We are not to be given a catharsis for our tensions, any more than the individuals in the Follet family get one—yet an additional service this novel fails to provide. Nor are the grown-up people any more transformed than the children. It has been said that Mary Follet becomes toward the end of the book less strenuously mystical, less given to pieties that have a way of being self-serving: all those to whom they are addressed are made to know how much they need to be told, to hear, to begin living up to. I am not so sure. At the very end of the book little Catherine wanders about her grandparents' house, grouchy and sullen out of fear and bewilderment. She hears her mother and Aunt Hannah speaking behind a closed door. They are praying. Rather, Hannah is going along with her niece's desire to pray—and pray and pray. Eventually, though, the very religious Hannah has had enough: "Mary, my dear, let's stop." No, the mother doesn't want to stop. But Hannah persists, sensing an overwrought religious inclination that will help neither the soul or the mind.

As for the others, they give not an inch, not during the long wait for news of Jay Follet and not afterwards, as his burial is prepared for, then witnessed. Agee is not going to let them mature in response to the adversity fate has brought. Mary's father is a doubter and will doubt even more when pressure toward belief mounts. It is in the very nature of intellectualized skepticism to mount when challenged head-on. That is why Pascal, in the end, gave up trying to win over by reason and argument those like himself and instead wryly used the almost sacrilegious image of the wager: everything to gain and nothing, really, to lose. Likewise, Kierkegaard could believe that a leap toward faith might mysteriously be made by anyone—and maybe was more likely by a man unattached to the stupefying, prideful religious routines that make a mockery, he believed, of true Christianity.

Perhaps Pascal would have persisted and got somewhere with old Mr. Lynch. Perhaps Kierkegaard might have one day had him capable of an Abraham-like kind of sacrificing resignation: you took my son, Lord; take my other son; take anyone and everyone— only know that I believe in you still. Certainly, Kierkegaard would

respect Mr. Lynch more than the Anglo-Catholic minister, Father
Jackson, who refuses to read the full service over Jay Follet's body
because he had not been baptized. And, alas, Kierkegaard would
likely have found Mary Lynch's faith unconvincing; she was helped
too much by the likes of Father Jackson, all of which Rufus comes
to appreciate in an important scene in the novel. The child sees
his mother go off with the smug but consoling priest, and ever so
gently the author suggests a kind of seduction. Kierkegaard never
gave any indication that he confused seduction with resignation.
One suspects, actually, that if Kierkegaard had to choose someone
in the Follet family as a possible candidate for the leap he talks
about—even to the point of "teleological suspension of the ethical,"
a willingness to do the impossible, the blatantly wrong, at God's
urging—the dubious (to a secular mind) honor would go to Aunt
Hannah, not because she seems so confident and believing a Christian, but because she knows anguish, experiences doubt, refuses
to cover up her sense of anger: that it should have happened, that
it should have been *allowed* to happen.[6]

The morning after Jay Follet hurriedly left to be beside his
ailing father, Mary Follet explains to her two children why their
father is not at breakfast: the old grandfather up in the hills is sick,
and there comes a time when "God lets you go to sleep and
you can't see people any more." The children respond with their
version of that kind of event. A cat named Oliver had died. Did he
go to heaven? Their perplexed mother says yes, to "a part of
heaven God keeps specially for cats." But then there were the
rabbits, what about *them*? Well, of course they died and went up
there, too. But Rufus won't let the matter drop. He reminds his
mother that the rabbits had died by violence, "all hurt and bloody,
poor things." Why do such things happen, why does God let them
happen? Rufus asks that question and his mother is prepared: in

---

[6]There is a valuable psychoanalytic and sociological literature devoted to the effect
of death on families, and especially children. Particularly important and comprehensive
is Sylvia Anthony's *The Discovery of Death in Childhood and After* (New York, 1972).
Anna Freud's landmark work during the second world war also ought be mentioned:
War and Children (New York, 1944). Of related interest is *Children and the Death of a
President*, ed. M. Wolfenstein and G. Kliman (New York, 1965). Needless to say, much
that these social scientists describe, Agee has his own (the novelist's) way of evoking.
The efforts are complementary, not antagonistic. Miss Freud's sensibility is very much
akin to Agee's: compassionate, yet knowing and without illusions about the child's more
demanding and vexing side.

essence the child is told that his ways are not ours, but he does have a design, a "plan" she calls it. Someday we will know, but not now, not ever as mere mortals.

The boy wonderfully, quickly, innocently, unpretentiously, correctly comes back at her: "What good would it do *Him*?" The mother parries the question, tries to get the boy to get on with his eating, insists that in time everything will become clear. The boy, out of respect for her, and maybe out of a kind of hopefulness and faith in God he himself cannot express to his mother or anyone else—certainly not himself—offers a way out of the dilemma, again with bold, direct concreteness: the dogs sneaked in when God wasn't looking, and killed the rabbits; had God been watching, he never would have allowed that flagrant injustice to take place.

But no, Mary Lynch cannot permit either her children or herself that line of thinking. God is everywhere, knows everything. But so is the devil, who tempts us, all the time does so. The children are not satisfied, though. They want to know what *tempt* means. They want to know why God can't overrule the devil. They want to know what the point of it is, all the suffering and misery, the rabbits killed by cruel dogs, the free choice their mother, in desperation, had to come up with as the justification for suffering. (The need "to know good from bad and be good of our own free choice.") The children sense all too clearly that even as dogs and rabbits have no choice in the matter—they are fated to be as they are, be strong or vulnerable with respect to one another—so, often enough, there is absolutely no choice involved in tragedy, simply its presence, abrupt, awful, and terribly confounding. Eventually the children elicit from their mother a declaration of pride, an expression of the Puritan ethic that would make both Pascal and Kierkegaard (for different reasons) smile: "God doesn't believe in the easy way," she tells them after they have told her that, really, it would be a lot easier, all around, if these instances of gross injustice and gratuitous brutality were banished by the all-powerful God. The narrator notes "a certain triumph" in the mother's voice as she tells her children what I have just quoted. But that is not the end of the scene. The children are relentless. They will not be content with abstractions. Whatever God believes has to be translated (by them, for themselves) into a human situation they can comprehend. Catherine suggests the analogy of "hide-and-go-seek" and in doing so makes her mother anxious. The mother also is silenced, because it is rather a startling and apposite analogy. Rufus now takes up his mother's previous posture and unwittingly but effectively caricatures it. No, something all that important cannot, must not, be reduced to child's play. "Hindnseek's just a *game*, just a *game*," he shouts. "God doesn't fool around playing *games*," he insists.

By this time Catherine is hopelessly destroyed. All she was trying to do was understand, and her brother has scorned that effort mercilessly. Nor did it help that her mother, for her own reasons, came to her defense. Perhaps she sensed that her mother was in fact scandalized by the analogy and by the new life Rufus had given it by the vehemence of his mockery. What he was denying and laughing at he was covertly saying might just be a sensible or fitting thing to think. So, in no time a daughter's tears also confront Mary Follet, and she quickly turns on Rufus, to his great surprise, and does her best to end forthrightly the entire breakfast table discussion.

Obviously a mother can enforce her will under such circumstances. But Agee does something rather interesting at this point. A discussion that revolved around the issue of violence ends with a kind of violence. The mother gets her son off to school, but he is full of anger at his sister and jealous of her because she has obtained their mother's sympathy if not favor. Meanwhile, Catherine is not about to pull herself together. All efforts at consolation fail, and the scene ends with "a roar of angry tears" from her and both of her fists brought down on her plate.

Animals inexplicably set upon one another. Among them the strong take advantage of the weak. Instinct prevails. Justice seems to be wanting. And among us there is a certain resonance to all that; one can even hear that resonance at a table in a decent, comfortable, God-fearing home. A conversation about God's purposes turns into a demonstration of man's nature: a mother's defensiveness, dogmatism, pride; a little boy's capacity to size up the grown-up world's confusions and use them craftily and provocatively; a little girl's hurt feelings, which can suddenly turn into unappeasable fury and which can stimulate retaliatory anger, not to mention a more chronic bitterness, anxiety, and sadness. We are not told how Rufus felt that day at school; Agee feels no need to insist upon explicit psychological analysis. But in a brief moment of the novel, a moment incidental to its entire thrust, we are made to look at an enactment, it might be called, of the issues that have plagued Christian and secular philosophers for centuries.

To make clear his intent, Agee follows that scene with another very much like it. Now it is Jay and his brother, Ralph, who work upon one another; and what we learn of them is a distinct echo of what we have learned about Rufus and Catherine and their mother. It turns out that Ralph has needlessly called his brother; their father is not yet ready to die. As a result Jay feels angry at his brother, but also sorry for him. The brother, in turn, feels angry at himself and sorry for himself—and in need of finding others to blame and feel blamed by. Agee is brilliant at getting into the head of such a person and narrating what goes on there. A monologue would have been easier, but he shuns it. The author's educated, sophisticated comments would have been welcome and appropriate, but he shuns them. Again, he sticks to his story at all costs. A textbook of psychopathology comes across in the alcoholic, self-defeating, hill-country mind of Ralph Follet. He is no villain, not even a full-fledged failure; simply a weak and occasionally stupid man who—we are back to Rufus and Catherine and their mother—feels he has never been loved enough by his mother, respected enough by his father.

The human nature Hobbes took for granted and Augustine confessed to meeting up with all the time in himself shows its powerful authority over this not especially unusual or even willful man from the eastern part of Tennessee. He probably struggled to write even a letter, never mind treatises and essays and long autobiographical confessions—or novels. But he knew how to feel envy and shame and lust and pettiness and rivalry. He also knew how to turn on his neighbor (by calling him a "poor-white-trash-son-of-a-bitch") and on his brother, too. As one gains a sense of this man, one wonders whether Cain was qualitatively any worse, only more driven, or, maybe, just less able to restrain himself than Ralph was. No murderer, he drinks to great excess, cheats on his wife, and takes care of the dead. Indirectly he is responsible for his brother's death. Jay was angry at being called for no good reason; Ralph was drunk when he made the call and clearly was hurrying his father's death along.

Against such a background the ride back home must have been taxing, much as Jay loved to be alone with his thoughts and speed through the night. One never knows with crashes, and James Agee is not the author to saddle us with an accident-prone personality, even to the point of indicating that anger can lead to self-absorption or to a kind of fierce wish, to be away from one place and near another, a wish that indirectly expresses itself in distracted, careless driving. All we can surmise, enough perhaps, is that a chain of events initiated by a sullen, resentful, death-minded (in several respects) brother ended up in Jay's fatal road accident. Where does one draw the line between outright murder and a murderousness of mind that leads to another's death? Obviously there is a distinction; only the least discriminating psychologist or psychiatrist will fail to applaud those who have learned to fight their wars, deal with their grudges and worse, within the confines of their own minds, as opposed to those who blatantly translate impulse into deed.

But as Agee's novel suggests, clear-cut lines are not so easily drawn. What seems as inexorable and unfathomable as fate itself can be traced down to specific, avoidable events—words spoken here, decisions made there, whole situations (dangerous, even lethal ones) produced when they needn't have been. And in desperation we ask where is the end of it all—and the beginning? What meaning do these apparently arbitrary and gratuitous events have? Who sets what in motion? God? Human nature? Infamous social institutions? And will God respond to our entreaties? Will human nature yield to the scientific advances ("insight," therapy) we make on it? Will our social institutions improve as we work on them—to the point that there are fewer and fewer harassed, denied people and, as a result, fewer and fewer acts of desperation, let alone murder?

At the very least Ralph's phone call was an act of self-deception; but by the time we have heard his mind out, we are entitled to refer to an act of desperation. We are allowed to take no solace, however, in the obvious limits of his personality. If he needs his white trash, we may well need the likes of him in order to escape notice of ourselves. Right after Ralph's story pours out through an almost uncanny mixture of his own and the narrator's words, Rufus is back before us; he has gone on a shopping trip with his Great-Aunt Hannah. "Ralph is the baby, Ralph is the baby" we have just heard spoken by none other than Ralph himself. Now Rufus shows us how dignified and grown-up a six year old can be; and, of course, we applaud. But rather soon we are let down. The child's unfailing good sense is not turned into an overworked foil, a means of showing how ironic things are: full-grown infants, like Ralph, and adults scarcely more than half a decade old, like Rufus.

Agee is intensely curious about people; and he is unwilling to see them as all-anything—only a mixture of characteristics, one that varies, but within limits. So, if we would only let him, Ralph can win us over with his honesty, his openness about himself. If he is a bumbling lush. who is tempted to be more calculatingly mean than he sometimes inadvertently is, he at least comes clean about himself as he grabs a drink, then admits his weakness, his various failings. No one would think to call him a hypocrite. Nor would anyone think to call Rufus the many bad things Ralph calls himself; but Aunt Hannah does get to think of the boy, even if only for a passing moment, as motivated by "fear and hypocrisy." Those are strong words for a loving and generous-spirited aunt to apply to a lovable and well-behaved boy. Rufus wanted a cap, and his mother wanted him not to have one. Aunt Hannah wants to buy him one, and he is by no means reluctant to take her up on her offer. The boy's willfulness is natural, his mother's possessiveness not uncommon. By the time Agee is through with the scene, however, willfulness emerges as something else, even in a child: at the very least, a prelude to possible evil.

The maiden lady and her young escort take the streetcar downtown and have a fine time together. We have another one of the novel's asides, a poignant spell rendered with humor, affection, and restraint by the author. (Nowhere in his writing career does Agee set himself up more directly for a moment of permissible sentimentality, only to walk away clear headed and in control of not only his characters but his own voice as well.) Rufus gets his cap, and it is full of color and extravagance of design. His mother, in a way, will not be disappointed; and for different reasons, his aunt takes somewhat concealed pleasure in the choice. If Mary would soon enough have "conniption fits" and then feel the pleasure of self-righteousness, Hannah had on her expedition with Rufus another kind of pleasure, the defiance of an authority felt to be, at least in this instance, unreasonable. Yet, as the two of them go their way—like in a ballet, they wander off for their own psychological purposes into their own worlds, then come back joyfully and gratefully to each other—there are moments for second thoughts. The boy is embarrassed by his own greed: he knows he wanted that cap, and all the talk and browsing about beforehand is necessary etiquette. When at last Aunt Hannah brings the subject up, Rufus is tongue-tied and blushes. On the other hand, his aunt notices something else, his coyness, the pretense he goes through as he first chooses a hat he knows she will like (whereupon "she smelled the fear and hypocrisy") and then goes on to his real preference, urged in that direction by her.

There is no point turning this touching moment in a novel that does its best to stay away from sermons into one of them. Nevertheless, in the midst of innocence and loving-kindness one encounters quite other emotions. The boy covets. He is stubborn. He shows guile, enough of it to make his aunt think the word *hypocrisy*. He is not beyond rubbing things in, testing authority already found lenient, if reluctantly so. And his aunt can find herself skeptical and distrustful; she sees all too clearly what the boy is doing, less clearly what the complexity of her own motives has brought about. She imagines the boy's mother angered and horrified at him and what he has chosen to have for himself. Nervously she presses on, lets the boy make his decision; but it is her own complicity that frightens her more than anything the boy may do or the mother object to. And such complicity, even in those quite wise, observant, and self-aware, can be expressed both unwittingly and deviously.

By the same token Rufus's bedroom—the boy is having trouble going to sleep, the father is devotedly at his side—would seem an equally inauspicious occasion for an analysis of the variability of human nature, yet that is what happens. Rufus has had a bad dream and has awakened crying. Relatives are there (this is a flashback scene, before the father's last automobile trip) and so both mother and father are impatient as well as concerned when they hear the child's cries. The father goes, talks with the boy, soothes him, sings to him, and shows how tender and patient he can be. The boy responds, and we seem headed for a quick end to an unexceptional but sensitively rendered moment. Once more, however, Agee won't let the matter drop at such a point. It is as if he wants to probe the very sentiment that tempts him. He has the father's mind wander back to his own childhood—a good novelist's way of doing things that at first glance promises us an occasion for legitimate nostalgia. But the result of Jay's reverie is that we are as surprised and jolted as he unquestionably was.

Jay's reverie begins sensually; he sees a great cedar, recalls the color of limestone and clay. He smells wood smoke. Then his mother's face appears, and he feels her hand on his forehead. He hears her voice, telling him not to fret. Now his mind goes back even further. *She* must have once been a child. One who comforts has herself or himself been comforted. As he tries to comprehend the succession of generations, mothers and fathers nourishing and soothing and encouraging children, who in turn become mothers and fathers, he goes back, eventually, to the beginning: "right on back to Adam, only no one did it for him, or maybe did God?" His next thought is this: "How far we all come. How far we all come away from ourselves. So far, so much between, you can never go home again." Well, he thinks, maybe you can, maybe there is one slim chance: "You have a boy or a girl of your own, and now and then you remember, and you know how they feel, and it's almost the same as if you were your own self again, as young as you could remember." But he changes his mind: that is not quite going back to one's *own* childhood; once we grow up, we lose forever the sense of security and timelessness that are so much a part of childhood, or at least the childhood many, if not all, children experience.

At the very moment Jay is most poignantly aware of what he has forever lost, the presence of his sleeping son notwithstanding, the narrator introduces a dramatic shift: "He felt thirsty, and images of stealthiness and deceit, of openness, anger and pride immediately possessed him, and immediately he fought them off." He tries to pull himself together. He will never get drunk again, he vows. He is so angry and upset with himself that he threatens to kill himself if he resumes heavy drinking. This oath, with its accompanying expression of a serious threat to his life, enables him to feel better about the future—and about himself. Interestingly, the narrator links Jay's recovered self-respect with his earlier childhood reverie this way: "He felt consciously strong, competent both for himself and against himself, and this pleasurable sense of firmness contended against the perfect and limpid remembrance he had for a moment experienced, and tried sadly, vainly, to recapture it." The effort failed, leaving him only with sadness. He stared into space, and when his wife came into the room to check up on things, he felt a "spasm of rage and alarm," which prompted shame in him.

Here, as mentioned, Agee has tempted himself with the sentimental and banal, only to skirt both and come up with an original, at times painfully uncompromising sketch that aims at presenting ourselves to ourselves, warts and all. Jay can have such fond memories, yet in the midst of them he gets thirsty, and soon his head is a jumble of bad, unsettling things. He recovers, but that recovery contended against the delicious initial moments of the reverie—to no avail. If Jay were going to get back to that home none of us can reach, once we have left it and grown up, he would yet again have to face the deterioration and near collapse he has for a moment felt and regarded and fought to a standstill, not for the first time, not (so far as he knows) for the last, either. He is, consequently, sad on several accounts: what seemed so wonderful wasn't only wonderful but a mixture of good moments and thoroughly upsetting, awful ones, and there is no way to separate such things, hold on to the one and bury once and for all the other; the better situated we are, psychologically, the less disposed is our mind to take the risk of going back, bringing up fond memories only to be confronted with painful ones. What applies to him applies to his boy, there asleep near him—one day he, too, may try for his own reasons to recapture the very moment they were both going through and, in so doing, feel as well in the grip of pain and fear and deep regret; and, finally, however well-composed we are, there *is* a continuing life (with irony at its core) that those long-forgotten experiences have. They enable a man like Jay to be his child's comforter, but they also interrupt him as he goes about doing so, cheat him of the fullness of pleasure he was experiencing and, worst of all, serve notice on him that they are around for good, even as his better side is a constant in his life and in the lives of his wife and children, hence that heaviest of sadness a resigned combatant finds himself feeling—when he isn't girding himself or simply going about the business of living, sure that he is, for the most part, a successful combatant, a winner not a loser, but a winner who knows he can't take too much for granted, because old enemies have a way of cropping up, out of nowhere it seems.

Agee can write long, long sentences, sentences that have a way of becoming a paragraph or two; and I am afraid I have just felt his influence. But there is in this scene I have tried to understand a certain connectedness or intactness that makes a reader want to respond similarly, shun the ordinary conventions of writing in order to draw together all the novelist has insisted must, inevitably, go together. The mind may crave distinctions, separations, a stop to this surge of emotion, a suspension of that line of thinking, but the mind also defies itself, insists upon what it tries to shunt aside, even runs amok just at the point it strives for coherence—and when it has found that coherence is detached enough, resigned enough, to realize only too well the price paid. Nor do I believe Adam's appearance in Jay's reverie to be only a historical marker, a name that means something like this: when you try to push yourselves and the rest of humanity back over the millenia, I am here waiting, a person whose name and reported existence can mean for you the beginning of things, the person beyond whom one can't go back any further. Jay not only goes back to Adam, he speculates about him. What was Adam's childhood like? Who caressed him, sang to him, looked at him with eyes full of parental affection, nodded to him, smiled upon him again and again as he hesitated, faltered, stumbled, picked up again and moved on? Agee knew his Bible, of course: "And the Lord God planted a garden eastward in Eden; and there he put the man whom he had formed." On the other hand, Adam is such an enigma to us not only because he lived so far off in time but because he was set down, all developed, it seems—in contrast to Jesus, whose birth and childhood and mother we know something about, enough perhaps to kindle our imaginations as well as reassure us that yes, God he was, but also a man, who was born, admired much, even resented, and so carried into exile by Joseph and Mary.

The word *formed* can be interpreted broadly—or overinterpreted to suit our convenience. Agee's religious training was considerable and his Biblical preoccupations ended only with his life. He knew that, at the very least, Adam received instruction from the Lord. He knew that Adam was taken by God, put in the garden, told "to dress it and keep it"; and was also told what *not* to do, under penalty of death. Still curious, apparently not told enough by Scripture, Agee kept wondering about Adam, who was so alone, given so much, given the whole world (the garden), but who was also warned sternly.

The childhood of Adam: the kind of speculation Kierkegaard would not shun or, in our time, Karl Barth. The childhood of Adam: something quite appropriate for Jay Follet also to think about as his mind moves from bliss momentarily recalled to a chain of disasters that were—how to make sense of them?—inextricably part of that bliss. No, one has to be more demanding about the way it is put, and say not only "part of," but a "necessary part of." All of which ought make us ask, with just as much ironic pointedness, what it was like for Adam, not only as a child, but much later on, after he and Eve were found out. The transgressor is that among other things. What he does wrong (apart from the suffering it can cause, for him as well as others) affects the life of his "goodness," makes demands upon a side of his mind and spirit that would have wanted events to turn out otherwise; hence the regret, the sorrow, the guilt, the wish to offer restitution and the sadness that often enough it is not possible to do so. And hence the resolve to make amends some other way, to be a different, a better person, followed by a continuing demonstration that one is not quite becoming that new person—and on and on.

Faith aside (for the sake of discussion, not because faith can ever be put aside, and there are many kinds of faith), it can be argued that Adam indeed didn't have a childhood, even as we are left by Genesis to wonder whether there would ever have been such a thing as childhood, had the Fall not taken place. To be a child, as Agee keeps emphasizing in this novel, is to need help, yet in time want to push aside that help. To be a child, any child, not only a boy destined to be a Jay Follet or, for that matter, an out-and-out alcoholic is to thirst: I want to taste life; I want to try this and this and this; and only for a while do I get filled up, so that I can sleep, or feel calm, satisfied and reflective (so grown-up!). In a flash I am ready again—for more. If I am denied I virtually succumb to thirst; all my considerable resources of mind bend to its satisfaction, and so the "stealthiness," the "deceit," the "anger and pride" Agee has Jay remember so painfully as they interrupt his nostalgic flashback.

As if to indicate that he really means business, Agee follows up Jay's reverie with the boy Rufus's actual experience: he lies in bed; he is sung to by his mother; he hears her "soft and shining" voice; he watches her "dear gray eyes." Once more we are offered a brief and disarming moment out of an author's largeness of soul. (I don't know how else to say it.) But once more an almost beatific vision is interrupted; the child senses sadness in the midst of joy. If there is a time when all is fine, when both parents are singing together or, alternately, when the world is immaculate, then there is also a time when "a feeling that things might go wrong" descends on the boy. He remembers. He has in the past overheard things. Agee, not averse to a good stretch of words to make things clear, gives us a one-word summary and sentence: "Whiskey."

After whiskey, after that scene in which we are a second time confronted with the mixed blessing that even the happiest moments in childhood turn out to be, yet another confusing situation comes up, this time with Rufus the intensely curious son who knows full well something is afoot, but not what. His mother has been behaving differently. The child has watched her in the apparently casual way children do and tried to reach his conclusions. "He felt subtly lonely," and so watched all the more closely: she could be unusually attentive one minute, then hopelessly withdrawn the next. He saw her grow, saw people either look closely or avoid looking with a degree of determination he could not miss. He wanted to know. He had been told it was a surprise, it was coming, he would soon enough find out. But he could not wait; he thirsted. He turned the house upside down, within his limits as a child, and brought his curiosity to his parents' attention. In front of him they disagree; they do not argue, but neither do they just converse. The mother refuses to tell Rufus, no matter how strongly his father says to go ahead, let him know. The boy is disappointed, still in the grip of his frustrated desire to find out.

A large black woman, Victoria, who had cared for him when he was much younger, arrives and begins to help the mother out. Victoria loves Rufus and is loved by him. So much loved that Rufus tells his mother that "Victoria smells awful good." He is told not to say anything like that in front of Victoria. Victoria is colored, Rufus's mother tells him, and colored people are sensitive. The boy seems to understand. He faithfully repeats words his mother asks him to say, as children do—as grown-ups do, too. Then he is left alone with her. His mother has gone off to get that surprise (his sister, Catherine), and he is told she will be back soon enough with it. The two go for a walk (headed for Rufus's grandparents). Rufus turns to Victoria, whom he likes so much, and asks her, "Why is your skin so dark?" He immediately thereafter feels her wince, feels her withdraw from him. He is saddened. She is silent. Then she gathers herself, turns to him, lets him know something about this world, about her world, and his world and the difference between the two and the effect that difference has upon the way people hear various remarks or questions, like the one he has just put to her. The boy tells her what she knows; he didn't intend any meanness. She reassures him. They draw close, but it is now a more complicated closeness: "A silence opened up around them in which he felt at once great space, the space almost of darkness itself; and great peace and comfort." As she talked to him "he felt she was not talking exactly to him." Yet, she *was* talking to him, and in her wonderful, untalkative way, her way with a gesture, a reach, a touch, she won him over—somewhat. Curiosity was Adam's undoing. Curiosity prompts defiance. Curiosity lives on; every child grows through it, and through it also stumbles and falls (and hurts people).

With that incident over, we are plunged relentlessly into the novel's actual event, a death in Rufus's family. At all costs Rufus has to be protected from knowledge of that, too; he and Catherine are not allowed at the funeral, though another outsider, this time a man and white, Walter Starr, does drive the children nearby and lets them catch a glimpse from a distance. Curiosity is the essence of childhood, Agee keeps insisting. Why did God tempt Adam and Eve with their capacity for curiosity? Agee knows enough not to answer such a riddle. But as a novelist he can evoke, rather than document, what might have happened, psychologically, long ago. Told not to do something when it is inexplicable to him why he should not, Rufus fairly soon disobeys. His dander is up. He has been made curious. He simply said something; had it been ignored he might have gone on to the next remark, and that would have been that. But no, he was challenged, and in a way he both could and could not understand. How many of us, of any age and in any decade, have known how to cross the barriers of racial etiquette, say what we honestly believe, feel confident that our goodwill is appreciated? Racially connected rhetoric, distrust, and malice may be out on the table now in American life, but that enormous and decent maid Victoria lets Rufus know that even a preschool child of four (his age when his sister Catherine was born) is not exempt from certain responsibilities and, if they are not discharged, certain penalties.

Without question Rufus not only indulged his curiosity, he asserted himself, defied his mother; and, I suppose I would have to add, expressed a certain bitterness at being left by her, especially under such mysterious circumstances. And when Victoria makes the boy feel she has turned away from him, hurt by what he asked and caused her unwittingly to feel, the boy appreciates what willfulness and maybe a degree of angry self-pity can set in motion. The analogy with Adam and Eve in the Garden of Eden is not hard to make, especially since the whole incident is so very much related to a mother's last days of pregnancy, her reluctance to discuss nature's secrets with a boy almost aflame with the desire to find out.

Agee goes back and forth between Rufus and his encounters with the world, on the one hand, and, on the other, the grown-ups and their various maneuvers in the face of a difficult set of circumstances; by the end of the novel one is not sure there is really any difference between the two modes of adjustment. The longest single section of the novel has to do with waiting. Is Jay alive or dead, and if alive, altogether safe or somewhat injured or badly injured? Agee uses that occasion to develop his characters; under the strain they reveal themselves and, to an extent, find out things about themselves they had not suspected. The family is genteel, respectable in a fairly relaxed way. They are not casually rich or once but no longer rich—shabby genteel; but neither are they nervously respectable, apt to become nasty or hateful if pushed hard by fate. They seem able to tolerate one another's individuality, a trait I have often seen in Appalachian hill people and those who live in cities near the hills, and a trait for some reason ignored in many psychological or sociological analyses of the region's people.[7] They are decent and kind to one another; they rally round as a family, and Agee is a master at showing courtesy, consideration, and affection as they come across in the smallest of exchanges. At the same time he wants to distinguish between Mary and her brother, Andrew, also, between Mary's father and mother and her Aunt Hannah, even as he wants, also, to show how chance (in this case, the worst of luck) can level people psychologically, bring out in them certain shared habits of thought and action. As a result the Follets merge into one another, but they also remain distinct, remain, in a way, types, though their peculiarities and inner contradictions, fortunately, rescue them from that fate.

---

[7]The Follet and Lynch families very much resemble the people of Tennessee and other parts of Appalachia I have worked with; in *Migrants, Sharecroppers, Mountaineers* (Boston, 1972) a Knoxville youth speaks at some length.

Much attention, necessarily, is devoted to Mary. She never loses faith; she may say she is "unprepared," she may at times look like "an astounded child," she may reveal her anxiety in withdrawal or plaintiveness or impatience, but she is the believer, maybe not Kierkegaard's, but the church's. And if one starts becoming condescending toward her, Agee has invited it—but also demanded a much more respectful appreciation of her strength and decency. The author refuses to turn on a suffering, beleaguered person who has caused no one any harm but seems singled out for the cruelest of life's blows. But the fact is that even virtuous people, caught up in an aching moment in their collective existence as a family, cannot for more than a brief spell sustain decorum or, for that matter, unblemished solidarity. Mary's faith begins to offend Aunt Hannah, to the point that she thinks to herself: "God is not here," then asks his forgiveness for what she has told herself. She is not repentant, though. A moment later she thinks even worse of her niece, whom she loves so very much: "Something mistaken, unbearably piteous, infinitely malign was at large within that faithfulness." She is appalled that she can think like that, declares herself (to herself) a person of no faith ("I believe nothing"). She prays hard, yet the "malign was still there, as well as the mercifulness."

As they wait for Andrew to return with news, the three old people and the increasingly desperate young wife and mother not only take each other's measure but begin to get voluble, a touch hysterical, and more and more like children: "Mary, whispering, 'Excuse me,' retired to the bathroom, affronted—humbled that one should have to obey a call at such a time; she felt for a few moments as stupid and enslaved as a baby on its potty, and far more ungainly and vulgar." She gazes in the mirror, as children often do, intent on seeing themselves for a change, subjecting themselves to the same hard look they give others, or intent on a bit of self-admiration after a period of self-doubt. She whistles in the dark, conjures up stories and situations that suit her fancy. Meanwhile her great-aunt does her one better: "Hannah, left alone, was grateful that we are animals; it was this silly, strenuous, good, humble cluttering of animal needs which saw us through sane, fully as much as prayer."

Mary Follet's mother is already so much a child. She is virtually deaf, cut off from the world, unable to deal with its moment-to-moment fluctuations. She is pampered, talked down to, held up on a pedestal, regarded as of very little help in a crisis, worried over and protected. As with children, so very often, her resources are grossly underestimated, and one of the results of her son-in-law's death is that her husband, at last, finds that out: "her immense and unbreakable courage." Nor is he immune to characteristics adults presume to ascribe to children. He buries himself in his own habits and concerns, enough so that his reading of the *New Republic* becomes not very much different from his wife's deafness. When alone they are enraged with one another, if jolted from their privacy and the protection it afforded; but they are invariably polite, and all the annoyance or worse gets turned into a further consolidation of the insulating arrangements that have worked so well in the past. They pout and fret and test one another. They feel desires to tease, resist them, turn impatience into carefully measured courtesy but fume underneath. Back to the *New Republic*; back to mending; back to their respective rooms and sanctuaries they send one another, each the child to the other.

Then there is Andrew, who goes to find out what has happened to his brother-in-law and brings back word of him; Andrew, who later on hovers over the mourning family, helpful and pleasant one minute, bitterly skeptical or critical the next. He possesses undeniable decency; but he also is shut off—restrained, one comes to believe, not only by the occasion, but by his grandiosity and self-absorption. Preoccupied with his own ideas, he makes the attention people give each other seem like an enormous waste of energy. Yet Andrew is the one who can spot in a flash what the rest never see or see only with the greatest difficulty and pain. Hannah gradually becomes aware of the excesses of her niece's piety; but she never loses sight of the precipitating event. Who is to decide what is appropriate for the extraordinary? Andrew, of course; he is not loath to decide many things, and all of those decisions have to run through the filter of his "cold and bitter incredulity," which manages to catch rather a lot. And God knows, the Folletts need his hard eye. If his father ever had the same eye, it is now, at the very least, turned inward. Let the editors of the *New Republic* find dishonesty and hypocrisy everywhere; and let Thomas Hardy brood about mankind through his various heroes and heroines.

Andrew is no misanthrope, however, though he is tempted. His struggle against cold self-centeredness becomes, at last, obvious and moving. And, finally, even he openly becomes a child as he walks home with Rufus and shares with the boy a sense of confusion that in Andrew's case is a welcome sign that the limits of self-righteousness and all too assured intellectuality have been reached, if not forced to recede. Even before the funeral Andrew has begun to forsake some of his proud rationality. As the Follets sit and face one another, certain now that Jay is dead, Mary feels his "presence." So does Hannah. Mary's father begins to talk about thought-transference, and her mother is too cut off to hear, let alone realize fully what they are talking about. Andrew guardedly gets interested—drawn in to a prevailing mood is perhaps the way to put it. He is not convinced, but he is not aloof, either. Maybe— maybe there are mysteries best appreciated even if not turned into objects of faith. Without any negative implication, it can be said that with Andrew's partial acceptance of what is now a family mood, the Follets are all for a while children: especially open to suggestion; able to wish for something and, one way or another, find it; tinder for one another's emotional sparks, which are by no means long in coming. Before a calamity they have become awed. They also have become appealing and difficult, as children are wont to be, sometimes simultaneously.

After we witness the child in full-grown people come forth in different guises, our attention is again diverted to children, this time a crowd of them, whom Rufus watches and meets up with and in several ways reveals to us. They are for him admirable and enviable: a little older, solidly in school, even if, at eight or nine not free of home. They have a swagger to them, an air of almost limitless confidence in their ability to take on anyone and everything. The boy isn't only caught up with them; even from a distance he sees the "hatred and scorn" in the boys—of a free-floating kind that is looking for a target. (He will certainly do!) But in them he also sees a forecast of himself, and he is captivated. He approaches them, gives himself to them, really. And they take him. They lure him, lead him astray, and with a kind of senseless enthusiasm betray him. It isn't just name-calling (his name, Rufus, earns him "Nigger," among other things); he recognizes a sinfulness in those children—no psychological word does quite so well. The children are not bigots. They are not maladjusted or disturbed.

Nor is Agee out to present us with a view of the evil youngster or the innocent one who only appears to be malicious but is actually playing a game.

I know I am supposed to say, at this point, that aggressive urges normally assert themselves in latency-age children, boys especially, and so that is the way it goes: now you suffer, now you inflict suffering. True enough, and important to know as true. But that is only one of many statements it is possible to make about such children. The same variation and complexity Agee provides for grown-ups appears among his children. Children, too, can become cannon for various ideologues who claim to know them, construct theories (or novels) about them. They are one thing. They are another thing. They have this drive urging them on. They are revealing that impulse or conflict in themselves. Even a beginning student in science, not too removed from his or her own childhood, might want to ask, which children, where, under what circumstances? And so would Agee, one can safely assume, on the basis of his way of looking at Rufus and the tormentors he involved himself with day after day. Rufus wanted the attention of the other children, maybe even was a touch confusing, hence provocative ("And so he remained very ready to do whatever seemed necessary to be liked.") Moreover, some of the children were "restrained, attentive and smiling," so it was not a matter of a united front. Rufus even saw shame on a face or two. He also saw indifference—boys who didn't care how cruel other boys were, so long as they did not become involved, bothered, or thwarted.

What does Agee intend here? It is a powerful scene, given a good deal of space but not turned into heavy-handed symbolism. In fact, the diffusion of right and wrong, the tangle of motives, feeling, and action presented make any larger allegoric plan hard to implement. I think he did have such a plan; he wanted to show that children, like the adults they will soon enough be, are given to numerous and sundry moods, dispositions, inclinations. He wanted to indicate that they build one another up (that crowd of cocksure boys, able to do collectively what few of its members would ever do, even care to do, alone) and tear one another down—and in so doing are confronted with themselves. That is, they have islands not only of awareness but assumed responsibility; hence they know moral conflict as well as the psychological kind we emphasize so strongly these days.

I mean, here, something beyond the kind of conflict a Superego puts upon an Ego, as both of them fight to keep pace with, and gain a little leeway over, the insistent promptings of the Id. Agee was not unaware of that picture of the mind and not averse to appreciating its very definite value. The children he describes, from Rufus to the nameless ones who beset him, are not, however, clinical specimens given the thin polish of everyday life, a polish we of this century are anxious to dismiss as inconsequential (no psychological ignorance, no illusions for us).[8] If such children behave as they do on Knoxville's streets, it is not because they are sick but rather are the sinners Augustine knew about a long time ago, the individuals Hobbes felt we all are (at the very least, capable, if not disposed, to be out for ourselves) and, as well, the human beings Rousseau wanted to restrain with his Social Contract.

However, Agee was never inclined to the misanthropic; if anything, he celebrated mankind's possibilities more or less the way Goethe or Beethoven did in their more hopeful moments. Even among the South's grim, hungry, thoroughly downtrodden tenant farmers he chose consistently to emphasize the honor and decency, the kindness and generosity he found during his stay. Still, we have this crowd of children on the way to school demonstrating not only indifference or callousness but deceit and a degree of persistent malice (every day, and for a good long time). The author wants to make a point, though not one he wants to run away with and turn into a whole philosophy of life; no particular philosophical or psychological formulation of man's nature, however valuable for whatever reasons, would attract him enough to do that.

No wonder the next scene contrasts so vividly with its predecessor. It is a rather well-known scene and is more readily associated with Agee's kind of sensibility. (We move from the apparently unavoidable and forceful presence of evil to a kind of pastoral innocence.) Rufus meets his great-great-grandmother, a country woman, a woman old beyond any meaning of age most of us know, a woman

---

[8]One need only compare Agee's view of childhood with the view that obtains in Golding's *Lord of the Flies* (London, 1954). We certainly have completed a circle of sorts when an age unwilling to look below certain surfaces of the mind gives way to an age that is inclined to think that all psychological truth lies underneath, bound there by repressions.

way up "beyond," up in those hills where a city like Knoxville may be vaguely apprehended the way some of us keep in mind distant countries and continents. The boy is the oldest great-great-grandchild, if such a status can be imagined by any of us. The encounter is one the author obviously savors, and he warms with delight at describing it. The lady represents all that is gone but in its own way lives on, stripped of the day-to-day demands that characterize the present. She does not care for herself. In a lovely passage we are given to know that she often is incontinent. She ignores much, even the presence of people, let alone their ideas or opinions. She does not, mind you, dwell on *her* ideas or opinions. Rather, she simply *is*; she sits there—the past that has its own way of offering itself to us. The boy is prompted and urged to approach her, and does so, and is told to kiss her, and does so. She responds, makes noises, ever so delicately indicates her "grave intensity"— a response to this child of another century paying her court. Then in a burst of self-initiated affection, Rufus kisses her again.

Will such a child, so kind and generous, one day join that crowd of mocking, teasing, cruelly seductive children? Rufus, who could be so suffused with love and thoughtfulness up there in the hills, to the point that his parents become a bit nervous and separate the two, lest the outpouring of emotion get to be too much for the lady, or perhaps themselves? Out of what psychological imperative does a child come to tease and be nasty? Need such a development occur? Is there some way of protecting the boy Rufus's mind so that his quality of outgoing decency and his tendency to be respectful toward people, to honor them quietly but without a doubt, are strengthened, made virtually immune to the assaults of various crowds? In the next scene Agee seems to say no, sadly but firmly. Friends of Rufus's parents, distant relatives actually, Uncle Ted and Aunt Kate by name, arrive on a visit from up North. It is another of those flash-back scenes that indicate, in essence, what kind of family it was that now has been brought face-to-face with death—and, maybe, what kind of family we all belong to as human beings. The uncle and aunt are strangers and come bringing gifts, though we are not going to find them traitors. They are different; they are not from Tennessee. They go visit the Smokies with Rufus, his sister and parents but are not impressed. As they all ride in the train things happen, minor and insignificant things, everyday incidents that are, finally, boring.

Why does Agee, who by this time has given us many such incidents in other, more important moments of the novel, give them to us now? Perhaps he is determined we remember how persistent and inescapable our psychological ambiguities are. Rufus's mother, so considerate of others, has to awaken Aunt Kate lest she miss an especially good mountain view. Aunt Kate promptly falls back asleep, perplexed that she has been shaken into an awareness she does not desire. Then the devoted mother compares her little daughter, Catherine, to Aunt Kate. Of all people, Catherine—who is not sleeping her way through the trip, merely looking a trifle *too* interested ("heavy and earnest") as she stares out the train window. The child does not like the comparison, does not like being made fun of. She begins to pout, look hurt. Her mother tells her she has to learn to be kidded without feeling in the grips of a disaster. But her father demurs. No one likes to be treated that way, he says. He comforts the girl, takes her on his lap. He does not say she ought never be kidded; he knows that is to ask too much for her; and, as we will shortly see, he may have known himself too well.

At supper it is Rufus's turn to experience a bit of gentle kidding. When he asks for more cheese Uncle Ted says, "Whistle to it and it'll jump off the table into your lap." The boy has not whistled before, but he is game to make the attempt. Eventually he fulfills his part of the bargain, causing Uncle Ted and Aunt Kate to laugh and laugh. Rufus's mother explodes with anger; she feels her boy is being deceived, tricked into a helpless, exploitable position out of his naïveté, if not gullibility, and also out of his desire to please and be thought well of. The vehemence of her anger takes everyone by surprise and makes a passing moment something more. The boy is being corrupted, his trust violated. He will indeed become a member of that crowd of school-bound children if he keeps on going through experiences like that one. Teased and fooled and made light of enough times, he will do likewise to others.

No, the others say; that is not how it goes. Uncle Ted and Aunt Kate, of course, want to defend themselves, and so does the boy's father, who has tried to stop his wife in no uncertain terms: "Come on, Mary, cut it out." The father wants to make peace, is embarrassed by the amount of emotion put into a seemingly innocuous event. He has even told his wife to be still after the philosophical significance of the event has been spelled out in no uncertain terms by Uncle Ted: "Why, Mary, he's got to learn what to believe and what not to." Is there some way that children can learn that without being hurt, made bitter, given a large appetite for vengeance? Rufus's mother at that moment is sure that the answer is yes: by treating our children with respect and devotion, instilling in them out of love certain values, we enable them to be not only "good," but also possessed of "common sense." Children who are trusted, not made to feel suspicious and self-doubting by the words and deeds of their elders, are children who grow up to trust. If they are played upon, hoodwinked, victimized, then that is not their fault; the devil is abroad, and his powers are notorious.

Though Rufus's mother doesn't spell all that out, she clearly believes it. Unfortunately, the logic of her position is easily faulted. Rufus did not demonstrate the common sense she claimed he had; on the contrary, he repeatedly tried to do the impossible and showed no sign of recognizing it as just that, thereby prompting his mother's loss of temper. She had been confronted with what she refused to admit: the absence of common sense in her son, given a certain set of circumstances. Rufus clearly did possess a good measure of common sense and, let it be granted, more than an average amount of the trust his mother claimed for him. We are not up against a deeply flawed family whose members, by their various actions, prove absolutely nothing except the extent of their own handicaps. The novel is about people above average in intelligence, as well as the breadth and depth of their ethical concerns.

Nor are they unsophisticated psychologically, Rufus's parents and Uncle Andrew and great-aunt and grandparents. Even his rather disturbed Uncle Ralph is no emotional simpleton. The power he has over the reader's sympathy and imagination comes from the shrewdness about himself his mind commands. Through him Agee can portray the not uncommon plight of the man who knows what ails him but has not the will to change things and can only make feeble vows, soon enough revealed for the illusions they are. He is no more a failure than most of us; it is his family's generally high standards of honor and deportment that set him apart so, even if those standards are themselves subject to strain, as the Folletts have yet again learned up in the Smokies.

Agee has avoided writing a novel with a particular psychological theory to urge upon the reader. He presents us with a series of vignettes, all in one way or another centering on a child's complicated experiences with members of his family. He pushes us neither toward their vices nor virtues. Against such a mixed psychological background he goes on to confront this family with a final, awful experience, whereby death becomes a living reality. At no point are we told what that experience will do for Rufus, or anyone else. The novel can be, has been, read both ways. Some see the various grown-ups becoming better people, more mellow and reflective, truly resigned to God's will or nature's rhythms, rather than desperate to placate the former or find some final explanation for the latter. Some see only omens of hope, counterbalanced by ample evidence that one person's gloomier side, another's more cramped, embittered side, or fanatical and self-righteous side, all persist, ready at a moment's notice to assert themselves, even take over completely.[9]

Everyone will agree, however, that Rufus has had to learn a lot about the world in the brief time of his life we know him and that at the very end of the novel, for all he has come to know, for all the sense of himself and others he has acquired, he is left with certain questions—tough, important, and unanswered. He has been walking "all the way home" with his Uncle Andrew, listening to praise of his father, anger against the arrogance and smugness of Father Jackson; listening, also, to the conflicted sensibility of an agnostic reveal itself in all its contradictory eloquence; and listening, finally, to a rather self-centered man, himself no Father Jackson, but enough like him to be made agitated and put on the defensive. The child senses all that, hears a hateful man being

---

[9]There is a small but worthwhile body of criticism devoted to the novel, which was published posthumously by McDowell, Obolensky (New York, 1957). I have already referred to Kenneth Seib's book. Peter Ohlin in *Agee* (New York, 1966) and Erling Larsen in his pamphlet *James Agee* (Minneapolis, 1971) devote considerable space to *A Death in the Family*. Dwight MacDonald has a fine essay on Agee, with loving and tender comments on the novel in *Against the American Grain* (New York, 1962). Leslie Fiedler has written an interesting review: "Encounter with Death," *New Republic*, December 9, 1957; also, Edward Ruhe, *Epoch* 8 (Winter 1958) and Michael Roe, *Twentieth Century Literature* 12 (October 1966) give the novel appreciative analytic attention. Less appreciative is George Elliot's "They're Dead But They Won't Lie Down," *Hudson Review*, Spring 1958. An interesting response to Elliot's review (decrying "sentimentality" in Agee's novel, among others) can be found in Gene Frumkin's "A Sentimental Foray," *Coastlines*, Autumn 1958. A recently published study of Agee that mentions the novel repeatedly but does not provide a sustained study of it is Alfred Barson's *A Way of Seeing* (Amherst, Mass., 1972).

condemned with gratuitous hate, feels that hate spilling over sense-lessly to others, his own mother and beloved great-aunt included: "His uncle had talked about God, and Christians, and faith, with as much hatred as he had seemed, a minute before, to talk with reverence or even with love."

The boy is appreciating inconsistency of feeling—more, the inconsistency of a person's character. He had appreciated the same in his father before he died: the book begins with a scene demon-strating how a decent and affectionate father can feel that kind of inconsistency and how his young boy cannot eventually fail to realize its influential existence as a fact of life, something to be reckoned with even when all goes as smoothly as possible. He had also appreciated his mother's inconsistencies: she could tease, then scream at a teaser, and she could be open and loving but also hope-lessly absorbed with her pious thoughts and at times lacking the common sense she told others *he* had. (She made his sister's coming arrival as much a mystery for him as the Virgin Birth has necessarily remained for all of us.)

It can be said that the inconsistencies heretofore sketched out and given a certain continuing presence are, at the very end of the novel, brought to a crescendo of emphasis. The child Rufus asks one question after another, and none of them will be answered by anyone—then or forever after, one can be reasonably sure. The questions are particular ones, asked of a particular person, but they are also particular instances of universally felt dilemmas, known to every theologian or philosopher (or, in our day, social scientist) who wants to understand human nature. Speaking to himself of his Uncle Andrew's relationship to the rest of the family, in the next to last paragraph of the novel, Rufus asks, "But how can he love them if he hates them so?" Then he switches and asks, "How can he hate them if he loves them so?" He goes on to wonder whether his uncle is angry or envious "because they can say their prayers and he doesn't." Then he reminds himself that Uncle Andrew could pray, too, if he wanted to do so; yet he doesn't. Why? So many whys about so many puzzling matters! Death, a funeral, a grieving family, a group of grown human beings brought to their knees by fate, and not all of them in that position out of any faith—all of these have made this child more than usually sensitive to the meaning of things and, to a degree, the lack of meaning.

As he grows up, he will only have the chance we all have: to
find a manner of facing those questions. They are questions, Agee
keeps pointing out, none of us can really answer. We try for a
degree of comprehension of them. We learn to live with mystery—
or, tricked by our mind's ambitiousness, we don't. Most often it
is a mixture we end up with. We treasure our willful intelligence,
its desire to know more and more; we also reluctantly come to
accept as *given*, certain psychological limits rather than see them
as next year's or another century's therapeutic challenges.

As I went through this luminous but unpretentious novel, with
its artfully disguised portrayal of childhood as a state of growing
recognition of truths ordinarily reserved (in the minds of many,
at least) for old age, I kept thinking of the psychoanalytic frame
of reference I have been educated to think about as pertinent to
any discussion of childhood. The longer Freud got to know his
troubled, mostly middle-aged and middle-class patients—like him,
late Victorians of the Viennese variety—the more he began to see
their daily behavior as adults to be very much a reflection of their
experience as children. Listening to them, hearing them complain
about this fear, that anxiety, he took note of where they grew up,
under what set of circumstances. He began to ask them questions
about those forgotten early years, even as he tried to make sense
of his own childhood—perhaps driven to do so by all he heard in
the office. As I mentioned in the Introduction, *The Interpretation
of Dreams*, his masterpiece, was a fusion of a clinician's experiences and a reflective writer's memories and dreams. Like Agee in
A Death in the Family, Freud presumed that his experiences as a
boy, properly formulated and presented, would have meaning for
others, and the result, in a way, was a new kind of psychiatry:
frankly self-critical and even at times Augustinian in its willingness
to look inward as much as at the patient's complaints.

The nineteenth-century doctor's aloofness, his not uncommon
hauteur, his prescriptive authority, sanctioned by society and not
only appealed to by all patients but believed in as holy writ by
many of them, gave way to what theologians would call a more
confessional and pastoral approach. Now the doctor, Sigmund
Freud, frankly acknowledged his kinship with his patients—all of
them, however bizarre or tormented. Now the doctor worked at
those long, arduous involvements with his patients, not only to
learn more about "them," but himself. Electricity and hypnosis,

pills and the drama of manipulative medicine gave way to a continuing and sometimes turbulent exchange between two human beings. The doctor was still the doctor—Freud never would give up his air of real and honest professional pride and competence, nor would his patients want him to do so—but the doctor was also a patient of sorts, carried back on a wave of his own free associations to his or her childhood. If the doctor's childhood was unlike the patient's in many ways, there was a limit to those differences. Freud never confused the issue; he knew the difference between himself and a raving lunatic. But he kept on insisting that in the beginning there is a child and a family that takes care of that child in certain ways, a mother of one or another temperament, a father who tends to behave like this or that kind of a person.

It is interesting to compare the psychoanalytic view of childhood, as developed by Freud and further refined and elaborated by child analysts like his daughter Anna Freud and Erik H. Erikson, and the uses to which a number of people have put psychoanalysis in the technologically advanced Western societies where Freud's work has become so influential. For that matter, more than a few psychoanalysts have given in to emotional demands that are only thinly masked as intellectual or cultural preoccupations. Analysts and their patients and more than a few interested observers, in Anna Freud's words, "ventured beyond the boundaries of fact-finding and began to apply the new knowledge to the upbringing of children." The hope was that a psychoanalytically influenced education for children would once and for all banish neuroses and provide children, then as they grow up, men and women, with a new kind of life, free of symptoms, full of something called "mental health." "The attempts to reach this aim," Anna Freud has observed, "have never been abandoned, difficult and bewildering as their results turned out to be at times. When we look back over their history now, after a period of more than forty years, we see them as a long series of trials and errors."[10]

[10]This and the immediately preceding and following quotations are from Miss Freud's *Normality and Pathology in Childhood: Assessments of Development* (New York, 1965). This book gives a fascinating and candid analysis, all the more effective because it is unassuming and brief, of the relationship between psychoanalysis as a particular field of inquiry and those upper-middle-class agnostic parents in nations like America, who have found in Freud's ideas (and various revisions of those ideas) a source of obsessive concern, if not an outright secular faith. I have discussed Miss Freud's ideas, and in particular this book of hers, in "The Achievement of Anna Freud," *Massachusetts Review*, Spring 1966; also in "Children's Crusade," *New Yorker*, Sept. 23, 1972.

At some length and in technical detail Miss Freud has documented those trials and errors, and in so doing indicated rather clearly how educated and established people in nations like ours have desperately reached for, and tried to offer their children, a near utopia: no anxiety, nothing to fear, no emotional trauma, no problems with authoritarian figures, no abandonment or overprotectiveness or lack of understanding or irrational punitiveness or puritanical restrictiveness. The child's needs have been respected. The child's drives have been understood and allowed sufficient leeway, lest too much repression give way to neurotic symptom-formation. The child's developmental anxieties have been respectfully heeded; every effort has been made to help him or her get beyond those anxieties, get into the next period or stage or phase. Sexual enlightenment has been offered. New kinds of educational techniques have taken into consideration the aggressive component of the child's personality; hostilities and death wishes and sibling rivalry were, thereby, supposedly given limited and safe expression and disarmed of their future power over the rapidly changing and developing mental apparatus, as some psychiatrists call it: our mind. "In the unceasing search for pathogenic agents and preventive measures," Miss Freud has commented, "it seemed always the latest analytic discovery which promised a better and more final solution to the problem."

What was "the problem"? The messianic dreams of proudly godless people, who, as Ariès has pointed out, saw in their children the only hope, the only possibility of survival? The grandiosity of professional men and women, who are themselves tempted to believe that finally and soon a whole new breed of human beings can emerge, given the judicious application of one or another kind of new knowledge? In a summary of what did happen to those reared and taught by psychoanalytically sophisticated parents and teachers, Miss Freud declares that "it is true the children who grew up under its influence [applied psychoanalysis] were in some respects different from earlier generations; but they were not freer from anxiety or from conflicts, and therefore not less exposed to neurotic and other mental illnesses." Though herself an active, hopeful, warmhearted, giving person, by no means inclined to pessimism or despair, she goes on to observe how dangerous if seductive a certain kind of "optimism and enthusiasm for preventive work" can be. The more sobering and ambiguous side of one's work—the mysteries that remain, the problems in patients that don't go away but simply take on a new form of expression— gets shunted aside, while successes, in the form of the acquisition of unquestionably valuable information, are allowed to color one's view of life itself. Even sadder is what happens to the particular field of inquiry; its specific purpose and the scientific and philosophical premises that form the underpinning to that purpose are both washed away, as one breakthrough after another is heralded and implemented.

Psychoanalysis, as developed by Freud and those who worked with him or followed in his footsteps, was never intended to be an answer to the riddle of human nature. The essence of psychoanalysis is its emphasis on conflict as built into life: conflict as an inevitable, indeed desirable, aspect of human development; conflict as a prelude to the exceedingly complicated organization of the mind that characterizes civilized man. The child of, say, one or two, at first gropes, then as he or she gets up and walks, wanders about in an effort to find out about the world. The little wanderer is also the person in need: of food, shelter, affection, reassurance, and control—control of his own body and control lest he die by stepping out of bounds before a car, into a lake, out of a window, and on and on. Tensions arise, as an explorer meets up with restraint or as a person already given much demands more than a mother and father feel they can, they want to, they ought to give. Soon those demands become even stronger before they are tamed. The child wants not only to test limits, to have the total freedom an explorer feels he needs, but to possess—this time a person rather than space or physical objects.

The whole oedipal drama is one of increasingly purposeful striving coming to an ambiguous conclusion, followed by, of all things, a kind of resignation that becomes liberating. And at almost every moment irony abounds. The child who is offered much, satisfied regularly and with great affection, can be for a while especially demanding and rather too full of himself or herself. The child who is least directed and put upon while being trained to have control over his or her body functions can often be especially commanding, assertive, domineering. The child whose mother or father is most considerate, attentive, and consoling at age four, five, or six can often enough have an especially difficult time breaking away, giving up enough parental attention to find a new world outside helpful and interesting.

Nor need such good parents be called neurotically possessive and worse; that way, of course, any time something goes wrong it is not the fault of the sophisticated and ultimately enlightened experts who offer supplicant and ambitious parents the definitive counsel Miss Freud has taken such pains to analyze and show to be, at the very least, unwarranted in the expectations and zeal it has inspired. (Rather obviously, psychoanalytic knowledge is not the only kind "applied" to our children and absorbed into our view of their nature. In recent years a whole range of political theorists, educational philosophers, sociologists have told us what to "do" with our children.)[11] That way, too, there is still hope: if only there were some parents who really knew themselves, really knew how to take advice, really responded appropriately to the various crises children go through as they get bigger—*then*.

Then *what*? Then Rufus would not have been teased by his relatives. Then other children in Rufus's neighborhood would also not have felt the need to tease. Then Rufus and his sister, Catherine, would have been less tense and hostile with one another, because Rufus's father and mother would have behaved differently in dozens and dozens of ways. Then the boy would not be seeing and hearing ambivalence in his uncle or listening to evasions about his mother's pregnancy or being fed incomprehensible talk about heaven and hell from people who, every once in a while, revealed to him, never mind themselves, how doubtful they were about any kind of divine justice, especially in view of what they were going through right there in Knoxville. In the words of A. S. Neill, whose *Summerhill* has not been without its influence on parents, "never must the child be made afraid or be made to feel guilty." Otherwise "anti-attitudes" and "complexes" develop. Bullying, fighting, dishonesty, teasing—they are evidence that a child lacks love and freedom. Such a child is becoming "anti-life" and should be "ad-

---

[11] Sometimes the "advice" has been valuable; sometimes one wonders who the authors have in mind as they predict Nirvana itself, given only one or another new attitude on the part of parents or their children. And I mean Nirvana quite literally: all the anger and envy and spitefulness that man is heir to will vanish—and a final emancipation of sorts will have taken place. Even a thoughtful book like Margarete Ruben's *Parent Guidance in the Nursery School* (New York, 1960) ends up with all too specific advice about "promoting healthy psychological growth in preschool children." Yet as Anna Freud has kept pointing out, we are far from sure what is "healthy" at what age for what *individual* child, let alone in a position to "promote" [*sic*] that knowledge.

vised to discriminate between those who are pro-life and those who are anti-life."[12]

Needless to say, an argument can be made that Jay Follet was antilife; and so with respect to his wife and her parents and brother and aunt. And how they all failed that boy Rufus upon occasion! The father was wrapped up in himself at a time when Rufus almost desperately wanted and looked for his attention. (Agee does not fudge; he makes quite clear at the beginning that Jay is not just casually or for a moment brooding but has had a long history of serious drinking, along with more than a touch of melancholia.) The mother had her own way of wrapping herself up so that no one, not even her children, could make head or tail of her mystical—let us now say *hysterically* mystical—ruminations. We have already spelled out enough of Uncle Ralph's psychopathology; we need only call him the names: depressed, a borderline personality, an alcoholic, maybe even a psychotic.

For that matter, who knows what dark and awful psychic conflict obsessed Jay? Had he lived might he once again have started drinking heavily, pulling away even more from his family, frightening an older Rufus, depriving him of someone with whom he might identify, a masculine image? As for Uncle Andrew, younger than his sister, closer to Rufus's generation, there is a lot Agee indirectly lets us know about *his* problems; if his sister is *obsessively* religious, he is *narcissistically* antireligious. One can only wonder about his irritability, his outbursts of impatience and anger, his cynicism, his lack of real trust in people or ideas, the intensity of the rage he directs at Father Jackson. Does he unconsciously see himself as a secular version of the priest—all too self-assured, ready in a moment to look down upon others as inadequate, foolish, duped exiles from his (rather than God's) kingdom.

One generation back there are those sad grandparents: Mr. Lynch, who acknowledges the serious flaws in his marriage; Mrs. Lynch, who for so long has been cut off, ignored, treated at best with condescension; or Great-Aunt Hannah, a maiden lady, a woman plagued with uncertainty and her own kind of resentments, a person who can be officious or mutely scornful one minute, sad

---

[12]The book is titled *Freedom—Not License* (New York, 1967), and I fear I went on a spell about it in "The Letter Killeth," *New Republic*, Nov. 4, 1967.

and self-lacerating the next. To call upon an all too familiar ver-
nacular of our time, they all had their problems, and the man who
created them, it can be said, has chosen to portray a serious, tragic
moment in their lives, a moment precisely when those problems
are most likely to loom heavily on everyone—like a series of in-
fections that bounce back and forth from person to person, never
doing them in but showing them to be vulnerable indeed and, in
time, wearing them down, too.

Even so, we have a right to assume that Rufus will not become
a candidate for the nearest child-guidance clinic. When he was a
boy, there was none nearby; but today I presume he would be rejected immediately even by the most eager and grim of Tennessee's
child psychiatrists, if not by Mr. Neill, who would be absolutely
right in claiming that here was a family that all along had its fair
share of antilife attitudes. On the other hand, though we are nowhere introduced to Knoxville's schools, it is safe to assume that
not all their teachers were as sophisticated and child centered in
their habits of thought as A. S. Neill has proved himself to be.
They may have assumed that every move of theirs was not all that
important, especially since by the time children have come to
school they clearly have more than begun to be distinctly themselves and so thoroughly different from one another in many
respects. Some of the more sensitive teachers may have worried
about the harm a boy like Rufus can experience on the way to
and from school, as well as inside; by the same token, those teachers must have wondered how much of what had already been done
in the way of damage to the children they taught could ever be
undone. Maybe they recognized that as teachers they were one of
many influences upon students and therefore not deserving of a
kind of criticism that makes daily efforts in the classroom, however
imperfect and even regrettable, a matter of life and death. Maybe
they recognized that the best teacher is to some extent helpless
before the antecedent experiences, thousands of them, a child has
gone through well before he or she ever steps foot in a school; and
those experiences keep on happening, day after day, while the
child gets an education.

One can always hope for a psychological transformation of
everyone: Rufus's entire family; the children who put so much
energy and ingenuity into heckling him and no doubt hurting him
psychologically; *their* families, too; the teachers who are in a

position to hurt boys like Rufus. I suspect Anna Freud would say that even if everyone in Knoxville had been analyzed by a large contingent of psychoanalysts flown over from Vienna in 1915 (a larger contingent would have been needed than existed then, and maybe now), there would still be plenty of pain and sorrow around, and not all of it "existential," and so inevitable.

Agee's view of human nature, as it begins to take shape in childhood, comes across as not unlike Anna Freud's; it is a wry and detached view, but one also informed by a mixture of awe and sadness—awe that in the face of so many hurdles the child often comes out rather sturdy, and sadness that those hurdles do indeed exact their toll. Most of all it is a balanced view, and one here uses the word not in praise but description. Rufus and Catherine, boys and girls everywhere, are at the mercy of the particular family that is theirs. The emotional tone in a given family becomes a child's heritage, all the time affecting in large measure how the world is seen and heard: on the whole, a good place to be, safe and rewarding and dependable, or on the whole a dangerous place to be, likely at a moment's notice to be offending and bruising. Each child responds to such a family life in his or her peculiar way—a function of the child's position in the family, sex, appearance, not to mention various accidents and fateful combinations of circumstances that can befall anyone, young or old, and set in motion untold numbers of psychological ripples.

Moreover, what is apparent at any given moment is not all that is going on. If the unconscious is a construct, an abstraction which explains the mind's ability to push aside thoughts, play tricks on itself, fend off urges felt to be threatening, and on and on, then it is also a way of looking at the cumulative character of growth: things build up, reveal themselves only gradually or, indeed, reveal themselves at one point, only to be discarded not much later. All of which is to say that Rufus is not Catherine; and neither of them is a replica of anyone in their family. We will never know exactly what kind of person each of the Follet children turned out to be, but it is Agee's purpose in his novel to underscore the complexity of the events they encounter in the course of growing up. Allegiances are there, to be grasped and found encouraging. Betrayals take place that were so meant—or were, in fact, utterly unintended. The unexpected, indeed, the extraordinary, brings out the banal. In the course of a dreary or boring day the children find a remarkable moment of vision that becomes for him or her unforgettable. The loftiest remarks can be ignored, but a commonplace observation somehow more than sinks in; it serves to rally hitherto divergent or unrelated attitudes or sentiments into something coherent, Agee's "way of seeing."

Over and over again Agee wants to indicate how indirect, surprising, accidental, gratuitous the child's really important emotional learning can end up being. There is a momentum, of course, to learning, and his view of the momentum is, essentially, Miss Freud's: the child relies upon certain people, watches them ever so closely, moves toward and away from them, appropriates as his own everything from their gestures to their modes of thinking and, as well, a manner of dealing with pain and pleasure. Still, the momentum, the energies of children as they get formed by their parents and relatives and later on teachers and friends simply cannot be appreciated by resort to categorical language. Miss Freud has emphasized in the strongest terms her conviction that "as our skill in assessment stands today, accuracy of diagnostic judgment seems to me an ideal to be realized not in our present state of knowledge but in the distant future."

She is not being pretentiously humble. She knows what she knows. Her "distant future" is not Judgment Day, but it may be closer to that moment in time than some of us would ever want to acknowledge. "In sharp contrast to former conventional beliefs," she has pointed out, "it is now well-known that mental distress is an inevitable by-product of the child's dependency and of the normal developmental processes themselves." At one point she talks about "a multitude of accompanying circumstances," the detection and analysis of whose significance in the child's life, she is frank to admit, are extremely difficult, if not impossible.

One must wait and watch, and as a clinician interfere only for certain quite specific reasons. Such a position of "distance" with respect to childhood is not one wanted or expected by many of us today, as Miss Freud has taken pains to emphasize in her own way, even as Ariès has more sociologically. Nor is her kind of "distance" to be confused with indifference or despair. She is enormously attentive to children, has given her whole life to their cause, and in the end come up with her own kind of hopefulness: in the very complexity of life, in its unpredictability, the child finds a haven of sorts—leeway to pick and choose, moments that are welcome, even redemptive, no matter how unexpected and even at times temporarily unpleasant. Death, the ultimate kind of antilife phenomenon, deprived Rufus of a father but may well have made him a more self-reliant, thoughtful person, even if prematurely so, than otherwise would have been possible; and once such a chain of emotional events is set in motion, further experiences can serve to strengthen a child who, one has to observe, might well under different circumstances have been weakened by those very same experiences.

For many of us Anna Freud's way of approaching the lives of children is both unsettling and unsatisfying; no wonder her books are not best sellers and, in fact, are ignored by large numbers of people all too ready for any bit of popularized psychoanalytic wisdom, usually (as Freud always knew would be necessary) watered down, stripped of the disconcerting clinical realism that does not easily lend itself to buoyant, confident promises or "applications." As for *A Death in the Family*, Agee did not live to see a message of sorts extracted from it and proclaimed, even to the point of being put into a play and a television drama: children are lovely, sensitive, knowing beyond our willingness to comprehend, fragile, vulnerable, tenderhearted, plucky, full of humor, sly social and psychological observers, so honest we cannot bear them. Not that the posthumous popularity of Agee's novel—as it has been interpreted—is an accident. The rest of us who are no longer children might be honest and admit our hypocritical desire to treasure children—but step by step teach them (if need be, *compel* them) to abandon their truthfulness and sincerity in favor of our kind of living, a kind that often enough amounts to Mr. Neill's antilife attitude, or goes under the name of "the politics of adjustment." To a degree the television version of Agee's novel is quite accurate. Children often are indeed as lovely and innocent as any romantic poet would have them be. As for parents, many of them have been brought up short by their children, brought face to face with how much we all give up in the way of candor, subtlety, spontaneity, and George Orwell's beloved "decency," as we slowly make those necessary accommodations to the demands of the neighborhood, the community, the whole range of social and economic institutions Augustine called the City of Man.

I remember treating a boy Rufus's age in the Children's Hospital in Boston. From a solid comfortable home in a suburb, he worried about others all over the world less fortunate than himself. Like Rufus, he had been set upon by a gang of children, mocked by them, made to feel weak, defenseless, and just as sad, gullible, and stupid. He was a bit too conscientious; he would get queasy before going to school, and worry lest he fail, even though he was, in fact, doing very well. His father was not dead, simply away a lot. His mother believed in social reform and psychotherapy, certainly not in God. The grandparents were not nearby; in keeping with recent American history, they were over a thousand miles away, tucked neatly in a community for the aged. The boy asked me if I ever made resolutions. Yes, I said I used to, but not recently. He said he made a few, now and then, but one in particular meant a lot to him: "I hope maybe when I grow up I don't close my eyes to the suffering of other people."

He wasn't being pious, sanctimonious, or self-righteous. He may have heard the resolution from someone else, but he surely had made it his own, having listened carefully and not forgotten what he heard. Actually, he wasn't even making a resolution; he was merely hoping. A teacher had called him depressed, and no doubt he was also somewhat fearful. But he had many promising things about him, not least the capacity to have concern for others. And he could be wonderfully tentative. He hoped, rather than knew, about the future. Maybe, but only maybe, he would one day resist the pressures exerted by a crowd infinitely larger, and perhaps more devious, than the ones that bother boys like Rufus or him. Nevertheless, I had to be solemn about the child's prognosis, not because I knew him to be in jeopardy, simply because so much would happen that might augur poorly for him—or might be the making of him. And I am not only, at this point, talking about what would happen in my office or for that matter within the strict confines of his family.

Agee above all shows his appreciation for children, mixed with a certain gravity he assumes as he describes them, a high kind of seriousness that also admits of humor—which can be deadly serious. Maybe I find such a stance not only reminiscent of Miss Freud's, and helpful in the course of daily work with children, but an invaluable corrective to what dominates our society: the elevation of childhood to an almost saintly state of being, cut off ever so conveniently from those later compromises and evasions, if not worse, acknowledged in other human beings (adults). One suspects no adult analysands, except the most naive, have ever thought that psychoanalysts, even the most successful one, would bring the kind of final solution to life's hazards, difficulties, and temptations Miss Freud describes parents (and even a few analysts) as expecting (hoping and dreaming for) in the case of children.

We have learned from Freud how important childhood is to our later years, how upsetting, even tumultuous, some of its moments can be. Even so, we crave a New Jerusalem, a city in which life will be decisively different, drastically better than it is and has always in recorded history seemed to be. And without faith in God, without any reason to believe that natural man will reappear, there are only our children to rely upon in visionary moments or moments of despair. We will not offer our boys and girls up to God, as did Abraham (for Kierkegaard, a test of tests), nor do we wish to rest content with the convictions of a Hobbes or a Locke, that our sets of checks and balances will offer each generation stability and the means for a reasonably quiet and unmolested life. Like Pascal, we would gamble for more; only we do so in a far different way than he dreamed of—looking not up to a hidden God but down to the concrete and tangible world of childhood that surely, we persist in believing, can somehow be brought to redeem us.

Rufus one day did redeem Jay and Mary Follet. All the malice and spite those two parents could not bear in themselves, all the sins a father tried to drink away and a mother confessed to God, begging forgiveness—all that and more did not escape the notice of a six-year-old boy. The death in his family was more than a trauma, more than an awful moment made all the worse by the presence of children as the ultimately helpless and innocent victims. Rufus is marked by the event, confused and saddened by it, denied a father he beyond question knew well and loved, within limits made clear to the reader. Rufus is also enabled to see things he might forever have missed; around that tragedy a new center of coherence and, yes even vitality and assertiveness begins to form. Sides of people up to now hidden are seen. Pretenses firmly defended collapse. Affections guarded or barely, politely admitted become more openly expressed, if not for the first time revealed: a distant, self-absorbed uncle reaches out a hand, a mother begins to pay an altogether different order of attention to her son—

reckon with him, really. Out of all that, we know from our other reading, a very particular Rufus will come, not the one who might have been, had Jay Follet lived,a full life, but no mere survivor: in fact, the man and artist James Agee.

III   Youth: Elizabeth Bowen's
The Death of the Heart

Not all writers choose, or even have a chance, to comment on their novels or short stories. Some Southern writers of this century, as if fearful of yet another Yankee invasion, this time by critics, have made a point of protesting a kind of innocence. Faulkner was not about to go into an extended discussion of the complex symbolic structure of his novels. One cannot imagine forthcoming from his estate the kind of notebook Thomas Mann kept as he worked on *Doctor Faustus*. Faulkner claimed only to be a storyteller, which is what Flannery O'Connor insisted she, too, was. Walker Percy has been similarly reluctant to come up with explanations of the meaning or intent of his three novels. He has admitted to a certain surprise (So that's what I've been up to!) upon reading those critics who have subjected his novels to thoughtful analysis. If novelists can evoke mystery, even celebrate it, and often use it to confront or startle people, critics can penetrate that mystery, thereby producing a few surprises of their own.[1]

In James Agee's case there is no hope for a reading of *A Death in the Family* from him; for one thing, it was published posthumously, and some of the most significant sections of the novel had to be fitted into the plot by his editors and friends. Nor was

---

[1] Needless to say, a dialectic of sorts takes place between novelists and their critics. Some of the casual remarks novelists make about their "innocence," their "simple" desire to tell a story, are perhaps meant to be self-protective. In any event, one can only contrast *William Faulkner: Three Decades of Criticism,* ed. Frederick Hoffman and Olga Vickery (Lansing, Mich., 1960) or Cleanth Brooks's wonderfully explicatory *William Faulkner: The Yoknapatawpha Country* (New Haven, 1963) with Faulkner's own comments on his work in *Paris Review,* Spring 1956. Similarly there is the growing body of criticism that Flannery O'Connor's stories have generated and, in contrast, her own disarming remarks in *Mystery and Manners* (New York, 1969). And in Carleton Cremeens's interview with Walker Percy (*Southern Review,* April 1968) a similar tension (by no means do I mean the word to be pejorative or psychiatric in implication) can be detected. In contrast, Thomas Mann certainly is his own willing critic in *The Story of a Novel: The Genesis of Doctor Faustus* (New York, 1961).

Agee interested in regarding his own writing, despite (in *Let Us Now Praise Famous Men*, for example) an almost Augustinean inclination for self-examination and criticism. He put in so much time, anyway, writing about the work of others (and enjoyed doing so more than some of his critics want to acknowledge) that there wasn't that much of his own work to comment on—hence, perhaps, the critic's understandable sadness or frustration: so much talent, so little to show for it, from the point of view of one who studies and writes about books.

Elizabeth Bowen, in contrast, has been a steady, productive novelist and short story writer. Like Agee she has also demonstrated an interest in literary criticism and a certain restricted but shrewd and powerful kind of social observation. She would never use her native Ireland the way Agee used his native South. (Alabama adjoins Tennessee.) She has wanted to go back and look, though—from an active writing life in London to Bowen's Court and her childhood memories.[2] Like Agee she draws explicitly on those memories, aware that they are rather different from the ones many of her readers are likely to have. I do not believe she has been victimized by nostalgia, though, as in Agee's case, the charge has been made. Both in style and subject matter she has stood her own ground, and for a number of critics of combined political and literary sensibility she has been a vexing writer to face.[3]

At least Agee's return to the past coincided with the interests and concerns of his generation's intellectuals: the Great Depression of the 1930s and what it was doing to America's people, among them the forsaken tenant farmers of the South and the Dust Bowl to the west. No matter that those three families get caught up in Agee's private ruminations and recriminations; that is the intellectual's prerogative to let happen—and, anyway, pages of *Let Us Now Praise Famous Men*, with their sophisticated political and social concerns and daring, if not experimental, narrative technique, most certainly spoke directly to Agee's neighbors and friends in

[2]See her "family history" in *Bowen's Court* (London, 1942) and *The Shelbourne Hotel* (New York, 1951). In 1962 she published some fine critical "pieces on writing" along with her earlier (1942) delightful series of "memories" of her Dublin childhood (*Seven Winters and Afterthoughts* [New York, 1962]).

[3]See, for example, Elizabeth Hardwick's essay "Elizabeth Bowen's Fiction," *Partisan Review*, November 1949.

Greenwich Village. Elizabeth Bowen, on the other hand, published *The Death of the Heart* in 1938, two years after Agee and Evans went south, right in the middle of Auden's "low, dishonest decade," when England was drawing nearer to an awful, second world war and had yet to recover from *its* depression. A conventionally wrought novel, utterly without experimentation, preoccupied with apparently trivial moments in the lives of people themselves easily worthy of being dismissed as trivial (not to mention politically reactionary and socially snobbish), it was hardly a novel to be celebrated as original, "deep," or in keeping with the requirements of the times.

Nevertheless, Miss Bowen had by then earned a reputation as a strong and persevering writer, and this novel could not be ignored; it would turn out to be her best, its subtle power slowly growing on a generation of readers, though one has to add that the novel was, too, an immediate success among a number of reviewers.[4] I compare *The Death of the Heart* to *A Death in the Family* because not only do the titles right away invite that response but because they are both, in a sense, quaint books. Agee's dwells on the small-town American home for readers at the time in the process of developing other concerns (with the demonic, the bizarre, the apocalyptic), and Miss Bowen's dares yet once more ask contemporary, twentieth-century readers to look into a Victorian

---

[4]The novel, published in this country by Alfred Knopf (New York, 1939), has stimulated a number of solid essay-reviews: Louise Bogan in her *Selected Criticism* (New York, 1955); David Daiches in "The Novels of Elizabeth Bowen," *English Journal*, June 1949; Graham Greene in "Two Novels," *Spectator*, October 7, 1938—wherein *The Death of the Heart* is compared favorably to Henry James's *The Awkward Age*; Raymond Mortimer in *New Statesman*, October 8, 1938; Sean O'Faolain in *The Vanishing Hero* (London, 1956); V. S. Pritchett in "The Future of English Fiction," *Partisan Review*, October 1948; John Strachey in "The Golden Age of English Detection," *Saturday Review*, January 7, 1939—and here, interestingly enough, *The Death of the Heart* is given a Marxist analysis, and thorough approval, perhaps because so much London "decadance" is obliquely exposed; and William Tindall in *Forces in Modern British Literature* (New York, 1947), in which the novel is compared to Katherine Mansfield's stories. A review I have found especially interesting is Mona Van Duyn's "Pattern and Pilgrimage: A Reading of *The Death of the Heart*," *Critique* 4 (1961). Another religious interpretation, also quite interesting and original, is Sister M. Corona Sharp's "The House as Setting and Symbol in Three Novels by Elizabeth Bowen," *Xavier University Studies* 2 (1963). And one more: Alison Heinemann's "The Indoor Landscape in Bowen's *The Death of the Heart*," *Critique* 10 (1968). Two full-length books on Miss Bowen's work ought be mentioned here: William Heath's *Elizabeth Bowen* (Madison, Wis., 1961) and, more recently, Allan Austin's *Elizabeth Bowen* (New York, 1971).

parlor, only a bit updated, and not in order to find it a shambles. Moreover, both novels approach the adult world through charac- ters not yet part of it: Rufus the child of six and Portia ten years older, the adolescent girl of sixteen. And, finally, both novels possess a psychological breadth and acuity that are not made much of but are quietly harnessed to the needs of a particular plot, and in each case the plot is not especially thick or dramatic, the story's ending neither eventful nor conclusive. If Agee was no Saul Bellow or Salinger, let alone a successor to Faulkner, Elizabeth Bowen largely wrote as if James Joyce or Virginia Woolf hadn't preceded her as innovators, nor Conrad, Forster and D. H. Lawrence, all of whom were quite willing to leave places like 2 Windsor Terrace, where much of the action, if such it can be called, of *Death of the Heart*, takes place, in order to view, and later write stories about, other situations, continents away.

Without, I hope, making too much of the comparison I have been pursuing, I would carry it one important step further by say- ing that despite a number of obvious differences between the two scenes, Rufus's life in his Knoxville home is not all that different psychologically from the kind of residence Portia has taken up in Windsor Terrace. Indeed, Portia seems to pick up where Rufus has left off. Like him, she is in the midst of a world she cannot seem to comprehend. She is older, of course, and not at the mercy of closed doors, concealed gestures or disguised attitudes; nor do street bullies entice and bother her—though her friend Lilian, more a schoolmate than anyone who really can be trusted, manages to confound her about as much as Rufus's street companions. She is a half sister to Thomas Quayne, and with the death of both her parents she has come to live with him and his wife, Anna, at Windsor Terrace. They are childless, in their thirties, and quite well to do, though not aristocrats by any means. Thomas runs an advertising agency, surely a suspect way to earn a living in the eyes of England's prewar gentry, if indeed *any* sustained effort at work, based on the crass necessity of obtaining an income, could have earned anything more than their tolerance. The novel is about Portia's way of getting along with those adoptive parents as well as their friends and associates: the novelist St. Quentin; Eddie, the up-and-coming business colleague of Thomas's and a self-styled artist in the broadest sense of the word; some longtime friends of Anna's, Mrs. Heccomb and her family, who live at a seaside place called Waikiki; a Major Brutt, who knew Anna and her onetime lover Robert Pidgeon years before she was married; and, not least, the Quaynes' maid, Matchett, brought to Windsor Terrace from her previous position with Thomas's family.

Miss Bowen has not only given her novel a suggestive title, she divides the book into sections successively called "The World," "The Flesh," "The Devil." Windsor Terrace is a proper but decaying world—not decadent, but sad, and at the edge of emotional deterioration. Anna is attractive, holds entertaining and lively dinner parties, but is aloof and known to no one, including herself. She has learned how to make use of civilization's routines, and they keep her afloat. She is not presently afflicted in any clinical sense of that word; she may once have been, but now has learned a kind of adroit emotional control that protects her even as it isolates her. She has married well, maybe "up." Her husband is passionately drawn to her yet seems to have little to do with her except in public. For him it is a marriage of fantasy as much as anything else—what they *might* do together if both of them were different.

The novel opens in wintertime; the emotional coldness inside Windsor Terrace is matched by the weather outside. Anna is walking with her friend St. Quentin, telling one writer about someone else's writing: Portia has been keeping a diary; Anna has come upon it and not resisted any inhibition she might have felt about reading it. In a house where man and wife have built a marriage around privacy from each other and where Matchett certainly knows the confines of her place, a schoolgirl's comments to herself turn out to be irresistible—and nerve-racking. Anna finds them "distorted and distorting," and tells her friend that "either the girl or I are mad." Particularly disturbing is the intensity and scrupulosity of the girl's commitment to observation. She misses nothing and records everything, and she does the latter in such a way as to confront the reader—presumably meant to be only herself, but now Anna—with those nuances and subtleties of speech, gesture, or facial expression that are as they are for a reason: were they to become more explicit, more nearly true to the intent of the various people involved, the result would be a wholly new manner of getting along, and for the observer and recorder, quite a different series of exchanges to set down.

St. Quentin is intrigued as a writer. He hints at the girl's honesty, or at least the possibility of it, by pointing out that "to write is always to rave a little," even in the case of experienced and thoughtful essayists or novelists, who know exactly what they want to say. He doubts Portia has any clear idea of what *she* wants to say, but he insists that if she did, if she were more tactful and controlled, she might on that account merely be "discriminating," and "not necessarily more honest." So right away Portia is established as a bit of a perplexing figure, who pushes people toward serious discussions in which their very nature and certainly their integrity is at question.

Her very existence, it turns out, was the outcome of a previous moral crisis. Thomas Quayne's father had, at fifty-seven, taken up with Irene, decades his junior. Eventually he was divorced by his wife, who managed to achieve an enormous psychological advantage by behaving quite practically and sensibly, allowing herself no demonstration of anger or jealousy. Old Mr. Quayne at the end did not want a divorce and felt drawn all over again to his solid self-sufficient wife; but she said no: what had happened could not be forgotten or ignored—and thus a broken marriage, a new one, and a child. They lived rather adrift and rootless, those three, mostly in the South of France, where there were "back rooms in hotels, or dank flats in villas with no view."

We are nowhere told about Portia's childhood under such circumstances, only the events that preceded a certain kind of marriage; however, such a marriage obviously offered its special psychological atmosphere to a growing girl. Portia became increasingly detached, one gathers, well before she arrived at Windsor Terrace. Detached, she looked at others from a distance. Detached, she felt less those strong demands that have to do with socialization. While other children her age learned to take as their own a particular way of living, with its assumptions, its rights and wrongs, she was at a remove and no doubt felt the anxiety and confusion of such a position (hence, perhaps, her later desire to look so closely at the world and put down on paper what she had seen, as if in writing she might find for herself a table of laws to obey). But detached, she could also find for herself certain special opportunities. Less tied to the world, she was somewhat free of its demand for accommodation, if not full-scale surrender. Less driven to surrender, she could feel more in command of herself. Less

implicated in the everyday hypocrisies that social existence toler-
ates and sometimes requires, she could feel herself entitled not
only to look at them, but look down on those who practice them.
It is only a step beyond that to self-righteousness, and one more
step to the raving, the thinly disguised (if that) preaching St.
Quentin describes as the writer's inevitable habit—both of which
tendencies, presumably, talent can turn to good effect.

After we see what a sixteen-year-old girl can do ("already not
quite childish") by keeping a certain kind of watch on the adults
around her, we are introduced to that world of theirs. Miss Bowen
is neither Sinclair Lewis nor Henry James, though more the latter
than the former. She has a keen instinct for the phony and pretentious, however solid and permanent in appearance. She has no
wish to run on and on, savoring the nice and entertaining moments
even a social order on its way out manages to offer. But she
respects her characters, does not want to wield them as instruments of social criticism or satire—even if she is not content to let
the novel's conversations and actions speak for themselves. She is
there, at critical moments, making sure that we get some glimmer
(and more) of her intent as a teacher and social observer. Authorial
comment is an old and established tradition, but it takes on a
slightly ironic form here, as Miss Bowen keeps a sort of diary of
her own while her story unfolds.

There is no doubt that to some extent Portia is meant to be any
adolescent. "She may become anything," we are told—by Anna,
who is revealed as not so happy with what *she* has become. Portia's
body was "all concave" and showed "jerkily fluid lines." Moreover,
"she had a habit of pulling and tugging at her belt which kept on
sliding down; sometimes in desperation she nervously gripped at
it." On the psychological side of things, she wanders about the
house, not only on the prowl for material to write up, but because
she is a growing person, desirous of being told as well as finding
things out for herself—and about others. She asks questions of her
halfbrother about history and human nature that are not those
Rufus would ask (at six or sixteen), and she makes comments he
would not think to make. But they are also not the comments or
questions that Thomas or others his age would ordinarily come up
with. She observes how "sad" history is, and Thomas cannot take
exception to that, only go on to qualify the observation by making
it more precise and less dramatic: "Bunk, misfires and graft from

the start." Not to be dissuaded, she asks whether once upon a time people weren't "braver." No, they were "tougher," Thomas insists.

This tension between drama and practicality, the heroic and the pedestrian, is not remarkable to Portia and her relatives. The author makes clear how a youth, a girl in the act of becoming a young lady, gets along in an everyday way with fully grown people. The effort of Portia and Thomas to get across to each other is not unlike a similar effort made by Jay Follet and his son in the beginning of *A Death in the Family*. It is an effort that both succeeds and fails; we call it these days a generation gap, but apparently in Knoxville during the pastoral summer of 1915 or in one of those years between the two world wars "while England slept," parents or those who stood in for them had trouble saying much of what was on their minds to their young or older children, even as those children had a disconcerting way of saying the wrong things or indeed not saying anything, only asking questions.

Rufus went to the movies with his father; Portia goes with her halfbrother and his wife. Rufus could only bask in the joyful mood Charlie Chaplin provoked in his father and also sense the significance of his presence there at a movie his mother found so vulgar and undesirable. Portia, in contrast, was not going to be grateful for an evening out. The Marx Brothers did nothing for her; indeed, "she sat almost appalled" as they went through their antics. Anna is made nervous. Why doesn't the girl yield herself, give in to a movie others find a temporary relief from the daily grimness almost anyone has to deal with? But that is just the point: Portia is not looking for an escape; rather, she knows herself to be on the brink of entering that very "life" Anna has found it necessary to manipulate, Thomas to regard so cynically. She perhaps was as appalled at the audience—its size, its devotion to such nonsense—as at the Marx Brothers, who after all were on celluloid and not so overwhelmingly at hand.

The Marx Brothers soon give way to a meeting with Major Brutt. He had gone on his own—he is on his own, through and through— only to be as disappointed as Portia with the Marx Brothers, "these chaps." Yes, everyone seemed to like them; "they're up to date," he realizes. But in his mind he harkens back to the old days, when vaudeville brought live people who addressed an audience directly and responded to its needs as a sort of personal challenge. Portia had told Thomas that people were braver in the past, and Major

Brutt agrees. Who is Major Brutt? Why do we meet him early in the novel and continue to meet him up to the very end? He knew Anna Quayne when she was Miss Fellowes, and he knew her friend Robert Pidgeon. The author arranges his encounter with the Quaynes so that Anna's past, with all its disappointments and insecurities, can be made clear; and, too, the Major is described as "this born third," a position Portia occupied with her parents and now with the Quaynes.

It is Major Brutt's arrival at Windsor Terrace late at night after the movies for a drink that makes Portia's presence (and the problem she represents for the world) more of a reality. Before, we have learned of her diary and listened to the way she holds a conversation of ideas with her halfbrother; now she is in action, so to speak. And with Major Brutt a sort of multiplier effect takes place; he is as homeless and lost as she feels herself to be. He is also self-engrossed, awkward, quite at a loss to handle himself in the sophisticated society that he looks at—gawks at, rather—yet can't quite understand, let alone enter and join. He finds it easiest with Portia, and she reciprocates. As civilities pass back and forth Anna notices Portia's "perfectly open face." Such a sight troubles her no end; she is made to realize "how much innocence she herself had corrupted in other people." She wonders whether the girl is "a snake or a rabbit."

The image is a suggestive one, and important, coming as it does in the first section of the book. I have said that Miss Bowen is not one to offer exegeses of her own work, but neither has she been silent about some of her overriding concerns. "It is not only our fate, but our business to lose innocence," she has remarked, "and once we have lost that it is futile to attempt a picnic in Eden."[5] Like Agee, who mentions Adam in his novel, she makes clear her interest in man's nature, and as a means of exploring it is not averse to Biblical imagery. What are we, like Anna, to make of Portia and, more broadly, how does her innocence fit into her larger self, still struggling to realize itself? What are the rest of us,

---

[5]The entire book from which this passage comes is to be recommended: *Collected Impressions* (London, 1950). Miss Bowen's remarks on other writers and on her own writing establish her as a sharp, intelligent, urbane critic. The particular quotation above obviously encouraged me enormously in the direction I have taken here—though she was *not* directing the remark specifically at the characters in *The Death of the Heart.*

grown-up, to do with that innocence as it gets expressed and works its way into our own moods and recollections?

By alluding to such issues early on, Miss Bowen serves a kind of notice on us: this youth will confuse and vex us as well as obtain our strong sympathy. We are going to be quite moved by Portia's situation, quite caught up by the magnetism and persistence of her energy. Moreover, she is not only innocent, not only as vulnerable as a rabbit, but she has been hurt. Her parents are dead and she is only sixteen. She was ill prepared for a place like Windsor Terrace. She is graced with intelligence and awareness, which can operate repeatedly to make a wound trying to heal itself open up afresh. She will only once be a full-fledged snake, and then she will strike at Major Brutt, thereby bringing us full circle round—and answering Anna's question: the young lady is capable of being both a snake and a rabbit. For the first part of the novel she at least appears to be a rabbit. But as we more and more see her involved with others, the image of the rabbit recedes. To be sure, in a flash she can reappear as the essence of a rabbit, harmless and for a certain appetite quite cuddly. But she also turns obstinately aloof and haughty, rather like the swans we first meet when they are watched by Anna and St. Quentin as they walk and talk about the recently discovered diary. We will come to see all that best when she is presented to us with her adolescent friend Lilian and with Eddie; for the moment, with Anna's mention of a snake and a rabbit, Miss Bowen has simply laid her cards on the table.

It is easy to dislike Lilian, perhaps too easy. She is a narcissist without inhibition—but without deceit, either. She doesn't even pretend to any interest in watching others; she finds herself most interesting of all. The two of them go to Miss Paullie's at Cavendish Square, an "imposing address." They are two of a dozen or so being taught to look up, straighten out, manage themselves correctly and appropriately. They have their "subjects," but most of all they have themselves—to know how to dress, to know how to handle: a commodity to be made appealing and one day signed up for life. Miss Bowen doesn't bear down too hard on the whole arrangement. She needn't. Just a few details help, and one of her brief comments: "No one had ever read a letter under this table; no one had even heard of such a thing being done. Miss Paullie was very particular what class of girls she took. *Sins* cut boldly up through every class in society, but mere misdemeanors show a certain level in life."

Portia had been reading a letter from Eddie, one proposing that they become friends. He had gone to visit Anna and met Portia. He is now at Thomas's firm, a bright young man in his middle twenties, out of Oxford but without "background." He has no money put away for him, no guarantee of anything from anyone. He is intelligent, talkative, resourceful; "alone" is the word he uses to describe himself and join his fate to Portia's. The two met because on his way out he was feeling somewhat harrassed by Anna's possessiveness—Portia had appeared before him with his hat. They had talked briefly and needed no more time to see what they had in common; it can be said that a good part of the novel centers on their efforts to explore that similarity of feeling more carefully.

Portia's first extended meeting with Eddie shows him not so unlike Lilian in character and temperament, for all the obvious differences. She is frankly sensual and self-absorbed, and no one for intellectual pretense. She wants to experience the world, worry later, if at all, about the consequences; as for the meaning of things, that will take care of itself. Eddie is in the commercial world, but he claims to be an avid reader. He presents himself as a poet manqué; he is sensitive, where others are greedy for money and power or, in the case of Anna, for him. He is not a man-about-town, or one easily recognized as a desirable and available lover; he seems flirtatious but not willing to become committed to anyone. One suspects Lilian, a bit older, would repulse him. He might claim that to be the case on account of her commonness— of a particular kind that the rich and well-brought-up can upon occasion demonstrate. He would find her no one to exploit (something he unashamedly does at work); she would really present him with a version of himself: attractive, knowing, sly, sharp eyed, quick to seize an advantage, unwilling to go long without using that briefest of words, *I*.

Lilian has been too easily dismissed in the small but valuable body of criticism devoted to *Death of the Heart*.[6] She does not figure throughout the book, and at times she is almost a caricature of a self-centered, melodramatic adolescent girl. But Eddie's behavior also caricatures adolescence, the more so because he should be out of that period and into another one. Not that Eddie is

---

[6]I find scant mention of her in the articles and books previously listed and no evaluation of her significance.

disturbed. He clings to what others can bid good-bye; he does so tenaciously and out of the fear a sense of desperate inadequacy generates. He is a retarded adolescent, an innocent who has not obeyed Miss Bowen's admonition that he stop trying to play about in Eden. But he makes his way in the world. He survives. He is able to do his work; Anna may have discreetly supported his cause at the firm of Quayne and Merrett, but he was able to take care of himself and more. Portia has words only for her diary; he uses them in his work and has some left over for a rich and complicated social life.

He also knows how to lie, to beguile, to elicit sympathy. He tells Portia how "alone" he is; he may well have indeed experienced that existential loneliness not very much talked about in 1938 when this novel was published, but, if so, we can be sure others were told about it. And not only in a frivolous or posturing way. Like Lilian he is driven. He has to talk about himself. But at his apparent worst he can be candid and winning. By the same token Lilian is a breath of fresh air—all those other girls are so anxious to put on their constrained smiles, agree to any and every demand for conformity asked of them. She dares break conventions and is no fool about why she would like to persist in doing so. Whether she will persist is quite another matter; at sixteen her behavior is perfectly credible on its own merits as the expression of a particular kind of adolescence. But to determine how lasting anyone's adolescent interests and predilections will end up being clearly requires the kind of follow-up we are not going to get with regard to Lillian or, for that matter, Portia.

Eddie, on the other hand, is all follow-up; we can only speculate what he was like when he was sixteen. It is dangerous, however, to assume that he was back then even more distraught, scattered, fearful of commitment, yet compelled to set up a succession of flirtatious entanglements. Maybe he was studious, reserved, ambitious to rise and affirm his parents through his success. Maybe he was the model of restraint—only much later to exact revenge on people he once only admired and attempted to imitate. Maybe some people enter an emotional kind of adolescence only when in their twenties; up to then they are virtually the same repressed boys and girls Freud described as typical of the latency years, ages five or six to twelve or thirteen. Lilian embraced sexuality when it came; but because it comes does not mean it cannot be fought off. Portia falls in love with Eddie and dreams of a sexuality she has not yet experienced, and never will with Eddie. Her curiosity is of the kind Freud described in those latency years; the child has learned about his or her strong (oedipal) affections, then subdued them as for the time futile, there being a limit to what he or she can do with them, and as a result passion directed at a person becomes diffused into a thirsty mind. Eddie flirts with Anna, with Portia, with Daphne Heccomb at Waikiki. He is closer than Portia to knowing exactly what he is missing—but in that respect way behind Lilian, who realizes exactly what she craves.

We have only the novel's *present* to draw upon—no flashbacks, no projections into the future. Miss Bowen is presenting us with an adolescent innocent, but also with variations on innocence, and, I would add, on adolescence, too. There is no reason for psychiatrists to behave like the majority of Miss Paullie's pupils; a descriptive term need not be made to fit human diversity into a straitjacket. Adolescence is a physiological state in that sexual capacity, involving hormonal changes and their effects, begins to take place at a certain age, and within a variable length of time leaves the person a full-fledged man or woman. What society decrees to be, and requires of, adolescence is another matter, all of which ought not come as a surprise to us.[7] There is always some room for differences, for various rhythms, for a uniquely individual pace. Both Eddie and Portia came to the world of Windsor Terrace ill prepared by birth and background for its rigors; and if Lilian is indeed prepared for them, she has chosen to set her own course. We might call her a precocious adolescent verging on an all too quick maturity, and not only of the sexual kind. We might call Eddie a late-bloomer, a very late one, with Portia perhaps headed in that direction. But by whose standards? A psychiatric version of Windsor Terrace's? I do not believe Miss Bowen has that kind of intent with any of these characters of hers. She is not out to offer a typology. Her characters are as they are, and to let them first be (that is, affirm themselves for what they are at a given moment in their lives) and then act upon one another in ways their respective natures urge is a job enough.

[7]Erik H. Erikson's *Childhood and Society* (New York, 1950) continues to offer the best analysis of the relationship between psychological growth and those various social factors that, in sum, make lives so different. I have made clear my sense of Erikson's importance in *Erik H. Erikson: The Growth of His Work* (Boston, 1970).

We are denied people who analyze themselves endlessly, with a boost now and then from their creator. It is as if we are asked to accept the fact that introspective adolescents have been known to the world a long time before psychiatrists came upon the scene to write about them, and have found things to *do* with psychological qualities like introspection (writing a diary, going through an Oxford with great success, taking on an Anna, not to mention an advertising agency's clients, with efficiency and shrewdness) besides using such qualities as a means of intricate, legalistic self-description. In any event, we are told that Eddie hasn't even achieved adolescence, so far as his writing goes: it is "so childish as to be sinister." No one's personality in this book is helpfully consistent.

The myths about children cling to adolescents. How innocent was Rufus? Was Portia capable of her moments of cruelty and spite? Do those moments preclude innocence? Does adolescent innocence, when it is at its height, as with Portia, surpass even the childlike kind we more or less take for granted as present, if with qualifications, even in our unsentimental moments? Surpass in what ways? Are there variables to enumerate about this mental state, or way of getting on? Miss Bowen's novel is a dissection of youthful innocence, and she has her own manner of cataloguing its nature and its various forms. But she will give us no clear-cut answers to the questions we are likely to have as heirs of Freud's estate. She does make plain her conviction that the mind never really forgets or gives up what it has once held dear. (Freud came to London the year this novel was published.) But, like Agee, she makes psychological generalizations on our part a risky business. Anna long ago trusted people more than she ought have, and her need to do so lingers on. She can too easily be dismissed as crafty, self-indulgent and dilettantish. Her meetings with Eddie reveal her to be all that, but also perceptive out of thoughtfulness and not for any self-aggrandizing purpose. She can be generous out of a sense of compassion. She has few illusions about Eddie, sees the vacuum in him; sees the talent being wasted as well as used; sees, in other words, a valuable human being who, like herself, is not nearly so jaded and perversely clever as he puts on. We are not to cry for either of them; they can take care of themselves. But they are not ogres, and if Portia's encounters with them make us judge them ogres then we had best look to ourselves. Again, what does innocence in its so-called pure or nearly pure form do to us in its presence?

That last question is rhetorical, since I am suggesting that blindness is contagious: the innocent misses some of the world's corruption, but we in turn miss some of the innocent's capacity for malevolence. The very word *innocence* can confuse us; one definition is "freedom from sin," another is "purity of heart," and still another, "guilelessness." In fact the very root of the word has to do with the idea of harm, *in + nocere* in Latin, meaning "not to harm." For centuries a young child was called an innocent; he or she is unsullied by the evil intentions older people constantly make known. Yet Agee has Rufus behaving quite without innocence from time to time; at the end of the novel he is actually a rather knowing boy, ready in a while to take on those bullies (who are also young children) and even join their ranks. Portia seems more fragile; she is a girl and living in a highbred world, even if somewhat an outsider to it. Still, like Rufus, she misses little. She is never combative or openly calculating, as he could be. But she is thoroughly willful, for all the veneer of confused helplessness she could display.

With Matchett and with the Quaynes, and especially with Eddie, and finally with Major Brutt, she has her own way of forcing herself: her interests and requirements, her obsessions, one feels occasionally in need of saying, are never really put aside in anyone's interest. With Matchett she talks at great length—about herself, her past and her present condition. Anna and Thomas are made to worry about her, and not just at the end of the novel, when she has strenuously pushed them into doing so. They think about how she looks, where she ought be going to school, whom she should be spending time with, what hour she must have as a deadline for returning home. They are limited people (who is not?) but able to reach out, and are encouraged by Portia to do just that. Why *doesn't* Portia enjoy the Marx Brothers, they wonder? For that matter, the whole novel turns on their perplexity—which is not directed inward, for all the licking of wounds each of them does, but extended toward Portia, whose diary confuses them, whose mannerisms and involvements eventually alarm them.

As for Eddie, he has at the very least met his match in Portia. For all the self-display he can't help finding necessary, the drift of the novel is toward Portia's hold on him; she never gets from him what she wants, or is struggling to want, but she does manage gradually to dominate their meetings, hence cut drastically into *his* time—for sounding off, for inflating his ego, advertising his current wishes or activities. Again and again, when they meet, he comes on strong, and she appears openly and without pretense grateful for his attention, but for one reason or another they end up talking about her, not him. It is no mean achievement for Portia, a test perhaps of whose innocence has more determination and staying power. And of course that diary, in this case the very essence of self-absorption, if of invaluable assistance.

Too often critics have had Eddie wounding badly the gentle, adoring, unblemished Portia, aided and abetted, it seems, by everyone else; and thereby, of course, we are told how awful it has been since Adam and Eve fell: the good in us falls prey to the bad. Eddie did take the initiative, seek out Portia, select her as a witness for the psychological Salome dance he liked to put on as a pitiable means of reaching out for people. But if he is virtually stripped bare and pathetic by the end of this novel, she is no more than momentarily upset. One way to give is to break down; one way to take is to make oneself obstinately at a loss about things, always in one or another condition of need—there waiting, if not with tears, then with bated breath. Since the Fall, Miss Bowen wants to show, it is not a clear-cut matter of falling prey; good and evil are hopelessly mingled or scattered. Portia's long conversation with Matchett is a case in point. The author shows us Windsor Terrace and its antecedents through a maid's eyes. Matchett tells Portia a lot about her halfbrother and his family and reveals along the way her own snobbery. No one can be more authoritative than a certain kind of family retainer, and even if the knowing retainer belongs to an old literary tradition, maybe too often called upon, Miss Bowen has not stumbled by taking the risk of making Matchett one of the most important persons in the story. She is wise, in her own way demanding and bossy. She has few illusions and great loyalty. She wants to be of help to Portia, who can be more like a child to Matchett than she would ever think of being in front of Thomas or Anna. Before long Matchett's willingness to talk, reassure, comfort becomes implacably swept up in a tangle of Portia's emotions. The girl cries. She asks why people are so "jumpy." She converts the maid's monologue into an excuse for one of her own. She is not grateful for the solicitude she is receiving, only able to reveal how much more of it she wants. There is a tug-of-war, ultimately, between the two, and not only over that letter of Eddie's hidden under the pillow and uncovered by Matchett. It is a measure of Portia's so-called innocence that she fears the maid capable of opening the letter. Or is it hysteria at work, making a youth inordinately suspicious?

Matchett has tried to justify her work, her life, the one being the other. While doing so she has revealed a measure of vanity: a sureness about her province, "them" and everything "they" have, from kin to furniture. Yet, Miss Bowen wants to establish the subtlety of this servant's pride; she is not officious and not a boaster. She dares level her criticism, but it is done tersely and always within the bounds of propriety. At her most critical, she gives the furniture voice—a wonderful stroke by the author. All those pieces in that fashionable, if not elegant, upper-middle-class town house: *they* see the unrest, the barely concealed nervousness, the "un-natural living." Matchett is quick to set things right again, though; she insists that there is an ethical code, a sense of honor in the family she has served so long and well. They did take Portia in. They are concerned about her, as is she.

Had Eddie been there, rather than Portia, the novelist in him at this point might have been tempted to throw aside himself and his sorrows or ambitions. There she was, that old Stoic, full of stories, a few secrets, too; a nudge or two and they would come tumbling out. She craved a listener and could find one only in Portia, still young enough not to be one of "them." When Matchett describes Anna's interest in "dolling up" a room meant to be a nursery (she has had two miscarriages), there is a flash of triumphant scorn in her manner: "*She* never filled it, for all she is so clever." The maid wants to indicate how locked up a barren woman can become. Anna has lost as well as won, suffered as well as inflicted hurt. She is now most at ease with things rather than people; she may even confuse the two at times: "Past that"— beyond her affinity with arranging and rearranging, buying and buying yet more—"she'll never go."

But Portia has her own interests to protect. Immediately she asks, "You mean she'll never be fond of me?" She is entitled to do so. She feels herself a stranger, unwanted. She has, anyway, been intensely interested from a distance in Anna and Thomas. What do they do? What do they say? How come they act like this or that? Here was a chance to learn more, to be a silent recipient of information clearly desired. One day, when tempted to self-pity, she might find such information helpful. But self-pity has its own demands. Why should Portia's sadness at her situation be brushed aside so that she might understand another's plight? It is possible to see the coldness that begins to develop thereafter in the maid as a kind of "arrogant rectitude," which is what Portia believed it to be. The maid felt jealous that the girl she was intimate with should at that very moment speak so plaintively about a third party—Anna "would never be fond of" Portia. Jealousy prompts withdrawal, and again it is the innocent one being unexpectedly rebuked, denied the simple affection she has every right to ask for.

Another interpretation would, also, make the ups and downs of Matchett's meeting with Portia less clearcut. Jealousy would be acknowledged, only its workings made a bit more complex. Matchett can be defended; she had a right to be jealous, not only of Anna, as the object of Portia's desires, but Anna as the one who, were she there at that moment, would have been allowed to go on: have her say, give of herself, be heeded for a change, rather than again be asked to do something—in this instance, take up the conversational tack Portia happens to have in mind. Here matters of class should be mentioned—though, arguably, dismissed rather quickly. Anna is the girl's sister-in-law, and Matchett is a servant, however long on devotion or high up in a household equipped with several of them. On the other hand, the most attractive side of Portia's innocence makes her little interested in those distinctions of class that everyone else seems to consider so important. She will never again in the novel have a chance for such a quiet and honorable emotional exchange; later on there will be explosions of rancor, confessions, passionate declarations, and rebuffs. She was drawing close to a person she liked and who liked her, for whatever particular reasons on the part of each. At a crucial moment, though, she becomes impassive, mentions a third person. "Past that," past a certain level of intimacy, Portia, like Anna, cannot go.

No wonder a little bit farther on the maid and the young lady are not only estranged but virtually on the brink of a quarrel. Had they kept up their own intimate talk, each of them, by sharing their respective visions of Anna's life, might have come closer to an understanding of their own difficulties. Matchett does not start out cold and legalistically, the classifier of who's where on the social ladder. There is an undercurrent of desperation in her as she goes back in time, tells all she knows, offers the girl a brief family saga. Though she denies herself at first, in the interests of going on and on about "them," as she naturally would, it is not for long that she can (or wants to) contain herself so. But innocence has its own momentum, perhaps can tolerate no interference; innocence asks questions, interrupts to notice what seems peripheral or accidental, pursues directions others find confounding.

Portia was disenchanged by what Matchett told her, yet never thought to inquire what the revelation might have meant to Matchett, who was the one telling all, so to speak—and prompted to, it has to be added, out of reasons of *her* heart. But the servant's state of mind is of no consequence. It is Portia we are likely to notice as she reaches out for Matchett and is once more rejected. Why does the old maid turn away so, we wonder, when the girl needs her? Surely the responsibility for the collapse of their "time" together belongs to the older person, already revealed as a thoroughly keen psychological as well as social observer. A fragile spirit has again been hurt, or so Miss Bowen at this stage of the novel allows us to think; unless, that is, we watch both her and ourselves carefully and think of Matchett's situation and rights as a human being in which case Matchett may well be the first victim of this novel's youthful innocent.

Miss Bowen next brings Major Brutt to Windsor Terrace, and for a very brief chapter allows herself a surprisingly large number of authorial comments. Portia unnerves the other characters and provides a focus for the story; Major Brutt is a middle-aged man whose appearances hint at what can become of Portia's innocence, when it is extended from adolescence into future decades. But the issue is not only psychological for the author; she sees society as also confused by its Major Brutts. Portia is a puzzle to Miss Paullie; Major Brutt is a puzzle to Thomas and, indeed, all England. He has never really found a decent or lasting position, poor man, and yet he utterly confuses those who have (the Quaynes of this world) because he is not in consequence bitter or suspicious. Like Portia, he asks questions, seems never cynical, can't quite negotiate his way through the thicket of emotions he comes up against but does not recognize, simply runs into and stumbles across. "What *does*

he want?" Thomas wonders as he looks at Brutt. The fact is that
the Major doesn't himself know, even as Portia isn't certain what
she is looking *for* as she looks and looks, then writes up what she
has seen, so that she can have a record of it and, presumably, look
at *that*.

A youth like Portia draws people back toward their own youth,
but not only out of nostalgia. Nor is regret the inevitable outcome:
if only—if only I had not lost what she now has in such abundance.
One can be made nervous by the sight of an old battle scene, even
if one is pleased with the way the battle turned out. But in case
there are any doubts on *that* score, Major Brutt is around to quiet
them, because neither Thomas nor Portia (nor Miss Bowen) had
any real regrets about the innocence he or she has lost—not if
Major Brutt is what they might have become, given an extrapolation of Portia's innocence into middle age. He is not a straw man,
though, an excuse for others to feel self-contented. He is observant,
kind, alert, outgoing. His loneliness is obvious, but it is not
grounded in sickness of the mind. Nor is he an early version of the
mid-twentieth-century existentialist, asking questions all the time
because he can take nothing for granted. Thomas sizes him up as
courageous, of "stolid alertness," and with a "pebble-gray direct
look" that was "morally hypnotic." That last phrase emphasizes
Brutt's lack of guile; he does not seem to have encountered the
serpent yet. And who knows why? Have his genes spared him, or
has a particular kind of upbringing? Is the serpent so busy that
not everyone gets corrupted—or, put differently, are there specific
social crises or experiences that turn us, finally, into grown-up
people rather than youths? Is age itself and the everyday demands
of living quite enough to move all the rest of us toward that guile
both Brutt and Portia so notably lack?

Thomas may be a little hypnotized in Brutt's presence, but he
is not made guilty; like his wife, he is made just uneasy enough to
become reflective. Anna's reflections carry her back to her earlier
years; she is a woman of the 1930s, the mistress of a splendid
home to which people come from out there in the world for good
food and wine, for witty company that lessens the strain of things.
Her husband's reflections, added to rather substantially by Miss
Bowen, move outward toward that world; he lives most of his
waking hours in it, and for all the boredom or impatience he
evidently feels at the Quayne and Merrett office, he has no fanta-

sies about some other working place or position—only dreams about Anna and himself: they escape to an uninhabited island under a warm sun that never gets covered by clouds and live there to the end of their days. Through his mind run sentences, phrases, all prompted by this unbitten Adam, Major Brutt, who drifts along, who is less self-centered than Portia, but very much like her in that he practically offers himself up to people, takes on the chin their rebuffs or frank scorn, and comes back for more, scratching his head, puzzled but not really offended.

"The *worry* of facing this patient man!" Thomas thinks to himself before he sees Brutt. In the major's presence, however, worry turns to hard practicality. "Society was self-interest given a pretty gloss. You felt the relentless pressure behind smalltalk. Friendships were dotted with null pauses, when one eye in calculation sought the clock." It is thinking worthy of Hobbes. A little later on Brutt candidly acknowledges feeling "out of touch." He knows "there must be something all you people get together about." It is Thomas he is speaking to, but "all you people" is "us"—is the society Thomas has just described to himself in his thoughts as he gazed at Brutt, an outsider if ever there was one. But Thomas wants to educate Brutt. There is nothing to "get together about." That was done a long time ago: the social contract has been signed, sealed, and put before everyone as a fact, and if Brutt somehow has been left out, then mysteries do happen. Thomas reassures Brutt that there is no conspiracy, there are no rules that get promulgated or rehearsed—again, no need for people to "get together." Life simply goes on, and not all that pleasantly. Brutt wants to be part of a world that can be rather unattractive; he doesn't have the sense, the ordinary push and cunning, to do so, force his way in as a member in good standing, and one uses words like *push* or *cunning* with no necessary implication of viciousness or deceit. (Christ suggested that serpents as well as doves are needed companions for those who would be part of the world enough to win others to his message.)

This is not a novel intended to dissect Windsor Terrace and find it wanting or even barren throughout. Miss Bowen assumes trouble everywhere, psychological limitations the condition of man. She makes no effort to cover up decay and rot in Thomas's home or office; he is aware of how bad things are in each place. On the other hand, Brutt's naïveté cannot go unchallenged: "I suppose there is nothing so disintegrating as competitiveness and funk," says Thomas to Brutt, "and that's what we all feel. The ironical thing is that everyone else gets thejr knives into us bourgeoisie on the assumption we're having a good time. At least, I suppose that's the assumption." He goes on to point out that "we weren't nearly so much hated when we gave them more to hate. But it took guts to be even the fools our fathers were." Anyway, in a gesture of resignation that is not Kierkegaard's religious kind but may be the nearest to it a man of property can find, Thomas concludes with: "The most we can hope is to go on getting away with it till the others get it away from us."

Major Brutt characteristically replies: "I say, don't you take a rather black view of things." He is no socialist. We have already learned he is not suited for the capitalist world. He is certainly not a psychological misanthrope, ready to enjoy someone else's gloom as a means of keeping up his own spirits. Given from Thomas the bleakest kind of honesty, given his searing social comment, at once general in its breadth but clearly personal as well, Brutt can only move back and say that the sun may only *seem* to be setting, so let's not be premature in our forecasts. Locke would admire such an exchange: one man has insisted that he and his ancestors have indeed carved out their destiny, and another man has replied that he accepts the fait accompli, and no recriminations, please. But has the major really understood Thomas? Can a truly innocent person comprehend the world's various evils?

Did Adam really understand what the Lord meant when he spoke to him so gravely about that particular tree? God himself put the serpent there in Eden—a fact of life, an inheritance of sorts for those two first ones of his. Who is to know why? All we know is that even then it was not merely their willfulness but his complicity. The setting for a disaster had been provided, not just the tree, standing there passively and warned against, but the serpent, that sinuously active agent in a scheme of things one can only guess at. Brutt is so characterized that he may well be imagined fending off that serpent, with an ironic reversal of the remark he directed at Thomas: "I say, don't you take a rather unduly hopeful view of things?"

As Thomas and Brutt go about their talk, they are interrupted by the arrival of Portia and Eddie, who have been to the zoo, one place in London where two such youths can gaze at many, if not every, "beast of the field" and "fowl of the air," and, like Adam, show skill at naming them. The two youths want to be by themselves, but Thomas for some reason unknown to himself can't let that be. He becomes, in Miss Bowen's word, a "bully," a role out of character for him. Explaining the transformation, the author says: "the diversion of a raindrop from its course down the pane, the frustration of a pet animal's will in some small way all at once becomes imperative, if the nature is to fulfill itself." In the barely apparent, polite, and disciplined way of a Thomas, the serpent strikes—suggesting something, pushing people toward something. Thomas has had enough of Brutt's kind of innocence; the arrival of two more kinfolk of the major's puts Thomas in a state of agitation. When Portia tries to stay with Eddie after the two of them are seen at the door, Thomas insists that "a minute won't hurt you." He then "pushed her ahead of him with colorless, unadmitted cruelty." Eddie had to follow. The poor, distracted Thomas at least had gathered all the innocents together in one room.

The picture Miss Bowen wants to portray of the world is now almost done. She need only emphasize a point or two through an exchange between Eddie and Portia, then go on to give us excerpts of that by now much discussed diary. When Portia and Eddie talk we find them drawing one another out. Portia is a relentless interrogator; if, as the author says, she asks her questions "without guile," she does not lack for pertinacity. Actually, she emerges as shrewder than Eddie, whose uninhibited brilliance often seems responsive rather than original. (He is a master at appraising a situation, then taking control of it.) Her character becomes defined as never before by what she asks says, really, through her questions. True, for a stretch Eddie pokes and pries, and she seems almost unaware of his purposes. Not that *he* is so aware of his reasons for wanting to be so intimately involved with everyone and so up to date about their thinking or experiences. As he undercuts his friend Anna, with a brief malicious comment or two, Portia shifts the discussion to a much broader moral plane. Eddie has said he's "several degrees worse" since knowing Anna; whereupon Portia wants to know if he believes himself to be "wicked." Nor is she satisfied with his clever "yes," meant by its dramatic terseness to bring her up short. "In what way?" she asks, undeterred.

Is she the innocent, dumbly pursuing one brazen inquiry after another? Has she simply learned to be as clever, for a moment at least, as her friend? One is asked to doubt both possibilities. She does glide like a swan right through her conversation with Eddie. At one point she has the considerable self-confidence (still without that guile!) to tell Eddie this: "I feel I shall always understand what you feel. Does it matter if I don't sometimes understand what you *say*?" Eddie disputes her claim; he tells her that she has "no idea what people are like." To that she replies, summoning the diarist's power of recall, that "Major Brutt noticed." She means she saw him silently observing (and enjoying—for him that is, one without the instincts of a jealous or possessive lover) the two of them as more than simply casual friends. Eddie quickly yields to her good judgment, one suspects without realizing he is doing so. He calls the major an "idealistic old warthog!"

As the two go on talking, Portia becomes not only troubled by Eddie's continued thrusts at Anna, but "exhilarated" by them. She is described as "a young tree tugged all ways in a vortex of wind," no compliment to Eddie and an interesting way of signifying what may well happen later on, since trees have a good chance of outlasting particular winds. There is an element of abandon in her; she is being led, played upon, fed ideas and stories, fed more than a touch of gossip, shown the mind's evil capacity by Eddie. But she is made for the role. The author calls her "his open piano." And so that we do not simply go along with the lightness of touch that the conversation between the two has to have (they are still getting to know one another and are not in any crisis or deep intellectual discussion), the author adds a long and sharply worded paragraph that spells out in the novel what she would much later write about more generally—the requirement that we make it our "business" to lose innocence, lest all too much suffering ensue:

Innocence so constantly finds itself in a false position that inwardly innocent people learn to be disingenuous. Finding no language in which to speak in their own terms, they resign themselves to being translated imperfectly. They exist alone; when they try to enter into relations they compromise falsifyingly—through anxiety, through desire to impart and to feel warmth. The system of our affections is too corrupt for them. They are bound to blunder, then to be told they cheat. In love, the sweetness and violence they have to offer involves a thousand betrayals for the less innocent. Incurable strangers to the world, they never cease to exact a heroic happiness. Their singleness, their ruthlessness, their one continuous wish makes them bound to be cruel, and to suffer cruelty. The innocent are so few that two of them seldom meet— when they do meet, their victims lie strewn all round.

The sixteen-year-old orphan and the twenty-three-year-old man of many interests are next called "two accomplices," not because they have any specific mischief in mind, but by virtue of their distance from others, their unrestrained and defiant willfulness. Portia's diary shows how removed, how willful, they both have been. It represents a considerable achievement for Miss Bowen; she succeeds in realizing beautifully Portia's youthful self-centeredness, her almost unlimited capacity to see anything, however trivial or passing, as somehow not only worth recording but worth connecting to her own life's momentum. For instance, a diarist who is mostly inclined to write one-sentence paragraphs chooses at a particular point to combine an observation, a speculation, and an apparently unrelated wish: "Tonight Thomas and Anna are going to dinner. I do wonder if Matchett will say good-night. I do wish my white rug would come back."

She misses nothing, draws everything around to herself, yet all the while does not come across as tricky or deceitful, as a boaster or a perversely calculating person. Wrapped up in her preoccupations, she moves along from day to day, diary entry to diary entry. She becomes almost alarmed when she misses writing down a few events, but when she makes up for lost time we find that nothing has changed: she is there, making her lists, drawing her distinctions, expressing her sense of wonder or chagrin in an almost deadpan prose that makes her seem less excitable and knowing than she is. "When Thomas comes in he looks as though he was smelling something he thought he might not be let eat," she writes on Friday. Who is the child in Windsor Terrace and who is the almost omniscient one? Thomas becomes easy prey for Portia's greedy eyes; and she is now at her most innocent—not yet at the seashore, where "The Flesh" is to be evoked, or back in London, having had her encounter with "The Devil."

One Sunday Portia writes this: "I wish someone liked me so much that they would come to the door when I was out and leave surprises for me on the hall table, to find when I come in." It is an apparently harmless fantasy of a lonely girl. Even the way she is to get the affection she craves is impersonal; the surprises are left on a table, not handed over to her directly. The remark is put in between mention of an afternoon service at Saint Paul's Cathedral. Portia had gone there with Matchett. They had sung "Abide With Me." Afterwards, on the way home, Portia learned that Thomas and Anna were going away for an April holiday. There is no doubt that to an extent the girl has recorded faithfully her reaction: they are leaving me, and I am therefore prompted to wish for those surprises from a someone more attentive than they wish to be. But she is not really gloomy, and I don't think she feels all that sorry for herself. She does indeed have Eddie in mind, as the rest of that day's entry indicates. In a matter-of-fact comment at the end of her train of thought she ponders whether he will eventually do just that, leave a surprise for her to discover when she comes home. Still, she is well cared for, and Matchett makes sure they enter the house through separate doors upon return from church; one uses the front door, the other goes down to the basement.

Portia is not a spoiled adolescent. She is never going to use a maid's basement entrance, and she knows that—tells it to herself as she writes down recollections that remind her of her relatively high position in the world, for all the sense of abandonment she happened to feel that day. Of course, an objective fact, no matter how clearly perceived, can be small consolation to a visitor, even if a relative: she will soon be *sent* off while others *go* off. But she does not let loneliness and disappointment make her truly introspective, self-critical, or mournful. She never veers toward humility; rather, it is defiance that comes out. They have taken her in, given her much, but not enough. She is not angry with them, only vexed that in the midst of much she feels unsatisfied. She does say she is sad, but she doesn't write as someone sad; she buoyantly describes Eddie in great detail, making him seem quite real and familiar. "When he was a child he knew pieces of the Bible straight off by heart," she mentions. Knowing that, committing those passages to memory, he was still "afraid of the dark," she goes on to say. And then the next thoughts about him have to do with food, money, love, possessions. He likes to eat this, he doesn't want to be *very* wealthy—only comfortably well to do, one gathers. He takes stock of people, senses what they think and want, gives them what they are after, is unhappy doing so, if a bit pleased that he is in the driver's seat, the one who is aware of what is happening and thereby not so taken advantage of as one might assume. And finally, he has a lot of things: though a youth who can feel sorry for himself at times, "he has thirty-six ties."

Neither of those two youths shows any intention of following Matchett's lead. Matchett goes to church, sings a hymn, and then lives it out. She does "abide"; she has been placed firmly in God's scheme of things, and so be it. She uses the basement door. Portia has been placed not here, not there; for her such an ambiguous fate is unacceptable. Not a woman's equivalent of Abraham or Job, she bursts with an insistency of sorts: I will have what I want, though by no means do I really know what it is or where I will get it or from whom—so right now I am prepared only to speak in vague and impersonal terms. And no doubt about it, in Eddie she has not another's (inevitably different) frame of mind to draw upon, thereby freeing her to some extent of herself. He is like her; as she so pointedly indicates with disarming resort to apparently stray and unconnected facts, he is not to be put in his place, either. "His father is a builder," she notes before she comments on Eddie's familiarity with the Bible. The builder's son ends up with thirty-six ties.

It is not that she is detached or has almost wicked insight into her own habits. Her capacity for the ironic is part of her insistence that life's restrictions and obstacles are not meant for her, or so she now insists and so Eddie, several years her senior, also insists. Major Brutt, who would never keep a diary like hers—or any other kind, either—and who would no doubt be contented with one or two ties, has his own way of showing a similar attitude. What prompts others to hesitate, turn away in pride or embarrassment, doesn't in the least upset him; more important, he plunges in, ignores hints from Thomas and Anna that they have no real interest in him, shows up again and again, all the while believing himself a guest very much wanted by them. It is not true that he simply stumbles into the Quaynes', acts like a blind fool. He curries favor, buys presents, energetically offers himself as a decided contrast to, and source of pleasure for, high-strung people who can profit from his imperturbability. If he is thick skinned it is because he has not wished to be otherwise.

Portia and Eddie demonstrate a similar inclination not to abide by the rules of the game. One can imagine some of Eddie's acquaintances calling him nervy, others wishing he had better manners, were more mindful of other people's feelings. As for Portia, she is mindful of others all right. But their *feelings*—does she ever really ask herself, and then write down, how someone else feels? Thomas, like a wayward child, worries he might miss out on some tea biscuits. She sees that—Thomas eyeing the biscuits—but never thinks to say he looks, as a result, annoyed or hurt or sad. The flatness of her narrative style, its dry, straightforward quality, its almost Kafka-like moments ("Today is Saturday, but nothing will happen.") give a semblance of indifference and aloofness, neither of which she really feels. She is very much interested in what is happening around her, insofar as it pertains to herself. When she *does* note directly the feelings of others, they have to do with her: "Then we sat in the drawing room, and they wished I was not there." She has offered not the slightest substantiation for the charge, and she is usually a great one for descriptions and enumerations that resemble lawyerlike briefs. At other times she can be appropriately modest about the limitations of her own perceptions: "Until I went out with Eddie I did not feel like this, unless I feel like this without knowing."

By the time Portia arrives at Mrs. Heccomb's place at Seale-on-Sea, we are prepared for the fate that befalls her, there and later, when she returns to London. From a well-bred home, where the lust and meanness we are all heir to get expressed indirectly, through rituals only a maid like Matchett can see for what they are, we are transported to a far more thriving place, emotionally. Despite its name, Waikiki is not what painters like Gauguin or Rousseau wanted us to see; but it is a lively enough place, and one would expect that here, at last, Portia might stop keeping her diary. She was kept busy, drawn into the whirl of feelings that, like the nearby ocean, pull back only to appear in full force again. Yet she maintains the continuity of her writing; indeed, the second section ends as the first does, with some of her daily entries.

Some critics have made a point of contrasting these two portions of the diary, and she is indeed more collected, less given to random observations, those guileless, deadpan remarks that in fact strike at the center of whatever target she is taking aim at. She also is upon occasion more reflective; softer, if by no means mellow. She has been hurt, found Eddie more shut off than she expected. The hurt is acknowledged ("Though things have hurt me since I was left behind here . . .") and allowed its effect on the tone of her writing. But though down, she is not out. She has had difficult and exhausting encounters with Eddie, found him quite willing to embarrass her, disappoint her, drive her to maddening confusion and despair. Given all that, given the provocative and even rude behavior she has seen Eddie capable of, one wonders why she has no desire to regard him more closely or, for that matter, take a keen look at herself. Why does an adolescent girl very much in love with an attractive man, now rebuffed by him, show such restraint toward herself in the privacy of her own written words? Even with Eddie, as he cries and shakes and seems at the very end of his tether, we are told that she keeps away: "Someone sobbing like that must not be gone near."

Portia is not nearly as cold or inaccessible as she seems in her diary. Anna was unnerved by the girl's distance from people, an observer's reserve that reminded her of her own. Rather, Portia is set on a course; with tenacity she persists. She burns with curiosity. If she were to stop taking such an overwhelming interest in people, places, things; instead, begin protecting herself somewhat from her mind's eagerness to see, her heart's desire to find a world worth joining and living in forever after, we would soon enough know: the diary would be more personal, weaker narratively but richer psychologically—or perhaps she would give up the diary altogether. This is no diary of a distraught adolescent who has come upon a cruelly callous outside world, hence the consolation of finding a literary form for her interior life, not to mention some companionship in her own thoughts as they obtain the kind of separate if extremely limited life pen and paper can offer.

Among the Heccombs Portia finds frank libido everywhere: not only sensuality, but all the envy, rivalry, anger, destructive possessiveness Freud took such pains to document in the course of his long clinical career. Waikiki is an adolescent jungle of sorts, in contrast to Windsor Terrace. It is still England, though—insecure middle-class England, with well-meaning people who are not about to be stripped of their dignity, whether by their betters or by an innocent who appears clumsy or rude. Daphne is appalled when Portia *mentions* what she saw, Eddie and Daphne holding hands as they all sat watching a movie. As Daphne hesitates and gets

ready to strike out, the author notes: "In that pause, the civilization of Waikiki seemed to rock on its base."

We know that Portia intended no condescension or harm. She
is once again her own vexing self: inquisitive, a confusing mixture
of awareness and seeming ignorance. Daphne's various ways of
describing her reveal much about her own background and state
of mind, but do tell us, as well, a little more about Portia. "I had
no idea at all you were so *common*," she says, quite angry at this
strange guest. Portia's strangeness, her peculiar way of *going on*,
not rising to self-defense, not striking out at anyone, not seeming
even to *need* protection, or anger, either—all of that elicits more
than displeasure and envy in Daphne. "Well don't just fidget: it
drives me crazy." Portia isn't even fidgeting. She is *there*, waiting,
looking, wondering. Daphne goes on to call her "mousy and shy."
Then she claims her to have "the mind of a baby—and an awful
baby, if you'll excuse my saying so." Finally, at a loss for words,
she says, "You're completely bats."

None of that is written up in Portia's diary, so far as we know.
Were Miss Bowen portraying someone else, it would of course be
interesting to learn how Portia regarded Daphne as a result of their
encounter. But Portia never did really engage with Daphne, never
did really try to justify herself or assert her innocence. *All* innocence (at least then), she has no psychological position within
herself from which she can look about and say, "*Then*, under *those*
circumstances, I was innocent." Nor does her conversation with
Eddie after his betrayal of her reveal any new side of her, any
depth. He is full of his desperate cynicism. He basically tells her
he cannot love her, not the way she wants, maybe not the way a
better side of himself would want, if it had any say over his behavior. "Life is so much more impossible than you think," Portia
hears. "Don't you see we're all full of terrible power, working
against each other however much we may love?"

No, she does not see that. To do so would require a degree of
self-scrutiny, a capacity for shame she quite lacks. Nor will Eddie's
vision easily become hers. She has her own way of resisting such a
view, and in the end her considerable reserves of ingenuity are
mobilized to that task. We shall never know how successfully,
because Miss Bowen (out of respect for the confines of her novel's
structure) has to leave unanswered our desire to know whether
Portia is *going through* something, a period in her life, or whether

she is and will be someone quite different from those she so un-
settles. We know she is different from others in Miss Paullie's:
they submit, whereas she drifts off, all taken up with her own
interests. She is not a protégée of Lilian's, either. Others her age
or older meet her at Waikiki, and they, too, find her a difficult,
maddening person. They can't figure her, put her into any of the
categories they have learned to find convenient and necessary. On
the other hand, who is to say what is normal about a time of life
full of change? In the last third of the book, Matchett sees Portia
upon her return home from Waikiki and observes: "I must say,
they've sent you back with a colour. I can't see that this change
has done you harm." There is the implicit suggestion that somehow, in some manner yet to become apparent, Portia will become
different: grow up, lose innocence, take up a particular position
in the world, rather than remain an uncorrupted onlooker whose
behavior unnerves and confuses—and hurts—a number of people.

As Miss Bowen prepares for the denouement of her novel, she
has Anna make an interesting observation about Portia. She and
Thomas have come home from their vacation, Thomas with a
headache and in a cranky, sullen mood, she a bit playful but also
tense. The subject of Portia comes up, and Anna comments: "Poor
child, oh poor child, yes. She stood about like an angel. It was we
who were not adequate. I wasn't very, was I?" Apart from Anna's
own problems, once again shown us, we have the image of an angel
to think about, maybe contend with, even as the Quaynes must.
If Portia seemed an angel to them, they have not been the first
ones to find a youth of about sixteen angelic.[8] Who *does* feel

---

[8] I suppose this moment is as good as any to make mention of the contrasting,
sometimes sharply conflicting, ways various social critics and social scientists regard
today's young men and women of Portia's age, or a few years older. The less said about
Charles Reich's *The Greening of America* (New York, 1970) the better—though it has to
be put down for the record: an archetype, perhaps, of schematic nonsense about what
Americans supposedly have been like and supposedly, in increasing numbers, will be like,
especially youths. More scholarly and sensible in his analysis of similar social antagonisms
as they become psychological ones is Theodore Roszak in his *The Making of a Counter-
Culture* (New York, 1971). And after that book we have his *Where the Wasteland Ends*
(New York, 1972), in which he loses all interest in looking critically at the counterculture; it is our last and only hope, one learns. I have to contrast these books, with their
heavily romanticized notions about certain young people—and implicitly or explicitly
negative if not insulting notions about other youths—with Edgar Z. Friedenberg's *The
Vanishing Adolescent* (New York, 1959). Professor Friedenberg has a warm and open
heart; he enjoys and wants to uphold the young people Reich and Roszak describe—and

adequate in front of an angel? Just as important, what is an angel?

The Death of the Heart was not written to expose the inadequacies of Thomas and Anna Quayne. They are not everyman and everywoman, but they will suffice as reasonably decent people whose grown-up lives are complex, occasionally fulfilled, occasionally miserable, though perhaps in a novel like this one the balance has to tilt toward the latter. Why upon their return from vacation does Portia remind them of an angel? During that vacation Portia herself changed; if anything she became less angelic, as Matchett noticed. She is a family's historian as well as its maid or maids, so she is on the watch for signs and omens others would miss. But clearly Portia has not changed all that much; she still seems defenseless as a child, full of a kind of youthful goodness, perhaps loveliness, that strike a tired woman, back from a not especially rewarding trip, as angelic. And angels have power, too. They are superior to the rest of us—wiser, but also able to do things we find impossible. Needless to say, angels are not the evil, sensual, finite human beings the rest of us are, nor is Portia actually an angel—just a certain kind of youth. Enough of an angel, though; she seems above and beyond everyone, hence she is a source of constant bewilderment and not a little envy.

Even the self-contained St. Quentin, thoroughly convinced of *his* superiority (a writer, he has gifts of intelligence, observation, and expression denied many others), is baffled by her demeanor, her intent and purpose as a youth who can command so very much attention without seeming to want it. Their meeting clarifies Miss Bowen's purpose and enables us, finally, to see what significance

---

they are not all that unlike Portia, given the inevitable corrections for time and place. But he has an open mind, too; he appreciates people enough to look at them honestly, not turn them into foils in a larger, ideological war. His vision is not unlike Agee's in *The Morning Watch* (Boston, 1951): young people who are awakening are threatened on all sides by those who have lost all faith in themselves and others. But it is acknowledged that young people have a few of their inner torments and demons to contend with, apart from the gratuitous meanness of any particular world: Regent Park, London, a university town in the United States, or a rural section of New Mexico, where communes adjoin the land of impoverished and suspicious Chicano people or Indians, not to mention the state's rather conservative "Anglos." Finally, another book that deserves quite as little discussion as Reich's is Lewis Feuer's *Conflict of Generations* (New York, 1969). Anyone who wishes to become acquainted with the way psychoanalysis can be used as a bludgeon against idealistic youth need only glance through this abusive, wrongheaded book—which finds as little good in certain young people as Reich does bad.

Portia is meant to have for *us*, for whom (whether we happen to like them or not) the Quaynes are stand-ins of a sort. St. Quentin can look as closely as Portia; he has a "distracted intensity" about him as he casts his glance here and there. Like Portia, he can walk "aimlessly," yet seem to pick up facts and thoughts all the while; later he writes them down, though his audience is far greater than a diarist's. (For that matter, Portia's diary has achieved a larger circle of interest than do many.) And in rather quick time he emerges, at last, as someone who can come to terms with her—really, is her match. For once *she* is made nervous, made to "miss one step, shift her grip on her case." She is tricked into admitting she keeps a diary by this "devil" who already knows she does. She stands "helplessly" before him—perhaps disarmed is the word, this time her peculiar power of no avail.

Satan and his other devils, lesser ones, accomplices of his, are fallen angels, originally created good but become evil out of their own free will. Cast out of heaven, they have become wanderers, outsiders, always on the lookout for others to join them as the tempted who succumbed. Some in the Christian tradition have portrayed Satan as responsible for the fall of Adam and Eve, though nothing in Genesis gives substance to the claim. In Job, however, Satan does figure; he is the one who collects information for that ultimate moment of divine judgment when good and bad are sorted out, weighed and given their due. He is also the one who wanted to be independent of God, apart and self-sustaining, free of the ties others (the whole universe) must accept. St. Quentin fills the bill. He is as quick and unpredictable as the lightning Christ associated with Satan. He keeps himself free of everyone, enjoys his own power. He has his suit of sheep's clothing: outgoing, affable, he quickly takes the measure of Portia, whose own childlike qualities have not lacked a certain winning charm. And his mind is quick, adroit, and utterly to the point. In a brief street conversation he tells Portia off, yet never with any intention of criticizing or reprimanding her. One can for a moment accept them as nearly coequals—two of a kind in communion and reflection—except for the fact that they clearly are not and, what is more, Portia is also a young and hurt woman, both vulnerable and compelling as a person, not at all herself the way St. Quentin has become himself.

In essence, St. Quentin the devil is also St. Quentin the educator, and Miss Bowen is not the first one to merge those roles in a given character.[9] Miss Paullie's school takes for granted the insularity of its pupils. Portia is exceptionally insular; having been all over the place, she can treat the whole world without exception as foreign territory and retreat to the only neighborhood she knows: her mind's memory. St. Quentin insists that the time has come for her to forsake that refuge—or else, like him, commit herself to it knowingly. "One's nature is to forget, and one ought to go by that," he tells her. To keep a diary is in that sense unnatural. If she used it to pour out her anguish, that would be quite all right. But she presumes to be Job's relatively silent, always discreet but observant recorder—taking note of everyone's steps and missteps and putting them down for the record. It's about time, St. Quentin implies, she put aside the diary and took a misstep herself. And anyway, the author St. Quentin says (maybe with another author nodding in agreement) "we remember to suit ourselves": all facts become part of someone's purposes, and even the most quiet and unadorned compilation of events in a diary leaves out much, for example, the noisy distractions and uproars which, if included, would constitute quite another kind of factual record.

From memory and its deceits he moves on to "connections," which he calls a "vice" when made indiscriminately, presumably to please the (devilish) appetite of the onlooker. "You're working on us, making us into something," he tells her. When life's drift, the things we do and say to each other, is always turned into a pattern, is given constant notice, even set down on paper as part of a daily record, then a drift becomes quite different—a closely watched sequence which for that reason no longer resembles other such sequences. People are on guard. They take care all the time, lest one thing or another be said of them, written about them. They are not being secretive, guilty, suspicious; they are human beings, entitled to their own mixture of self-scrutiny and spontaneity.

God in his heaven watches over all of us, but presumably he is one of a kind. So even though what Portia writes may be quite "silly" rather than momentously psychological, she is "taking a liberty." She is setting a "trap" for those around her. She is under-cutting their "free will." She may hide from others her intentions;

---

[9]Mephistopheles is always with us. Even Fagin was an educator of a kind. Today we tend to internalize our devils; they are psychological drives that urge us on to wicked ways, but also mold our character, make us much of what we are, educate us.

maybe she doesn't clearly know them herself. Nevertheless, by design or out of some mad series of accidents, she has become "God's spy," and that is "unfair." Even if she has a loving nature, it is one *"in vacuo."* She loves everyone and so no one. She is infinitely tolerant—submissive, almost, to whatever happens around her; only determined, it seems, to keep in mind everything that can be seen or heard. She is the whole world's lover—with Eddie more a representative of the world than a potential suitor, adored and sought on his own right.

Portia now reacts. For a moment she is still the plaintive questioner, uncertain why this shrewd and cynical man would want to bear down so relentlessly and mercilessly on her, a mere sixteen-year-old girl, even if a secret diarist who has been found out. Then she is briefly a new person: "Pushing her hat brim further back from her forehead, Portia turned and sized St. Quentin boldly." She is up to the meeting with him, up to his kind of worldliness. She can give as well as take, surmise as well as await for others to declare and make obvious. She soon falls back, though. She becomes "dazed." She becomes compliant, a little mousy, all too grateful for St. Quentin's initiatives. She is back to her questions, innocent questions, galling because they are not intended to undo that innocence—rather, keep it intact.

If she is to be a writer, make a career of being curious, she will need "some key to why people do what they do." St. Quentin attacks frontally a certain implicit quality of her mind that all others have felt but not been able to recognize in any accessible way—her position as a critic, a person who reproaches, intimidates others by her presence. "You think us wicked," he says. She demurs. He insists; oh, he doesn't mean that she is a censorious person always ready to find fault. She simply fails to supply a context to the feelings and doings she meets up with. She does not consider that what seems unpleasant and compromising, wicked even, may be "our little way of keeping outselves going." One has to overlook as well as look. One has to save another person's everyday face, or, at the very least, not deny another's right to do so to a third party. St. Quentin is not pleading for mercy or rationalizing away evil. He is no moral hypocrite; as a jaded old novelist he knows full well what he shares with Portia. Eventually the two come close; they are companions of sorts, each presumptuous enough to dare find words for all that goes to make up life.

Tactfully he gets to the heart of the problem of pride: "It takes people in a lasting state of hysteria, like your friend Eddie, for instance, or people who feel they have some higher authority (as I've no doubt Eddie feels he has) to break every rule every time."

Their conversation is not conclusive; St. Quentin is arrogant and self-serving as well as a thoughtful person whom Portia is intelligent enough not to dismiss out of hand. But toward the end, as they ready to part, he makes a point she finds persuasive: "One thing one must learn is how to confront people that at that particular moment one cannot bear to meet." It can be said the advice was gratuitous; Portia had certainly managed to confront and deal with *him* in the past few minutes. St. Quentin may himself have realized that, because he follows his pedantic bit of advice with a somewhat apologetic "I suppose you're sorry we met?" No, not entirely; she replies, "I suppose it's better to know."

From that moment on Portia really begins to change. Until now she has been static, psychologically. Others have acted upon her in one fashion or another, only to be absorbed in her characteristic watchfulness. Now she does indeed continue to look around, but in a more active manner; she responds to what she sees directly, though not consistently by any means. A few days later, when in the company of Anna and Eddie, their clever talk, so false yet freighted with significance, wears her down. She flees into sleep right in front of them, and they envy her the abrupt honesty. It is a way of confronting what is unpleasant. St. Quentin might not approve of the choice, but better any choice than none at all. She has told those two how very tired they make her. She has also told them that she is beginning to know what they are up to. No longer is she the wide-eyed girl who listens intently and records faithfully but with no capacity for analysis or judgment. (As for Eddie, Anna lets him know her estimate of his overinclination to analyze and judge, through a sharp comment some of us in psychiatry ought regularly read over: "I don't think you ever know what is happening: you are too busy wondering what you can make of it.")

Later on, as the novel ends, Portia's active, engaged spirit becomes even more manifest. Anna notes her not "nearly so shy"; also, "less spontaneous." In fact, she is more spontaneous, less predictable. Her detachment had been almost studied; she would leave it to reach out, but quickly return. Now she is on her own. She takes off "the ingenuous little hat" she'd formerly worn. She weeps openly, even at the risk of being fawned over and consoled by the likes of her girl friend Lilian, for whom anything that happens is an excuse to get further self-absorbed. She meets Eddie, and she begs him, throws herself at him, takes issue with him, questions him, and indirectly reproaches him. When he pretends ignorance she mocks him, is described as speaking "coldly." By the time she is through with a confrontation of sorts, he remarks upon how "different" she is. Once she was "much gentler, much more sweet." Now she seems to have more than a glimmer of his number. Her new self-assertion can best be measured by Eddie's mounting panic. As she bears down, he becomes self-justifying, then truculent. Then he tries to take her with him, make her a full-fledged citizen of his world, all the while talking like a spokesman for St. Quentin's world: "You've got a completely lunatic set of values and a sort of unfailing lunatic instinct that makes you pick on another lunatic—another person who doesn't know who he is. You know I'm not a cad, and I know you're not batty. But, my God, we've got to live in the world."

He is by now speaking plaintively, and soon they will say good-bye, one assumes for good. She has managed to "know" by getting him to tell her. He *is* a cad, maybe a touch crazy if not a lunatic. She is starting out, and might well be headed, in his direction; but then, there is an increasingly good chance that she may not be, that she may collect her wits and become a grown-up person rather than Eddie's version of the "eternal adolescent." Anyway, her next and final stop, which is as far as the novel can take us, is the Karachi Hotel and Major Brutt. It is a sad and dreary place where the major lives, and once and for all any illusions we may have had about him are shattered. He has been the kind visitor, a bit pitiable, but also one who listens and has an odd kind of strength—none of Thomas's covert despair or Anna's edgy and brittle sociability. A waitress slights him. He is to the end decent—and unaware. No one can really insult him or manipulate him; he has constructed a steady view of others, and in so doing forgotten about himself. He is all innocence; if anyone tries to demean him, he can only fix the person with a certain surprised stare he is capable of and go on to the next situation life unaccountably will present. It can be said he is a living diary: always ready for the next day and the one after that; prepared to take in faithfully the world of others but not carve out any for himself; a shadow of a life rather than a part of it.

Suddenly Portia arrives, looking like "a wild creature." She is not only uncomposed; she is full of ideas of her own—and she is also full of purpose. Now it is Brutt who is acted upon, made to feel surprised or confused, moved to ask questions. She wants to be with him. She has been hurt by what Eddie has turned out to be; her very hysteria shows how clearly she has glimpsed him—now she is stripped of the illusions she was formerly prepared to have, and he prepared to make sure she had. Brutt calls her a "hysterical kid," but he is only half right. She is shrewd and demanding, no longer a kid; and when rebuffed by him she is not simply bold or saucy, but manipulative and, finally, another St. Quentin. She tears away at Brutt's illusions: all the warmth and coziness he has felt at Windsor Terrace have been imagined, because "they groan at each other when you have gone away." She offers him solace: "You and I are the same." But there is already a gulf between them, and it is not one exclusively made up of time. She is didactic and forceful; he submits, as always. True, he will not have her, take her in, bend to *that* wish. But he is no match for the "startling authority" she now possesses, and "ruthless as a goddess" she goes about her business—raging at Thomas and Anna, declaring herself and Brutt both betrayed, setting down all she at last has come to understand. ("That made all three of us funny, I see now. I see now that my father wanted me to belong somewhere because he did not: that was why they have had to have me in London.") It is not only *what* she sees, but *that* she does. She keeps on saying, "I see now"; the words end one sentence and begin another, for obvious authorial emphasis. One guesses Portia will not be writing down what she has just gone through.

She even manages to unsettle Brutt. For a moment he, too, seems converted. ("He saw what a fiction was common sense.") But the most he can do is shake himself out of his lethargic accommodation to the world and give expression to a kind of resigned generosity that is almost saintly (or angelic), but leaves him as vulnerable as ever: "When people seem to give you a bad deal, you've got to ask what sort of deal they may have once got themselves." For Portia such words are meaningless. Brutt himself has added: "But you are still young enough—." He breaks off; were he to continue he might contradict himself, indicate how right it is that one learn to protect oneself against, as well as understand, predators of various kinds. Moreover, Portia has already shown how well able she is to give as well as take. She is young enough to do so; he has never learned to and is now so old there is no point trying. The author speaks about both of them—what one is right in the middle of struggling with and the other has spent a lifetime firmly refusing to acknowledge: "Childish fantasy, like the sheath over the bud, not only protects but curbs the terrible budding spirit, protects not only innocence from the world but the world from the power of innocence." Brutt has not for a long time, if indeed ever, needed much curbing; Portia now is virtually unleashed, a typhoon upon the Karachi.

Soon enough the storm subsides, and then there is a deathlike silence. Brutt is not destroyed; a life so locked up is almost beyond assault. Portia looks like a "drifting object." Her passion has been spent. Betrayed, she has come to full life, fought on several fronts, retired in seeming defeat. But the willingness to do battle represents an all-important step for her: she looks dead but of course is not. Her heart seems dead, not her mind and not her soul—and, really, contrary to the book's title, not all of her heart, either. Miss Bowen won't simply let us say good-bye to a betrayed innocent. We are sent back to Windsor Terrace, where Thomas and Anna and St. Quentin are shown to be not at all betrayers—killers of a girl's honest, touching dreams.

They look at themselves as closely as Portia ever did, more openly and honestly than she could have once dreamed possible of them—or of herself. They are still in many respects small, wretched, foolish people. This is no novel intended to justify them circuitously and after much sly hemming and hawing. But it is absurd, Miss Bowen insists, to make them either devils or their disciples. Anna is as candid and self-accusing as her worst foe might wish. Thomas is poignant rather than shifty and cynical. St. Quentin is true to his position as a novelist-colleague of Miss Bowen's. (Portia herself may someday turn from diary-keeping to the writing of short stories and novels.) If these three and countless others are devils, it is about time Portia came alive to see them for what they are. In so doing, she will see a good deal of herself. Only Brutt and Eddie are denied that kind of self-scrutiny; the former scarcely knows how to do the looking; the latter sees so much he sees almost nothing.

As for Matchett, she may be exploited, abused, ignored, or taken for granted by a caste-ridden society, but she also helps hold together those so definitely above her; and, whether we like it or not, she will likely be deterred from that position by no one. After one reads her long monologue, carried on as she goes to fetch Portia on behalf of those sitting in some bewilderment and sorrow at Windsor Terrace, one is left with much respect for her—clearly intended by the author. She is tough and obstinate, proud and sensitive. If she has illusions, they are the kind sociologists and political scientists study better than psychologists. The book's last word is "authority"—a servant's on behalf of a family that is imperiled but not without some strengths. Portia's awakening, her frantic and outspoken search—from St. Quentin to Eddie to Brutt—has had its effect. She is in the center of things, not an onlooker or at most acted upon, but a forceful participant. Others take notice. St. Quentin may be sent scurrying to his notebooks, rather than a diary. Anna at the very least will look more closely in the mirror; and Thomas may be driven to a *new* run of fantasy. One doubts that Portia, whom Matchett with her "air of authority" gets ready to approach, will come home with an incurably broken heart.

In this novel Miss Bowen is an unflinching realist and, I suppose, easy prey for those of us who want the Portias of this world to fit our image of them. The novel ends inconclusively; we don't know, because we're not told, whether Portia will even consent to go back home, presumably for further growing up, a cold and banal term these days, used in its injunctive form at the slightest discretion of those who, quite baldly, want others to be like them— or suffer the consequences. On the other hand, the novelist might have easily, and to considerable dramatic effect, left us with a Portia fatally wounded by her beloved Eddie or a second time betrayed—now by Anna who could have plunged St. Quentin's knife just a bit deeper into that heart. Instead, spring weather is upon us, and a girl has shown herself able to demonstrate a grown woman's decisiveness, initiative, momentum.

She has also shown cruelty, vengefulness, spitefulness, a thorough lack of consideration for others. Brutt survives, but through no effort of Portia's. What has happened to this tender girl of mystery? Why her outburst of arrogance and the indulgence of her extreme self-regard at the expense of someone like Brutt? Are we to believe that she acts as she does out of desperation—the response of one whose heart has died? If so, the psychological assumption is interesting: meanness, rudeness, and worse can at any point in a life

arise, *de novo*, following a severe enough betrayal. Out of the
heart's death comes an unprecedented kind of life—the mind's
capacity for evil doing, now given substantial energy and direction.
If that holds, it is nothing short of miraculous. If innocence is a
puzzle, its relationship to evil becomes puzzling beyond comprehension when that relationship is predicated on death. Or is it that
evil has all along been in Portia, tied very closely to her innocence?
When the latter begins to fade, the former becomes more evident.
The issue is not one of the existence of evil but rather its emergence: when, under what circumstances?

Miss Bowen has said as much; I suspect, however, that many of
us, despite her asides, are not disposed to get the message. We are
tempted to echo Anna, see Portia as virtually angelic, or at least
that until the very end, which again we can dismiss as gratuitous,
an author's editing of life. *Tempted* may be just the word—in the
religious or philosophical as well as the psychological sense of the
word. Satan wanted to be God's equal; and though we think of the
devil as an evildoer, one who prompts others to act against God's
laws, there is another side of that fallen angel's ambition we are
likely to forget. God is not only ultimately the Maker, the Moving
Spirit, he is also the Knower and, of course, without sin. Satan
wanted that, also: God's perfection, his omniscience, his immunity
from the faults and blemishes the rest of us either admit to or
spend a good deal of energy denying. If man's pride has to do with
our never-ending wish to win—to obtain power, get esteem, be
recognized as important or valuable, and on and on—that pride has
an additional dimension, one perhaps less subject to criticism these
days: we want to know and be transformed by what we have
learned—made into better and better human beings, to the point
that we are just about faultless. Every utopian movement partakes
of that ambition, be it a political, messianic effort or the kind of
social and intellectual development Miss Freud in essence was describing when she reflected upon the uses to which various people
have put psychoanalytic knowledge in recent decades.

If only, one is implicitly told over and over again, and what
follows varies, of course: if only we bring up children this way;
if only we educate them that way; if only young men and women
are allowed to find one direction or are encouraged in another
direction; if only the nation were run under the following principles or by these or those individuals; if only people made a series

of changes in their lives, in the arrangements by which they live, the assumptions they hold dear. (If only we might all be—and remain—like the Portia we tend to perceive in the first part of Miss Bowen's novel: a youth who is sensitive, observant, thoughtful.) One has no right (speaking of sins) to throw heaps of cold water on all those dreams. For one thing, some of them do indeed promise substantial alleviation of human misery. Moreover, pride can take many forms, not the least of which is despair or cynicism. In that respect St. Quentin hovers on the brink. If Christ himself had to have his time of betrayal and abandonment, a man like St. Quentin can justify his scorn of his neighbors, his doubt that anything good will come of them. That temptation is the obverse of the secular millenarian fantasy. And I think Miss Freud would, in her gentle but firm clinical manner, be willing to use that word, *fantasy*—because it *is* a fantasy that is indulged when one or another side of man's psychological development is ignored or brushed aside as a remediable accident of history; for instance, a mere product of given social or economic circumstances.

At this point, with Portia in mind, one turns again to Anna Freud, a London neighbor of Miss Bowen's. One has to keep insisting that Portia is no prototypical adolescent and Miss Bowen is not trying to describe the strictly psychological vicissitudes a girl goes through as she gradually becomes a young woman ready (with all the inevitable hesitations and equivocations) to join the particular world she has been fated to be part of. *The Death of the Heart* dwells on those longtime members of London's Windsor Terrace as well as their recent guest. And the author has a social critic's eye as well as a psychologist's ear. Nevertheless, I believe Miss Bowen in the 1930s was struggling with some of the same issues Anna Freud was, and at the same time. Here is Miss Freud trying to set down some of the seemingly "incomprehensible and irreconcilable contradictions" that youths of both sexes present those who pay them close attention:

Adolescents are excessively egoistic, regarding themselves as the center of the universe and the sole object of interest, and yet at no time in later life are they capable of so much self-sacrifice and devotion. They form the most passionate love relations, only to break them off as abruptly as they began them. On the one hand, they throw themselves enthusiastically into the life of the community and, on the other, they have an overpowering longing for solitude. They oscillate between blind submission to some self-chosen leader and defiant rebellion against any and every authority. They are selfish and materially minded and at the same time full of lofty idealism. They are ascetic but will suddenly plunge into instinctual indulgence of the most primitive character. At times their behavior to other people is rough and inconsiderate, yet they themselves are extremely touchy. Their moods veer between light-hearted optimism and the blackest pessimism. Sometimes they will work with indefatigable enthusiasm and at other times they are sluggish and apathetic.[10]

One can, of course, make too much of those swings, those alternations that make no sense and can drive a theorist to the use of more and more adjectival phrases or to making the most of a dilemma by converting it into the basis of yet another definition: adolescence *is* those very things that puzzle or enrage us, the ambivalence, the cyclical episodes of self-indulgence, the swaying, to-and-fro movement of the mind's emotional life, all due to the arrival of new libidinal energy at the door of the psychic apparatus. But Miss Freud is less interested in theoretical definitions than in direct observation, followed by a scrupulous write-up of what has been seen. Maybe that is why her description evokes Portia—who, by the way, not once in the novel considered herself, or was considered by anyone, a candidate for psychotherapy. Nor would Miss Freud want to take the young lady on as a patient at Hampstead Clinic, not all that long a trip from Regent's Park, presumably the model for Windsor Terrace.

The problem is one of normality, not pathology, as Miss Freud strongly insists in the book she published in 1936 but went on to document even more thoroughly in a later book.[11] Cultures vary, and anthropologists have documented how provincial some of our psychological formulations are. Portia is, again, no universal adolescent, nor is Miss Bowen a disguised philosopher or psychologist, intent on rivaling Augustine, Kierkegaard, or Freud. But no culture can avoid the problems of innocence and worldliness, of life and

[10]Miss Freud's lengthy descriptions of adolescence in her *The Ego and the Mechanisms of Defense* (London, 1936) are fitting companions to Miss Bowen's book. From an altogether different vantage point Miss Freud comes to see the Portias of this world in quite the same light Miss Bowen does.

[11]The first is *The Ego and the Mechanisms of Defense*, the second *Normality and Pathology in Childhood*, both referred to previously.

death, of rising expectations and failing health—the problem of succession, really. Portia hopes for something. The Quaynes regret a host of things. Already they and St. Quentin feel shadows over their lives; and Portia for a spell doesn't know what a shadow is, which makes her absurdly ignorant at the very least. Were she to persist in such ignorance, she would risk becoming fatuous, and Major Brutt is more that than anything else; he endlessly bases his expectations on a reality constructed by his mind—and it is a mind that does not think to check out its conclusions with a little of Anna Freud's direct observation. That phrase was meant to dissuade psychoanalysts from their own kind of naïveté. Theory-building can be as perverse as diary-writing: in both instances the mind is tempted to go its own way, apart from the world or the flesh and maybe to the enhancement of the devil's power. Portia leaves out no more that is important than many other social or psychological observers have managed to do, and they with less excuse.

Unlike Portia and those psychiatrists whom Miss Freud has gently but continuously chided with her admonition that we need more looking and fewer conclusions, Miss Bowen tries hard not to leave things out. Portia is decent, thoughtful, unaffected; Portia is calculating, provocative, wrapped up in herself, capable of unmistakable cruelty. The Manichaean heresy was no temptation to the author of *The Death of the Heart*. In fact the novel reads like a subtle twentieth-century fictional echo of much Augustine struggled against and, later on, Pascal. Drawn to God, those two could not fail to notice the presence of evil in themselves and others. Augustine uses himself to describe the psychological ambiguities a particular youth eventually had to find bearable—because they are resolved, as we put it today, only in the City of God. Pascal may have been more drawn to Satan; Jansenism was strongly inclined to sort people out into the clearly saved and the quite definitely condemned. Yet he had an ironic temperament and was no Calvinist at heart. In any event, to this day, and under innumerable guises, the Manichaean heresy lives on. *The Death of the Heart* can be read as a novel that flirts with that heresy, then firmly rejects it. Some psychiatrists and social observers are no less subject to the obvious appeal such a heresy can have, though, God knows, these days, that particular heresy has taken on new, highly secular forms.

Put differently, it is not only certain Christian theologians who have wanted to set Satan apart from the other angels—and thereby distinguish in the most emphatic and categorical way those who are good and those who are evil. We crave order, and there is no reason to believe we will deny the mind that order, especially when it is the mind in the first place that wants such order. Why wouldn't we turn that desire back on itself, so to speak—submit man's psychological life to man's psychological urge to straighten things out, tidy them up, put them in their place? In so doing there are fringe benefits: we become seers, if not God. To confront man with his sticky, messy self, sprawled all over the moral and psychological spectrum, is to appease no one's pride and quite possibly is to risk offending the vanity of any number of people.

Nevertheless, Miss Bowen is not afraid to show Portia contending with most of those seven deadly (capital) sins: at the very least, pride, covetousness, lust, anger, and envy. One could even make a case for sloth, and leave gluttony to Lilian. Many of us have no trouble recognizing the presence of a few such sins in ourselves; we may even have spent years with a psychiatrist learning how pervasive and influential that presence can be. When we are through our apprenticeship in self-recognition, we then quite understandably feel less saddled with illusions; we remember all of them we have painfully cut away. But illusions have a way of going underground; perhaps the unconscious, very much part of nature, also abhors a vacuum, and so new illusions slip in when old ones are made to leave. Miss Freud's descriptions of the chronology of an illusion (that childhood can be made an almost heavenly experience) is but one of many such chronologies.

All one need do is read some accounts of youth to find a similar trend: the young might be, or ought to be, or are on the verge of being freed of whatever ails or limits or even discomforts the rest of us—*if only* a certain kind of social or political change takes place, or *if only* they all get to have some psychiatric experience, or *if only* they make for themselves certain living arrangements. Once they were *this*, now they will turn into *that*. Besides, as *youth* they have these traits, while *we* are characterized by this other bundle of characteristics. Needless to say, the particular adjectives or nouns vary with the proponent's theoretical orientation, or maybe his plain biases, admitted or not. Youth are our only hope: they are idealistic, decent, honorable, the world's seekers, the one segment of our population that demonstrates this kind of consciousness or that quality of mind and heart. Alternatively, youth are an increasing danger to us: they are selfish, turned in on themselves, demanding, spoiled, naive, dangerously ignorant and susceptible to the blandishments of—well, dozens of dangerous propagandists or ideologues. On and on the lists get drawn: who is what, and why.

Kierkegaard wrote every one of his books in order to save us (and, or course, himself) from those lists, however sophisticated and (he was careful to point out) inevitable they are. He had nothing against Hobbes distrusting people or Locke thinking the best of them. Were he alive today one suspects he would smile approvingly at the efforts of social scientists or psychiatrists to insist upon one or another aspect of man's inner life. And if children have "envy or gratitude," youths have more of both, and that "more" certainly requires analysis and portrayal. It was Hegel's intellectual ambitiousness that drew Kierkegaard's anger and fire: the nerve of presuming to plot out the entire human drama, as if he were God.[12] No wonder *Either/Or* is a final statement on final statements, such as those that end with an *either/or*. Kierkegaard ultimately argues that before God all is mystery; yet each of us has to keep on trying to fathom the world. To maintain such a position is to walk a tightrope, and he knew the dangers. One can surrender and ask nothing—become dumb, unconcerned, a caricature of the faithful believer. Or it is possible to try so hard with one's grasping mind that one not only believes what has been assuredly and seriously studied but elevates it to a much higher order of significance. Here generalizations become something else, those age-old articles of faith that men have constructed for themselves, then gone on to worship vehemently and possessively: Saint Paul's "tables of stone."

The word *youth* is, of course, an abstraction; it refers to millions of individuals. They are no more privy to Arcadia's secrets than the children they once were or the working men and women they soon enough in most cases will be. Rufus and his sister, and Portia, too, will not save us, provide us with all sorts of lessons: what to

[12]Kierkegaard is rather clearly Johannes Climacus, who appears on the title page of both *Philosophical Fragments* and *Concluding Unscientific Postscript*, each stock full of attacks on Hegelian speculation and theory-building.

do, what not to do. Both James Agee and Elizabeth Bowen want to let go of their characters, give them their due but not ask more of them than any human being (or "age-group") has to offer. As novelists they by and large speak their minds by implications; they also put the reader through a trial. We are moved; our sympathies are strongly engaged. Rufus is a sturdy, lovable boy, and his predicament awful; that he seems destined to survive it is reason to add admiration to an already strong affection. Portia is a fragile and impressionable girl, who, under difficult conditions of her own, has retained some qualities many of us have lost or never really had in any great quantity: honesty, thoughtfulness—in Miss Bowen's imagery, open-heartedness. That she fights the devil so hard and long and at the end is still fighting may tempt us to make the hope we feel for her part of a more general hopefulness of our own: hearts may die, but they needn't—and someday the devils of this world, the whole Windsor Terrace crowd, residents and visitors alike, will be seen for the killers they are, and summarily banished, or at the least stripped of their considerable authority over the lives of the world's Portias.

Without in any way denying our right, even the obligation we have, to think along those lines, one has to hold out other grounds for the attachment and regard we feel toward a Rufus or a Portia: the sense of camaraderie they inspire in us. However idiosyncratic their lives, we recognize ourselves in them. They were fated to suffer—from a father's death, from a society's corruption become the corruption of individuals—but they were also fated to suffer at the hands of themselves, as we all are: not as neurotics but as particular, finite human beings. There is no great drama in such daily moments of suffering. Yet the best novelists have recognized in them the greatest challenge. One suspects the rest of us have a similar recognition. Rufus grows after he has experienced the drama of his father's death and begun the kind of life that will follow it. We have reason to think Portia has contrived a dramatic moment in order to put an end to something, then begin a new and important direction in her life. The reader may feel cheated in both cases. What *will* happen—to the boy, to the youth? Both novelists say, finally: as with life, the answer is never in until the end, so beware of those, whatever their calling, who claim to have advance knowledge.

IV Maturity: George Eliot's *Middlemarch*

W<small>HAT</small> <small>WE</small> *can* predict is the advance of age, barring various disasters that extinguish the lives of children or young people. Yet who feels satisfied with that kind of prediction: the statement of the obvious? There is, after all, a sequence of events in this life, which must have a certain cumulative effect. Why not, then, declare Rufus likely (at least) to be a man of *this* quality and Portia a woman who can be characterized as *such and such* a person? The question is rhetorical these days; the social sciences have come into their own and beyond question enable us to make rather educated guesses about what is in store for certain psychoanalytically defined character types or for those from certain socioeconomic groups. Childhood is destiny; or background is destiny—so plausible theories strongly suggest. All a novelist can do is stay with certain individuals, in the hope that what is imagined and presented in a story has its own special value; even as most clinicians learn that no matter what they have learned about a person's psychological and sociological past, the present and future are mysteries still, because each person has the freedom to use his assets, however limited or stunted, and yes, his liabilities, however considerable, in an altogether singular way.

We are fixated by fears or anxieties or obsessions. We are poor or rich, white or black, American or European or Asian, educated or illiterate. Within such limits, substantial and often enough overwhelming, we have a range of possibilities that deserves emphasis and appreciation. Accidents, fateful encounters, unexpected arrivals and departures of certain people, surprising incidents that elicit wholly original or unforeseen turns in a person's thinking or behavior—these are the stuff of life. It is a stuff those intent on measuring traits or putting labels on things (or people!) ought have the good sense to respect from a proper distance. It is the stuff of prosaic or momentous psychological changes, for the good or the bad.

If childhood, class, and race are factors of enormous significance in our lives, so are those chance meetings, those mishaps, those utterly casual or random or indeterminate or uncontrollable happenings that make all the difference in a life. Whom do we meet, then marry? Where were we sent while in military service, and what happened there? What did an illness do to the way we thought about life and even lived life thereafter? Then, there is that word *if*. Again and again we· say that if it hadn't been for him or her or them—and on and on. What psychological or sociological theory really takes into account such developments? They cannot be tabulated, calibrated, foretold, explained. Shall they be called "other" in someone's list of causes—to the apprehension of those of us who want life firmly under control, wrapped up in tidy phrases and formulations?

Meanwhile, Agee tells us that a father's death is not simply a loss, or the occasion for a family's grief reaction, but an event likely to make for new lives, saddened for a good long while, different always from what they might have been, but not only in a negative or pathological sense. And by the same token, Portia's encounters with her half brother, his wife, his young associate, Eddie, not to mention Matchett, St. Quentin, and Major Brutt, represent something more than an adolescent adjustment reaction, to draw upon a clinical phrase one has a right to use as medical shorthand, provided the decided limits of such a phrase are acknowledged. From each of those particular human beings Portia took something; through her involvement with them she was enabled to shift and realign her posture toward both herself and the world around her—to the point that she may well at the end be ready to turn into a somewhat different person in many respects. Had her parents lived, had she stayed with them and struggled to grow up in that rather different situation, one can imagine her becoming quite another person, though exactly what kind still would be an unsettled matter: there, too, in Switzerland or Southern France or wherever, things (as we put it with fitting vagueness) would have happened.

All of these ironies, riddles, and enigmas of life do not seem to bother James Agee or Elizabeth Bowen; and as for George Eliot, she has built the whole novel *Middlemarch* around that theme—of life's *indefiniteness*, a word she stresses in the book's prelude. It is a prelude often analyzed, and one especially of interest today, when women are asserting their individuality and humanity against customs and laws (and generalizations) as embarrassingly irrational and insulting as they are instructive. (One century's, even one generation's, conventional wisdom is the next century's or generation's appalling stupidity.)[1] Usually critics emphasize the connection between Saint Theresa of Avila and Dorothea Brooke. Both are women very much curbed by the spirit of their time yet gifted with energy and intelligence that, given other circumstances, might have been differently—in greater measure—put to use. The author intends no slight of what Saint Theresa did accomplish— rather a lot—even as she has throughout the length of her novel extended the fullest of sympathy and respect to Dorothea. It is more a matter of recognition: some souls are passionate beyond the norm, and on that account fated for frustration. The destiny of such men or women may never suit their psychological and spiritual endowment. George Eliot was also haunted by those who never even come to be seen as limited by a particular historical era: "Here and there is born a Saint Theresa, founders of nothing, whose loving heart-beats and sobs after an unattained goodness tremble off and are dispersed among hindrances, instead of centering in some long-recognizable deed."

She can be even more ironic, and in awe of life's unpredictability. Not only have there been those thwarted and disappointed who might have lived "an epic life"; some "born a Saint Theresa" have ended up living "a life of mistakes." And the reason? She will side neither with nature or nurture; perhaps some internal flaw, some "tragic failure" undercuts such would-be individuals of distinction, or perhaps it is the "meanness of opportunity" all too many indeed the vast majority, of this world's growing children must accept, like it or not, as their inheritance.[2] Still, she is not quite satisfied

---

[1]No matter how gifted and analytic his mind, Freud could go only so far—could free himself only so much from his era. That fact of life becomes especially apparent in his remarks on women. In that regard, a recent article that does justice to the injustice of much psychoanalytic theory, without in the process overlooking the integrity and sincerity of Freud's effort, is Paul Schwaber's "Women and Freud's Imagination," *American Scholar*, Spring 1972.

[2]One can go on and on, trying to walk the tightrope of nature-nurture. Melanie Klein in *Envy and Gratitude* (London, 1957) places the origin of our lusts and rages so close to birth that the issue of what, in fact, causes such emotions—the workings of genes or a particular society—begins to fade in importance. If, as she suggests, infants

with that rather broad and flexible way of looking at human growth and development. Are women, for instance, afflicted with an "inconvenient indefiniteness," God-given most likely? She asks the question, and naturally has no answer. She herself is rather comfortable with "indefiniteness"; it is a psychological fact of life: "the limits of variation" to human behavior are rather broad—perhaps an unpromising way to start a novel that is called "a study of provincial life."

Nevertheless, for all her appreciation of life's uncertainties, George Eliot was very much interested in the scientific method. She had spent a good deal of time studying medicine and biology in connection with the writing of *Middlemarch*, and she had a strong interest not only in philosophy but psychology.[3] In that brief prelude, a page or so long, she speaks of "scientific certitudes": how are women, or men for that matter, to be understood with any exactness in the face of the psychological "indefiniteness" she speaks of? And how is a study done of individuals when they are

---

struggle in the first few months with complicated psychological reactions (as opposed to needs, for food, warmth, protection) then a whole generation of new anthropological-psychoanalytic observation will be required to supplement books like *Childhood in Contemporary Cultures*, ed. Margaret Mead and Martha Wolfenstein (Chicago, 1955). All the variations reported in that book, so clearly tied to cultural forces at work among parents and children, may be preceded by the kind of psychological uniformity Melanie Klein postulates. On the other hand, it has to be added that Anna Freud and D. W. Winnicott, two child psychoanalysts who are English colleagues of Klein's, are by no means inclined to go along with her formulations. Miss Freud's work, and Winnicott's, written up in *The Child and the Outside World* (London, 1957), place greater stress on the subtle interplay between a child and his or her environment: people, places, values, or customs handed down. From another direction, however, one is again asked to question the emphasis on cultural relativity. Of all people, an anthropologist, Colin Turnbull, has shown in *The Mountain People* (New York, 1972) that social pressures at a certain point reveal capacities in human beings that can only be considered demonic rather than aggressive or adaptive. His field work in a curious way dovetails with a recent novel of Cormac McCarthy's, *Outer Dark* (New York, 1968); and both the anthropologist and novelist can be considered kinsmen of those Greek tragedians who emphasized fate—certain forces at work that defy classification as social or psychological. Here is a biologist coming close to a similar (heavily ironic—I suppose, too, tragic) outlook: "There can be no immortal cells. Indeed, Leonard Hayflick has found in careful experiments that by the time a cell has divided about fifty times the clone of cells formed from it all fail to divide. *The machinery of life ensures the death of individuals.* But exactly this machinery also ensures the evolution of new forms. *The errors that destroy the individual are also the origin of species*" (J. Bronowski, "New Concepts in the Evolution of Complexity," *American Scholar*, Autumn 1972; italics are his).

[3] See Asa Briggs's "*Middlemarch* and the Doctors," *Cambridge Journal* 1 (Sept. 1948).

so frustrating in their complexity—never mind the world they belong to, which can be (sometimes simultaneously) so obstructive and discouraging, so enabling and encouraging?

Throughout *Middlemarch* George Eliot seems unable to forget that word *indefiniteness*. The novel's plot, its characters, its psychological and philosophical themes—they all resist clear-cut definition. In the eight books that make up the author's study, stories give way to other stories; and unattractive individuals to our surprise demand our sympathy while those we have felt close to suddenly are found wanting. No central argument prevails, even as no one person dominates the narrative. It is a world of refined gradations we have to comprehend, a world where political reformers, bent on doing what obviously needs to be done, are shown to be, at the same time, foolish, frivolous, or uninformed. It is a world where hypocrites are not segregated and scoffed at; we meet one of them, get to know him well, and before we are through knowing him we have learned of his thoughtfulness, his sincerity, his genuine capacity for moral introspection. It is a world where well-meaning idealists falter and reveal severe mistakes in judgment. It is a world where neither abstract social forces nor historical conditions nor individual initiatives dominate; they all are mixed so subtly into a particular narrative, into a *story*, that they resist the critic's desire to extract them and weigh their separate influence. It is the world of England's Midlands around 1831 and 1832, just before the Reform Bill was enacted; and there is no doubt that the values of every one of the individuals portrayed reflect that geographical and temporal fact.

On the other hand, various individuals (and not just the ones we meet at greatest length) are capable of being very much themselves. With a determined assist from the author, they say things that transcend any era's confines, and they not infrequently act in ways that jolt the reader; he has not been prepared by the author for what he learns has been said or done. It is almost as if George Eliot is determined that this long and ambitious story *not* be any one thing, but rather combine elements of fiction that other novelists are perfectly willing to sort out and use separately for particular novels.[4]

---

[4]F. R. Leavis, in *The Great Tradition* (London, 1960), points out how broad George Eliot's sensibility was, how hard it is to pin down her novels, fit them under various categories. At this point I should mention some of the books that have helped me think

Critics have noted that the prelude, with its mention of Saint Theresa, seems to indicate that the novel will center itself on Dorothea Brooke, a sensitive and willful lady who has her own ideas and aims to have her own way, a contrast indeed with her conventional sister, Celia. Yet if that was for a time George Eliot's intention, she soon enough moves on to other characters and their private worlds. Since they, too, are casting about for a situation in life that will be worthy of their energies and since they are men as well as women, one gradually realizes that these parallel constructions of character and predicament are meant to connect Dorothea to others. True, she is a thwarted woman, a kinswoman of Theresa, a lady rather more "definite" (imaginative, competent, conscientious) than a particular era's prejudicial eyes, belonging to men, of course, were willing to acknowledge. On the other hand, her life affects other lives powerfully. She is not abandoned for other characters and the interests or problems they present. She is with us to the end; the novel's first paragraph introduces her to us, and its last paragraph mentions her and no one else we have met in Middlemarch. Through a series of connections the author makes, her subject's ardent, striving nature is given its definition, freed from the "indefiniteness" social and cultural restraints would place upon such a woman.

Miss Brooke wants to know more than others thought seemly, do more than a woman even of her position was encouraged to do. She is all taken up with hopes—not only for herself but the world. She dreams of intellectual discoveries and, later on, good deeds that will make for a better Middlemarch, a reformed and more nearly just society. But her struggles are shared; the obstacles she

---

about *Middlemarch*. Not every novel has a critical *book* devoted to it, but this one does: *Middlemarch: Critical Approaches to the Novel*, ed. Barbara Hardy (London, 1967). There are some fine essays in that volume—it is as if George Eliot's depth and range of mind inspire in her critics a similar breadth of view. Also of value are Barbara Hardy's *The Novels of George Eliot* (New York, 1959), *Critical Essays on George Eliot* (London, 1970), and *The Appropriate Form* (London, 1964). Clearly, without her work scholarship on George Eliot would be substantially less than it is—and also more scattered. A recent book of great interest is Calvin Bedient's *Architects of the Self* (Berkeley, 1972). The author does not forsake literary criticism for psychological analysis but knows how to draw sensibly on the latter—no mean achievement these days. Very useful in view of George Eliot's "preoccupations," is U. C. Knoepflmacher's *Religious Humanism and the Victorian Novel* (Princeton, 1965). Also, the same author's sensitive and suggestive *George Eliot's Early Novels* (Berkeley, 1968). Finally, I found Jerome Thale's *The Novels of George Eliot* (New York, 1959) stimulating to go through.

faces turn out to be more common than one might have expected. Lydgate is a man and a doctor; on two accounts he is free to use his intelligence and determination, in ways denied Dorothea. She has her own mind, yet is expected to fall prostrate, gullible, and grateful before any suitor. Not so with him; he is a suitor. She has a mind that is alert, curious, attached to specific interests and wishes; however, she lacks a profession to give shape to all that. Not so with him; he is a physician. Nevertheless, his difficulties are substantial, and ultimately his life has to be judged tragic. Not so with hers.

Nor does Ladislaw's fate help matters along—or Bulstrode's, or even that of relatively minor characters, like Fred Vincy. They are all men; yet in each case the same indefiniteness mentioned in connection with Dorothea comes to be a problem—to the point that, in comparison, Saint Theresa seems to be very much the exceptional person she in fact was: for most of us, man or woman, doctor or person with little education and no profession, life leads to no such dramatic, vividly circumscribed but distinctly memorable achievement—to sainthood, speaking of the exceptional. Rather it is a matter of rise and fall, spells of murky confusion followed by really luminous periods, contradictions that never get cleared away, failures coupled hopefully with real moments of affirmation— indefiniteness lived out, but no doubt about it, offset now and then by those periods in which a person shows himself or herself to be sharp and clear about what is at stake.

At one relatively early point in the novel the young and idealistic Lydgate is talking to Middlemarch's vicar, Mr. Farebrother. Lydgate wants to help change a sadly ignorant and corrupt profession. This is no idle fantasy on his part; nor is he the shrewd, self-serving kind of reformer who is simply waiting for the right moment to be bought up, lock, stock and barrel, by some representative of the status quo. His honesty is beyond question, his beliefs long held and well thought out. He has no interest in showy or dramatic gestures; for some time he has tried to figure out how to bring about the changes he has in mind, and as he tells the vicar of his plans he sounds sure of himself and no fool. On the other hand, as the vicar keeps reminding him, it is no easy task to win over people, never mind deflate the pomposity of a professional group that can always rely upon the life-and-death fears of people. As they talk along Lydgate asks the vicar, Farebrother, about a mutual acquaintance of theirs—a man with whom, actually, the former, as a doctor-in-training, had shared an apartment in Paris. Trawley by name, "he was hot on the French social systems, and talked of going to the backwoods to found a sort of Pythagorean community." The answer is quickly offered: "He is practising at a German bath, and has married a rich patient."[5]

The vicar has no desire to be gloomy or sarcastic; he is a quiet man, inclined if anything to self-criticism. ("And I am not a model clergyman—only a decent makeshift.") He cannot tolerate Bulstrode's evangelical Christianity, so full of intensity and moral sureness: do this, believe this, act this way and the kingdom of heaven is, beyond doubt, a hop, skip, and jump away. Yet he has grave doubts about the practicality of Lydgate's ideas; and those doubts get across to Lydgate and reveal a side of him otherwise not easily apparent: the activist's self-righteousness, especially summoned when already stiff odds become even higher. In essence the doctor says that he always knew he had the right way of seeing things. Let his former roommate fall astray; he, Lydgate, will persist and succeed. In reply the vicar answers: "Your scheme is a good deal more difficult to carry out than the Pythagorean community, though. You have not only got the old Adam in yourself against you, but you have got all those descendants of the original Adam who form the society around you."

Doctor Lydgate does not want to hear that kind of talk. He is full of not hope but expectation. Given time, effort, and his self-acknowledged intelligence, Middlemarch will have a much needed new kind of medical practice, one that will be a model for other communities all over England. The vicar persists, but not too forcefully. Nor does the author choose at this moment to enter with one of her comments; there will be plenty of time for them further along. As a novelist she has to show us through the experiences of her characters what those two men are trying to say. She does, of course; and nearly five hundred pages later we are all too aware of Lydgate's struggles, the limits he has found in both himself and Middlemarch, the particular society the vicar has mentioned. I think it is no accident that in the early stages of her novel George Eliot, like James Agee and Elizabeth Bowen, makes

---

[5]The analogy to Dick Diver's fate in F. Scott Fitzgerald's *Tender Is the Night* is rather striking.

mention of Adam and the inheritance it is claimed we have as a result of what happened in the Garden of Eden. She also brings up references that have nothing to do with the Bible—"the French social systems." A woman of broad philosophical and religious interests, much influenced at one time in her life by Rousseau, she was fortunate enough never to be certain what to emphasize as a matter of her intellectual faith: the destiny individuals find for themselves as a result of the force of their character or the fate those individuals meet up with whereby particular intentions become transformed by the workings of a given social and economic system into something altogether different.

She paid close attention to human psychology, so close that she anticipates Freud in important respects by a good thirty years; quite simply she knew of the unconscious mind and, even more significant, knew exactly how that part of the mind works. She also paid close attention to the gradual and subtle way that money, power, and social position work their influence on the unconscious. *Middlemarch* is indeed a study as well as a story, an effort on the part of one novelist to answer those riddles Tolstoy posed just a year or two earlier in *War and Peace*. The two novels have often been compared; both are the products of minds unwilling to rest content with the usual intellectual categories. Tolstoy refuses to call *War and Peace* a novel. George Eliot refers to a study, and is not being pretentious or coy when she uses the word; before and while she wrote about the people of Middlemarch she investigated the medicine, the politics, the whole cultural climate of a generation that preceded her own.[6] Her aim, like Tolstoy's, was to recreate the history of the immediate past, and to do so she summoned more than her imaginative powers. *Middlemarch* is not only full of a social observer's comments and a historian's acquired facts but a philosopher's passion to find coherence for apparently diverse or unrelated phenomena. Tolstoy, similarly motivated, has his second epilogue waiting for us; George Eliot scatters her analytic and interpretive remarks throughout the book.

---

[6]Jerome Beatty has done a first-rate job of documenting her various preparations in "History by Indirection: The Era of Reform in *Middlemarch*," *Victorian Studies*, December 1957. And, of course, there is George Eliot's own account in *Quarry for Middlemarch*, ed. Anna Kitchel (Berkeley, 1950)—the notebook she kept while writing the novel.

In *Middlemarch* the questions James Agee implicitly posed about Rufus and Elizabeth Bowen about Portia get directed at grown-up people, rather than children or adolescents. Dorothea is a worthy successor to Portia, if one may reverse literary history in the interests of another kind of chronology. If Rufus has been misunderstood as the wholly sensitive and impressionable boy cruelly hurt by events, and Portia as the wholly open and decent youth, cruelly hurt by people, then Dorothea Brooke, Dr. Lydgate, and Will Ladislaw can. all too easily be seen as their fully grown equivalents: each is innocent, uncorrupted, strangely at the mercy of the world's evil. And in all three novels one has to fight hard to keep open to the author's intentions, even as they themselves as novelists indicate the dilemma before them. How to write with sympathy and compassion, even open partiality, about the goodness in people, their capacity to show loftiness of purpose, unselfishness, good faith and clean hands—and at the same time show another side of life, a side that no one can ignore or feel removed from?

Sometimes one wonders whether all three novelists haven't been a bit wicked; in each case the favor felt for an important character in the story is made to be so strong and apparent in the beginning, and the reader is consequently so won over, that he has a difficult time coming to his senses toward the end, even in the face of a good deal of evidence presented. As for the critic or essayist, he risks becoming cranky and picayune—always pointing out those negatives about obviously vulnerable children or innocent youth or high-minded adults. None of these three novelists makes it easy for us to dislike their principal characters. None of these three novelists is an out-and-out satirist, though each is tempted; and, interestingly enough, the common source of temptation is someone or something connected with religion. In both *A Death in the Family* and *The Death of the Heart*, the church does not come off very well. Agee has no great use for the Anglican priest, and Miss Bowen largely ignores explicitly religious matters until the second section ("The Flesh") when Portia goes to church with Mrs. Heccomb—and the lack of significance such attendance has, its ironic inconsequence in the face of Waikiki's larger (that is, utterly trivial or self-indulgent) preoccupations, becomes all too obvious. As for George Eliot, she not only invokes Adam, but Noah, too, and in this way: "When the animals entered the ark in pairs, one may imagine that allied species made much private remark on each other, and were tempted to think that so many forms feeding on the same store of fodder were eminently superfluous, as tending to diminish the rations. (I fear the part played by the vultures on that occasion would be too painful for art to represent, those birds being disadvantageously naked about the gullet, and apparently without rites and ceremonies.)"

She is getting ready to describe a Middlemarch funeral procession, including what she devastatingly calls "the Christian Carnivora" who formed it. A substantial sum of money was left by Peter Featherstone, and the result is obvious: envy, jealousy, rivalry, hatred, artifice, pretense, hypocrisy—a procession of emotions that directly parallels the procession of human beings in mourning. For the most part, though, she resists such temptations to scorn the people of Middlemarch. Certainly Dorothea is at all times a genuinely decent person. Often in the novel she wins the reader's strong sympathy as a victim. Her suitor, then husband, Casaubon, is so obviously pretentious and humorless. She is the woman desirous of doing good—good by her husband and good on behalf of the world. He is the dried-up pedant whose appetites are larger than his capacities. His pride is immediately obvious; his meanness becomes obvious only later. His marriage seems like a travesty when it begins, and becomes a living hell for both parties before it is ended by death. When Casaubon dies he is a jealous, melancholy man who has not finished his "Key to All Mythologies," the very title of which would no doubt set Augustine into one of his rages.

And yet; there are always those "and yets" in store for George Eliot's readers. By emphasizing the pitiful and stupidly grandiose quality of Casaubon's pride, she makes Dorothea's kind of pride, conveyed only by indirection, seem a far greater issue, if not problem, for us. Miss Brooke was not kidnapped, after all. One feels that at first Casaubon himself was not pleasantly surprised but, rather, startled by her persevering interest in him. He had long since wrapped up whatever liveliness and spirit he had in that scholarly quest of his. Suddenly an attractive and intelligent young lady from a good family has turned him into a demigod. By the tenth chapter of the novel's first book, the author is ready to disabuse us of temptations she feels sure we, like some of her own characters, have. "I protest against any absolute conclusion," she says; she has in mind the various prejudices held by the people of Middlemarch against Casaubon.

No one had a good word for him. She does, however. She indicates that anyone who works for so long on a book with the title "Key to All Mythologies" has perseverance, dedication, and imagination, as well as pride. Moreover, she insists that we place the man's failings in the context of our own. ("This trait is not quite alien to us.") He was a lonely man, a desperate man, even; time was running out, and he might soon be found out as vain and unproductive rather than the great scholar he hoped to be. Who was defenseless before whom when Dorothea's Theresa-like soul met up with his tired, declining nature? We are given a hint with this authorial comment: "But something she yearned for by which her life might be filled with action at once rational and ardent; and since the time was gone by for guiding visions and spiritual directors, since prayer heightened yearning but not instruction, what lamp was there but knowledge: Surely learned men kept the only oil; and who more learned than Mr. Casaubon?"

Dorothea never is made to be calculating or brash. She is only willful with her own family; when she marries that learned man she continues to hold him up high for a long time. Even at the end, when his sharply exacerbated narrowness and aloofness are but preludes to his death, she respects him, is a model Victorian wife: submissive, attentive, hurt and puzzled by her husband's moods but not about to challenge them. A woman with all sorts of hopes for herself, a woman intent on doing things in the world rather than (like her sister, Celia) sitting back in sweet but servile domesticity, she nevertheless becomes the obliging caretaker of a dying man. However, she also ends up using Casaubon even as he uses her. The author tells us how in the passage just quoted. Like Portia, Dorothea becomes perceived by many in the world as a wounded one, unfairly taken advantage of. Celia knows otherwise. She saw what would happen, though not because she was all that prescient. For her own selfish and spiteful reasons she says to her sister well before her marriage to Casaubon becomes an immanent reality: "You always see what nobody else sees; it is impossible to satisfy you; yet you never see what is quite plain." It is a comment easily applied to Portia. It is also a comment that many in this century would find no difficulty using to evoke childhood: the child's extraordinary openness; the child's eagerness to meet up with and know the world; the child's innocence, that makes him or her miss so much of the world's all too obvious banality or worse. Rufus, too, catches glimpses of things others miss, has an insatiable curiosity and appetite for experience—but fails of necessity to notice or understand what others are thinking or doing right in front of his eyes.

We can have our sorrow for Dorothea, but we are leveling the worst of insults at her when we deny her motives of her own; and once motives come into question, we are indeed, as Miss Bowen has said, at a point in time after Adam and Eve have taken their Fall. As for the people of Middlemarch, George Eliot makes sure that their provincial life is never mistaken for a completely pastoral one. On the contrary, nineteenth-century idealist that she was, hopeful of the possibilities an increasingly scientific and secular society could offer, the novel is, nevertheless, guarded indeed about human nature and what it has to offer, even through its finest examples. The best people in the novel, those we most identify with, either come to naught or are badly shaken so far as their original hopes and ambitions go. Furthermore, speaking of ambitions, the idealists, Dorothea and Dr. Lydgate and Will Ladislaw, turn out to be ambitious as well as possessed of ambitions, and that particular difference is one we are not allowed to ignore. Dorothea not only wants to help others, she proves herself willful, sometimes obstinate. Lydgate is genuinely honest; his integrity as a physician makes it hard for us to think about his messianic, sometimes arrogant conviction that a whole profession will ultimately pay him heed.

In many ways Lydgate is the best realized of the novel's characters. Again, we have to be *told* that Dorothea set out to use Casaubon, so cannot be counted the wholly innocent one she at times very much seems to be. Lydgate's struggle is more subtly rendered, especially in its important early period, when he is all hope, energy, and confidence. It is clear to us that he married the wrong woman; Rosamond elicits little sympathy from the author. But we are left with the puzzle: why does so shrewd and well-intentioned a man choose Rosamond Vincy for a wife? Yes, she is attractive and charming; a well-bred woman who spotted the doctor and made after him. Nevertheless, she turns out to be a rope around his neck, and at the end the author makes no effort to conceal his ironic fate. He died a conventional London doctor, who put in time, besides, at a "Continental bathing place." He was "what is called a successful man"—meaning in his own terms, a complete failure. He died at fifty of diphtheria, and his widow promptly married another (and, of course, wealthy) doctor.

Though all was superficially placid in Lydgate's last years, there can be no doubt of his misery and despair. He has tempers to the very end, and they are directed at his wife. He refers to her as his basil plant, explaining that "basil was a plant which had flourished wonderfully on a murdered man's brains." To which his lovely and always composed wife could only ask that all-important question: "Why then had he chosen her?" It is a question other novelists have asked; one thinks of Dick Diver in *Tender Is the Night.* Why indeed? A mistake? (Don't we all stumble now and then?) Or is it a matter of innocence once more being betrayed by an agent of the devil? The doctor was busy, constantly trying to effect important changes in medical practice; he was also a relative stranger to Middlemarch. Was he thereby easy prey for this scheming young lady, who is herself no monster, simply a stubborn bourgeoise who will not be deterred?

Rosamond is more than that, though. She is intelligent, shrewd, well educated, sure of herself. Her neighbors may think of her as an attractive housewife who at times has to hold on for dear life while her husband goes through his "idealistic" stage (that is, a spell of extreme impracticality); but she is in her own way as inordinately ambitious as her husband. She wants to move up, *way up*, on the social and economic ladder. She is a cold, vain woman who puts on a sweet face indeed—while at the same time her eyes make their appraisals. She is, in a way, a variant of Lydgate. He pushes aside the vicar's gentle reminder that the best of intentions can be undone by one's own unrecognized flaws. It is for others to fail—his former roommate, for instance. He, Lydgate, knows what he is up to and sees no reason to be warned by a village vicar, who is all too evidently wedded to the status quo, hence eager to rationalize the basis for such an existence. Like his wife, the doctor has set his mind on something and aims to win.

Nor are they all that incompatible, psychologically, from the very start. Rosamond is self-adoring and shut off so far as the feelings of others go. She offers herself as a sight, and hopes her beauty and refinement will be enough. There is nothing more for anybody to have. Dr. Lydgate wanted what he saw and got it. True, we see him hesitating a bit, made guilty as he doesn't plunge immediately. But was he simply trapped by a woman's cunning—

entertained, given time and admiration, then practically summoned
to marriage? And did he say yes because he was so innocent, so
decent, so responsive to the offered affection of a very nice young
woman? One can say yes; but the puzzle remains. What kind of
sympathy or sensitivity or innocence is it that leads a man to the
guillotine or, in this case, the basil plant? Why, of all people, was
Portia so taken with Eddie? These days the temptation is to come
up with hidden and not so hidden self-destructive urges or else
something called masochism. Yet neither Portia nor Dr. Lydgate is
masochistic, and Lydgate never really seems bent on undercutting
himself.

Miss Bowen clearly indicates the affinity between Portia and
Eddie; they speak of it to each other. More indirectly, with enormous patience and skill, George Eliot shows how two people are
drawn to each other because they have in common a number of
qualities, face comparable predicaments—not unlike what happened
in Genesis. Adam, lonely among all those others, the animals and
birds he knew and felt (correctly) superior to, finally is enabled to
come upon someone he can really *be* with, feel a companion and
ally. Told certain limits, Adam and Eve go along and live, do not
worry about hazards or possible pitfalls. They find themselves—
the two of them together as a newfound reality—quite sufficient
and indeed entrancing. They are all. God's warnings recede into
that other world that includes everything outside of their joint
sphere of preoccupation—again, themselves. Never were Rosamond
and her Tertius Lydgate that enthralled with each other; their
folie à deux was less momentous. But a subtle psychological bond
was forged, and it would prove unbreakable.

One persists with whys. Why didn't Lydgate extricate himself,
either before the marriage or later, when he saw full well how
demanding his wife was, how contemptuous of his purposes? Is
the answer once again Victorianism—the confines of a historical
era working on a particular pair of human beings? That is, was the
upright doctor trapped by the demands of society? Once having
paid so much attention to a lady, there was the obligation to follow
through with marriage; and once married, always married. At
moments, especially late in the novel, when Lydgate is indeed a
tragic figure and his tragedy is for a moment joined to Dorothea's
and Bulstrode's, we are tempted to go back and see a plot:
Rosamond the seductress, Lydgate the victim. Yet the author has

warned us in the book "Three Love Problems" that human nature is inconsistent, and so our persistent effort to resolve those inconsistencies, as they one after another make themselves felt in various lives, ought be more the issue than the presence of the inconsistencies themselves. And George Eliot is really rather sharp, if not devastating, when she gives us her warning—it is one of the few times Dr. Lydgate does not come off as at all appealing:

In warming himself at French social theories he had brought away no smell of scorching. We may handle even extreme opinions with impunity while our furniture, our dinner-giving, and preference for armorial bearings in our own case link us indissolubly with the established order. And Lydgate's tendency was not towards extreme opinions: he would have liked no barefooted doctrines, being particular about his boots: he was no radical in relation to anything but medical reform and the prosecution of discovery. In the rest of practical life he walked by hereditary habit; half from that personal pride and unreflecting egoism which I have already called commonness, and half from that naïveté which belonged to preoccupation with favourite ideas.

Pride, unreflecting egoism, naïveté—enough to undo anyone; and especially vulnerable are those who are self-confident and high minded: educated, dedicated, discerning, no fools when it comes to sizing up the world and charting a course whereby it is to be changed. It can be argued that, in fact, Lydgate was not trapped by his own susceptibilities, or even Rosamond's willful charms, which later wore him down so. Middlemarch is portrayed as provincial in several senses of the word; its people are by no means open to new ideas, and they are determined to frustrate this dangerously assertive doctor who has all sorts of new and unproved ideas. Actually, Middlemarch's citizens are not really interested in proof; they have their loyalties to various doctors and are unwilling to have familiar and comforting beliefs upset in the name of scientific progress. Here George Eliot does a brilliant job (a *learned* job) of showing how the state of a particular profession affects the lives of those who practice it, and are practiced upon. Lydgate is the reformer who has to fall back on his prophetic vision. He has not ironclad proof that his intuitions are correct. Medicine at the time was a hodgepodge of superstition, magic, and common sense, with the last not always prevailing. If George III could find himself bedeviled by doctors, whose remedies he found it almost impossible to resist, even when he knew enough to try, one can sympathize with the Middlemarchers of the early 1830s.[7]

If Lydgate's colleagues had nothing else, they had gall and that cocksure fastidiousness that make the presence of ignorance seem out of the question. Patients were bled nearly to death and given all sorts of useless, even harmful substances. They were also bullied and threatened as a matter of course. Lydgate appeared on the scene as an advocate of both rationality and humanity. Even as political reformers wanted more people in Middlemarch and elsewhere to have a say in what their government did, a medical reformer like Lydgate wanted to treat people with unheard-of consideration. He preferred to do nothing rather than put up a smoke screen of routines and regimens that deceive and injure already ailing people. But of course people so often want what they already have and fear what an outsider offers, however tantalizing it be. Especially in the matter of sickness, fear even today brings out a host of deceptions and self-deceptions in what transpires between patients and their doctors, to the point that one wonders who is fooling whom—the patient who gets the doctor to be more grandiose or deluded than he ever consciously intended being or the doctor who plies the patient with false messages as well as nostrums or, these days, futile if showy gestures that promise everything and deliver very little except a sense of action, with all the exhilaration that a performance executed with bravura manages to produce.[8]

George Eliot is not one to come up with unqualified causes to explain the direction of lives. She has written this novel to show how history limits not only would-be Theresas but Lydgates as well. She is interested in how psychological flaws lend themselves to history's hand; and, in particular, she is after an understanding— she knows it will always be limited to her own kind: those who think a lot and, as Celia (not a likely spokeswoman for the author) says, miss a whole lot. So Dorothea and Lydgate merge thematically. The latter has not just naïveté, plain and simple, but a version of it:

[7] An especially good study of George III and his experience with the doctors of his day is Ida Macalpine and Richard Hunter's *George III and the Mad Business* (New York, 1971).

[8] Recently a number of psychiatrists have begun to show how macabre such encounters between overzealous doctors and their patients can turn out to be. See Avery Weisman's *On Dying and Denying* (New York, 1972).

he is unsophisticated enough to be so preoccupied with his own ideas that he overlooks Rosamond's. His condescension and attendant openness to psychological exploitation are not on the surface; I do not think they can be characterized as unconscious, either. There is, quite simply, a limit to what any mind can hold. Lydgate's, as the author tells us, is intensely preoccupied with the strategy for a virtual war upon certain customs, upon human fallibility and credulity; under such circumstances he had no time to bear down on other issues—and no capacity to do so. We are not only motivated to do things, or ignore doing other things; we make choices, and having done so, we have, as George Eliot puts it, a "preoccupation." As a result, things happen to us and we are, psychologically, elsewhere: thinking, planning, dreaming, conspiring. An obsessed doctor has only so much time to analyze his would-be wife. The issue is not intentionality, open or disguised, but the range of experience that a finite human being can deal with. (God told Adam and Eve there was such a range, and it seems they had to find that out for themselves.)

As for Dorothea, she is no less fully occupied mentally. We feel close to Lydgate, and we are terribly moved by her predicament. In Middlemarch's struggle between the children of light and the children of darkness, she is clearly on our side, the side of those who read novels like *Middlemarch* and try conscientiously to apply its message to a later century's problems. Still, we have been forewarned with respect to her, also, and when George Eliot wants to exert caution on us she doesn't mince words: "Her mind was theoretic, and yearned by its nature after some lofty conception of the world which might frankly include the parish of Tipton and her own rule of conduct there; she was enamoured of intensity and greatness, and rash in embracing whatever seemed to her to have those aspects; likely to seek martyrdom, to make retractions, and then to incur martyrdom after all in a quarter where she had not sought it."

Dorothea's is the mind of one who knew by heart many passages of Pascal's *Pensées*. It is the mind of one who recognized and scorned the banalities and superficialities of provincial life. It is also the mind of one who—moving from irony to blunt critical comment—"retained very childlike ideas about marriage." And at this point "childlike" is linked with an interesting illustrative sequence: "She felt sure that she would have accepted the judicious

Hooker, if she had been born in time to save him from that wretched mistake he made in matrimony; or John Milton when his blindness had come on; or any of the other great men whose odd habits it would have been glorious piety to endure; but an amiable handsome baronet, who said 'Exactly' to her remarks even when she expressed uncertainty—how could he affect her as a lover?"

Is it childlike to want to "save"—in this case, people from what seems to be their foreordained fate? When George Eliot wrote *Middlemarch* she had herself given up an earlier evangelical religion (her father's) and now preferred to talk of "human lots" and our "destiny," which in her mind has its own unfathomable momentum. It could be that for her *childlike* means ignorant or untutored or naive: to think that one has lived so little, or lived so long yet still so little, as to think that one can undo what has been fated. On the other hand, there is the issue of presumptuousness; and children can be that, too. Linked with presumptuousness, rather often, is self-righteousness.

A clue to the author's interpretation of Dorothea's "childlike ideas" comes much later on, when she has the thoroughly honorable and untainted Caleb Garth wash his hands of Bulstrode when his dubious past begins to be revealed. Confronted with a troubled soul, Garth rather too quickly passes judgment, missing thereby a great deal of moral complexity that the author takes pains to provide—and connect to everyone, Garth included. Here Garth is being childlike. Bulstrode rushes to save, willy-nilly, and himself needs saving. Garth rushes to escape the presence of corruption, blithely unaware of his own complicity as a fellow human being and neighbor. Garth's childlike behavior is not without obtuseness and malice, and both stem from a version of the author's often mentioned preoccupation, that of the self with itself. Charity is lost, because it requires a gesture outward. Common sense is lost, because it requires the same thing—a look at what is reasonably possible, as opposed to what is dreamed of or insisted upon. Those who designed the "French social theories" might not find such a conception of *childlike* congenial.

In fact the author might well have substituted *childish* for *childlike*. The words have different connotations. The latter suggests the admirable qualities children often have, their directness, their charming and affectionate side, their lack of so many of the disguises it takes years of living to develop. The former refers to the petulance children can show, as well their undeveloped mentality, their ignorance, and, even more, their inability to understand much of what is happening around them. Further, children love to pretend, build castles in the sky as well as on a nearby beach.

I write this as I work with Pueblo and Indian and Chicano children in New Mexico. As I was going over *Middlemarch* yet again, trying to gain some sense of George Eliot's intentions, so to speak, toward her various characters, I thought of a girl of eight I visit in one of the Pueblos north of Albuquerque. Once I asked her what she pictured her life like in the future. She was in a lively and frolicsome mood; maybe a teasing mood, though she would have denied that allegation. She thought for a minute, then told me she wouldn't mind "rescuing people." Well, of course, I wanted to know whether she had any people in mind. Yes, there is an uncle of hers, who has a bad leg and can't walk well. And there is her grandmother, who feels tired all the time and gets chest pains when she exerts herself. There are also those various dead people she has heard about; some of them had very difficult lives, and she wonders whether "by some magic" they won't come back again, so that they can have an easier, better life. If so, she would certainly be right there, anxious to help them, busy "rescuing" them. In a final summary she looked me right in the eye, a touch defiantly, and said: "Rescuing people is the best good you can do, if you get a chance." There followed a more historical discussion, initiated by her: the Pueblo Indians, she reminded me, have been helpful to other Indians—have rescued them by teaching them how to raise crops and live a less nomadic, more settled kind of life. I suppose I could have tried to push us both back to a more psychological line of talk; though it could be that she, like George Eliot, knew a lot better than I how to integrate her particular imagination—her reveries, her aspirations, the "night-pictures" she speaks of seeing while asleep—with her people's historical experience and their ongoing social and cultural life.

But ought I turn that child into an all-knowing authority, someone we must uncritically look up to? She can be silly and impractical. She can vex her parents no end with her peevish, obstinate ways. She can also ignore her younger sister's crying, her immediate needs as she goes about her own moment-to-moment play. Her mother has often had to warn me about something, and I will let her tell what it is: "She's wise, like you say. But she's not always wise. There will be times when I get so angry at her I have to fold my arms and grit my teeth, or else I'll hit her, and I don't want to do that. She'll be talking so nice, and meanwhile her sister is in trouble, and she hasn't helped. Or she'll be playing, and I'm in trouble, and she won't lift a finger—and it's she who's done the spilling or the breaking. Children have to learn to grow up, I guess. I tell my children that things don't just appear on trees, and meals just don't happen, and a house doesn't just become clean. You have to train yourself to pay attention to all the little things. You can't just be sitting and dreaming about rescuing people, like she told you, and all that. I rescue her every morning—from those hunger pangs she has when she wakes up. And let me tell you, I don't dream when I do my everyday work—cook and clean up and get the whole house organized so all of them are ready to go to work or school."

This is the one deviation in the direction of my own present everyday work that I will permit myself here. I do so because I believe the tensions George Eliot tries to bring alive in a Dorothea or a Dr. Lydgate are shared by those who never become as singular as they each did (by virtue of being made the center of an author's attention, in contrast to all those other Middlemarchers who are in the background), never mind as saintly and thereby historical a figure as a Theresa of Avila. And it is ironic that one like Pascal (were George Eliot writing today, Kierkegaard might replace him) becomes so influential to Dorothea. For all his force of mind, Pascal knew that religious faith had to be grounded, ultimately, in each person's ordinary, dreary perhaps, often boring, certainly undramatic daily life. There is a conflict in Dorothea and Lydgate, also in Ladislaw, between their secular faiths (which prompt their ambitions) and their everyday lives. That is, they feel the antagonistic tension between the prophetic and pastoral modes of living. Dorothea and Lydgate are heavily inclined toward the former; Ladislaw would like to be, but lacks the fierce will those other two possess.

Dorothea's "theoretic" mind, Lydgate's dreams of a new form of medical practice have an enormous effect on their lives, not to mention the lives of others. Yet at times that quality of her mind, those dreams of his seem to be dispossessed, in a vacuum almost. We occasionally wonder what they do when they are not trying to implement their ideals. The author is tempted with the romantic hero—full of special and all too glamorous aspirations and headed always for spectacular affirmation or an apocalyptic decline. Only at times, though; George Eliot wants to fix those two and everyone else in the world and show how Middlemarch sets limits on any mind's ingenuity or expansiveness, shapes even the most original of dreams. Of course she was tempted as a Victorian storyteller simply to let Dorothea loose, spring free Lydgate and his aspirations, and offer us their dramatic, not seriously impeded fulfillment. The two of them are memorable, and insofar as they become so, page by page, they obtain at least a share of the distinction each fervently sought, urged on by a mixture of egoism and moral uprightness that no one in his or her right mind can ever sort out into percentages.

The novel obtains momentum, however, because the novelist chooses to indicate the antagonism I mentioned between the pastoral and the prophetic. Even as a Pueblo mother can contrast her child's dreamlike (childlike?) state with the demands that a given society makes on a girl of eight, never mind her older sister and brothers or her mother and father, so George Eliot begins *Middlemarch* by contrasting Celia's accommodating spirit to Dorothea's rebellious, at times almost agitated state of mind. We are disposed to scorn Celia; she questions no one or nothing, is willing to be dominated, taken for granted, denied her rights as an individual human being. On the other hand, the preface, with its mention of Theresa, is followed by a great deal of favorable comment on Dorothea and her aspirations. If Middlemarch or any other part of England is going to change, people will have to be brought to think more like her, less like Celia.

But nowhere does George Eliot make us feel that if Middlemarch is going to change, she and Lydgate will be the kind of people who do it. Nor is it that the two of them were a shade ahead of their time. Lydgate was; but he needn't have stumbled as he did. Dorothea might indeed have lived a different life, as the preface tells us, had she been born in some other place, at some other time. However, one cannot simply make that kind of extrapolation; in fact, the whole point of *Middlemarch* is to make clear what it means to be born in a particular place, to live at a certain time. There are traits that transcend place and time (one moves from Theresa to Dorothea to that Pueblo girl), but the setting for those traits is crucial and (as the length and complexity of this novel demonstrate) ought never be taken for granted. As for who or what does cause social change, the author seems to feel that the answer is to be found not in character portrayal so much as the vast yet detailed social portrayal, mediated through her characters, that is *Middlemarch.*

Middlemarch starts out with the words "Miss Brooke," whereas Agee's novel begins with a long evocation of Knoxville, and Elizabeth Bowen's with a less intense, more measured description of the correct and ritzy world to which Windsor Terrace belongs. The provincial world of the Midlands is almost assumed; for a while we get little formal description of it. Rather, the general atmosphere as well as various particulars of a sociological nature come through in the minor characters, whose various distinctions of speech and attitude have a cumulative effect as instruments of representation and analysis. And even more insidiously, as it were, Dorothea and Lydgate, Ladislaw, Bulstrode and Rosamond are made to reflect that same atmosphere.

Chapter 46, for instance, opens this way: "While Lydgate, safely married with the Hospital under his command, felt himself struggling for Medical Reform against Middlemarch, Middlemarch was becoming more and more conscious of the national struggle for another kind of Reform." But within a paragraph that transition from the life of Dr. Lydgate to the more general life of England in the years immediately preceding Queen Victoria's ascension is reversed; we are back with Mr. Brooke and Ladislaw having their conversation, and a little later with Rosamond, all decked out and sitting proudly at her tea table. The ebb and flow of talk comes around to social issues and a nation's political struggle, but in no overwhelming or didactic way. The author's comments can sometimes be intrusive, arch, overly extended—if never without interest; but she is a master at converting abstractions into the rhythms of everyday language, and the nuances of individual expression that a novel requires (in contrast to an essay by a social scientist).

Interestingly, the main characters, for all their force of personality and idealism, lack the larger view that is occasionally possessed by some of the minor and more humble people (socially and intellectually) of Middlemarch. George Eliot knew out of her own life not to romanticize the peasantry or the rural bourgeoisie. Still, from Caleb Garth and his daughter Mary we obtain spoken integrity and philosophical detachment, the latter of a kind Kierkegaard would find thoroughly appealing. As Mr. Featherstone nears death Mary watches over him, and like her father with respect to Bulstrode in a later chapter, she is meant to be a contrast: the faithful, incorruptible servant or working person and the selfish, skeptical, mistrustful rich man, more alone than he can either realize or bear, and alone amid all those who hover over him and curry his favor. And if Mr. Garth can be a touch priggish, his daughter is a tenderly depicted representative of all that is fine in observant but un-intellectual people. Here is how she is presented at one point: "She sat to-night revolving, as she was wont, the scenes of the day, her lips often curling with amusement at the oddities to which her fancy added fresh drollery: people were so ridiculous with their illusions, carrying their fool's caps unawares, thinking their own lies opaque while everybody else's were transparent, making themselves exceptions to everything, as if when all the world looked yellow under a lamp they alone were rosy."

One cannot imagine the author saying that about Dorothea or Dr. Lydgate. They are introspective, bold, reform minded. Mary Garth is none of these, even the first. She can spot illusions, size up her employer better than his prospective (and soon to be disappointed) heirs. But she does not really look inward; her eyes have been trained to respond to the directions others give. The author is keenly aware of the social lines that often determine what psychological characteristics we assign to people. She believes that Mary Garth is as entitled to be compared with Saint Theresa as Dorothea Brooke. She believes that Mary Garth is in certain respects more knowing than Dorothea, even without exposure to Pascal. To turn things around, Dorothea has never been able to overcome the limitations of her background. Brought up to feel free and of some importance, even when orphaned (Miss Bowen's Portia has had the same upbringing, the same set of expectations), Dorothea has never had a chance to see the Mr. Featherstones of this world the way Mary Garth has. Dorothea has learned to order, not take orders; to feel responsible, not an agent of execution. Her eyes are directed up and beyond and over there; Mary's down or level with the stove, the furniture, the hedge, or the door.

As for ears, it is rather apparent that Dorothea has been listening to the voices of the world's greatest thinkers, dead or alive, while Mary Garth has had to learn how to distinguish Mr. Featherstone's various moods, anticipate what he will say, respond to what he doesn't even bother to say, simply assumes to be heard, then acted on. The movement of Dorothea's mind is toward herself—and so with Celia's, too. Both of them had ideas about how they would live; and each felt able to make a very considered choice as to where and with whom that living would take place. Mary Garth no doubt had some choices as she grew up, but the movement of her mind was in quite another direction; she had to learn how a self becomes (for pay) subject to another's beck and call. True, all women who married (or for that matter, didn't) in that period of Middlemarch's history can be described as so subjected. But quantitative differences can become qualitative ones, and economic pressures have a power all their own.

In this novel ambition never fails to be connected with vice. Neither Caleb nor Mary Garth has any pretensions, or hopes for a rise on any one of the scales a society implicitly presents all its members for their perusal and knowledge. The Garths are not without sin; they are tempted, and at moments their good judgment or rectitude seems to be narrowly secured—made evident only when enabled by another's downfall. One wonders whether they would be so upright were they ever able to conceive of themselves as the relatively free agents people like Dorothea or Dr. Lydgate were, or believed they were. Of course, Raffles is also poor; yet he is ambitious, sometimes in a clumsy manner, sometimes with cunning. The issue is never *only* class. But Raffles certainly was no yeoman or servant. As for Dorothea, the strength of her personality and its capacity for good are hopelessly entangled with her self-possessed side. She may subject herself to Casaubon, but he never for a moment overcomes her sense of who Dorothea Brooke is, what *she* thinks, what *she* hopes to accomplish. Given such an attitude toward herself, she spends little time looking wryly or with resignation at others—or up toward the heavens, if not God. Her attitude toward herself is serious and demanding; Mary Garth's is respectful but casual.

Those contrasting attitudes work upon the two women and to an extent determine whom they are to marry. The author never connects Dorothea's fate with Mary's, but they look upon marriage quite differently, and it is a major irony in the novel that Dorothea, who has so much, can be at critical points in her life so self-effacing (if still proud), whereas Mary Garth, far lower down in Middlemarch society, is robustly protective of her independence. Dorothea almost throws herself at Casaubon; she wants to care for him, do whatever tasks he might deign to offer her. Well-to-do and well-educated, she feels contemptuous of many around her but virtually worthless in the face of what she has imagined Casaubon to be. And her interpretation of him, really her construction of him, is an act of self-portrayal. It is not only that somewhere in the back of her mind she realizes how thwarted would-be Theresas like herself feel; she has more than enough doubt about her capacity to be a Theresa even under the best of circumstances.

Theresa had no easy time in her effort to revitalize Spanish Catholicism. Powerful clerics opposed her. She fought hard and long, developing in the process a blend of practicality and mysticism that worked. But she had to battle tenaciously for what she wanted, and often had to do so alone. Dorothea for a moment struck her uncle and sister as strong willed, even impulsive, and maybe someone at twenty-one ready to find a crusade of her own. Yet her marriage in a way was a renunciation of her own self, from which she never really recovered. She felt herself lucky to be accepted by Casaubon; and at the end the reader has his doubts about her second husband, Ladislaw. He may have been elected to Parliament, but he is hardly going to be her Saint John of the Cross. The last chapter, the novel's finale, makes it quite clear that she is still floundering somewhat, for all the happiness the author endows her with—a little gratuitously, it can be argued. She still had an interest in social and political change, and was glad to have her husband fighting things out in London. On the other hand: "many who knew her, thought it a pity that so substantive and rare a creature should have been absorbed into the life of another, and be only known in a certain circle as a wife and mother."

Mary Garth would never be pitied. She gave herself only after hesitation and careful consideration to her ardent and longtime suitor, Fred Vincy. He was going to prove himself worthy of her expectations, or not have her. She is not, in that regard, another version of Rosamond. Her demands of Fred are a reflection of her satisfaction with her own self. Satisfaction of that kind is not to be confused with arrogance, pride, or the lust of ambition, each of which can convey to the outside world an appearance of sureness or decisiveness. Mary Garth simply had a decent set of values and had learned how to live by them. Their essential worth is best demonstrated by the young woman's application of them to her own life: she regards herself as entitled to demand of others as well as wait on them. A servant, she will be served. Dorothea is surrounded by servants, but aims to please, if not serve. Life is ironic because, among other reasons, social class cannot determine one's attitude toward others or oneself.

No wonder in the novel's finale that Adam and Eve and the Garden of Eden come up once again, and repeatedly. "Marriage which has been the bourne of so many narratives, is still a great beginning," we are told, "as it was to Adam and Eve, who kept their honeymoon in Eden, but had their first little one among the thorns and thistles of the wilderness." Fred Vincy and Mary Garth, so far as that bourn goes, "achieved a solid and mutual happiness." Whereas Dorothea is left giving her husband "wifely help," we get no sense of a *mutual* relationship, let alone the happiness granted Fred and Mary Vincy. For minor characters those two are accorded exceptional notice in the novel's last pages. Almost a half of the finale goes to them. Interestingly, they have three sons to the one Dorothea and Ladislaw have; and, of all things, both Fred and Mary write books—his on agriculture, hers a children's book, modeled on Plutarch's *Lives*.

Also of interest is the author's decision to show how warm, affectionate, and accomplished a mother Mary Garth was, and how independent she was, too. One wonders why that is done in the limited space allowed for pulling strands together, tidying up the story in the tradition of the nineteenth-century novel. Especially sad, in a way, is the comment about Dorothea's marriage. We are told how social snobberies and family tensions worked their way out somewhat. Celia's husband relented. There was some end to the conflict between the brothers-in-law. ("Where women love each other men learn to smother their mutual dislike.") But nowhere are we given a hint of how Dorothea took to being a mother. Nowhere do we really hear from Dorothea. She is referred to, described; and in the last paragraph the author comes full circle round by using her as a symbol. Her voice, however, is denied us, as is Ladislaw's—after we have just been given a revealing exchange between Fred and Mary Vincy and also been told that their children "like nothing so well as being with their mother."

The author, no stranger to the Bible, has begun her farewell to Middlemarch by reminding the reader in general terms that from Adam and Eve on, some have fared better than others. Cain and

Abel were different individuals. God's response to that first transgression was to move the human drama out of Eden and into the
"thorns and thistles of the wilderness," yet Fred and Mary almost,
but not quite, seem like candidates for Eden before the Fall,
whereas Dorothea and Ladislaw are unquestionably not spared a
whole range of psychological difficulties, made no easier by the
wealth and high social position they have. Moreover, as Henry
James puts it in the delicate but suggestive way he speaks of
Ladislaw,"The impression once given that he is a dilettante is never
properly removed, and there is slender poetic justice in Dorothea's
marrying a dilettante."[9]

Perhaps not poetic justice; but *Middlemarch* was written to show
how devious and inscrutable history is, not simply the history we
study in books, with all those kings and prime ministers and
generals, but the broader kind we all share in as human beings set
down here briefly and asked to give an account of ourselves. George
Eliot may have wanted to offer Dorothea and Ladislaw a lot. (She
obviously at one point thought of making Dorothea even more
prominent in the novel, and she never really turns her critical
powers on Ladislaw, as a result of which, of course, he suffers as a
character: he is given too much, *spoiled* the word may be.) But she
knew she could give way to her generosity only at a high cost;
nothing less than the consistency of her viewpoint was at stake.

Had she strengthened Ladislaw, and dwelt more on him and
Dorothea toward the end; had she endowed the Ladislaws, finally,
with a triumphant happiness, she would have abandoned herself to
sentimentality and made a mockery of her earlier psychological
(and, too, theological) sophistication. I would insist that Ladislaw
had to be kept relatively weak: if not a dilettante, then a somewhat
elusive or nondescript character who *seems* to fail (though not
disappoint) Dorothea—so that she yet again proves true to herself.
She is never going to write Theresa's sharp, forceful letters nor have
the self-awareness that comes across in that Saint's autobiographical
writing, shot through as it is with canny psychological and sociological appraisals. And that side of Theresa's never needed any
opportunity ("equal" or any other kind). Nor did Theresa write
sure in the knowledge of an attentive posterity. She wrote out of

---

[9]Henry James's laudatory essay first appeared in *The Galaxy*, March 1873. It has
been reprinted in *The House of Fiction*, ed. Leon Edel (London, 1957).

her heart. Her words do not deceive us so far as her temperament goes.

By the end of *Middlemarch* we have been shown the power of a given social system; but Eliot's power as a novelist never wanes. She has created a character as well as evoked a rural scene at a given moment in history, and she remains faithful to her imaginative life as well as the world of Middlemarch. If she fails with respect to Dorothea, it is in denying her the intensity of scrutiny given Bulstrode. We are expected to accept Dorothea's personality as a given; she *is* idealistic, she *has* the reformer's zeal, she *believes* in certain principles of justice and equality, stripped (one is to gather) of any divine sanction. She is never carried back in time, though, as Bulstrode is. The complexities of her life are those that grown-ups have to face, but because she is carried *forward* in time (inevitable in a novel like George Eliot's) the problem of repetition comes up. Why does she choose the men she does? What about her prompts such peculiar and recurrent self-abasement, a contrast indeed with the haughtiness she also keeps revealing?

Are those questions that belong to another age our questions? Even though the author is quite aware that we have to contend with an unconscious (she speaks of "invisible thoroughfares which are the first lurking-places of anguish, mania, and crime"), we may demand too much of her when we notice a little petulantly that she has not sufficiently analyzed those "first lurking-places" of Dorothea's. Yet in the case of Bulstrode she shows herself willing and able to do more than take note of such places. She goes into an extended analysis of what made this man what he has become; and for the most part her emphasis is restrospective and psychological rather than descriptive and sociological. From Bulstrode's tormented life, years in the making, we learn to think about people in one way. From Dorothea's persistent if flawed effort to make something of herself in relationship to a given society (and through the agency, it might be put, of two husbands), we pick up a quite different perspective. No portrayal in *Middlemarch* is exclusively psychological or sociological, but Bulstrode's motives get astonishingly intense scrutiny, and Dorothea's life to a considerable extent prompts us to think about provincial life in the first part of the 1830s. (I differ with Henry James, when he describes Bulstrode as "too diffusely treated.")

George Eliot operates out of a tradition of fervent moral Puritanism, with the Christian underpinnings considerably weakened,
but by no means abandoned. It is a tradition still alive; D. H.
Lawrence and Faulkner belong to it. It is a tradition that takes
seriously man's peculiar position on this earth, and concerns itself
with judgment. There is nothing neutral or detached about D. H.
Lawrence. He may despise elements of Christianity and the middle-
class commercial world that embraces the institutional church for
its own purposes, but he has not lost interest in heaven and hell, in
the saved and the damned. Nor is he afraid or undesirous of con-
demning or uplifting, if not rendering worthy of worship. Faulkner
may be a little less explicit, but the message still gets across: there
are good and evil, personified as well as distributed randomly; and
the novelist must center his attention constantly on the struggle
between the two.[10] I suppose their attitude, very much George
Eliot's, is one of moral earnestness. Sometimes in this century that
earnestness takes on a decidedly psychological cast; and sometimes
a cast of mind can become an obsession. But self-scrutiny was not
invented in Vienna around the turn of this century, nor the
psychological observer's ability to keep himself or herself substantially removed from a particular subject, though still of opinion
about the person's worth.

In Bulstrode George Eliot had a chance to put her own religious
experiences to work. She was, anyway, a moralist first, a romancer
later. The man is thoroughly pompous and self-serving, also manipulative and power-hungry. When he first enters into a crisis, and
begins to appear even more wicked and unsavory, we merely take
note of the fact and feel further educated about the facts of life:
Middlemarch, like other areas of this world, has its fair share of
hypocrites and deceivers; bad has gone to worse under the careful
tutelage of this student of provincial life, and we, most likely eager
to rejoice in the demise of at least one fraudulant man of influence,
can only feel satisfied.

Suddenly a remarkable shift occurs in the novel, and soon enough
we are deprived of a good deal of our pleasure. Satire is foregone.
Mockery is lacking. Sympathy appears unexpectedly; but, even
more telling, Bulstrode is connected to all of us, not with a pointed

[10]See the excellent critical essay by Harold Douglas and Robert Daniel, "Faulkner
and the Puritanism of the South," *Tennessee Studies in Literature* 2 (1957).

finger, but in an almost offhand manner. We are ensnared when we had expected to stand removed and gloat. Bulstrode is in that sense quite definitely treated "diffusely." But when Henry James says "he never grips the reader's attention," his criticism might well be accepted only with a proviso: with good reason, because no reader accepts such a shrewdly and powerfully launched, such a penetrating critique of his own nature as a human being, alive in a Middlemarch of his own, without an effort to let go and run.

In certain respects Bulstrode is the most powerfully drawn character in *Middlemarch*—the strongest person, the one we struggle with most, perhaps the one from whom we learn the most. Even in the prelude we are told that Dorothea will never quite live up to her possibilities. Dr. Lydgate wins our admiration; later on he disappoints us, or we cover up our impatience toward him with pity. Ladislaw is indeed weakly portrayed; if only he *were* a first-class dilettante—anything to give some direction to his personality. Casaubon is not so easily dismissed, thanks to the author's stubborn sympathy for everyone she creates. But an old, tired man obsessed with obscure philosophical points is hardly the one to capture our imagination. He, too, becomes pitiable—and maybe at times defended by us as an object of exploitation: it is no joy to become an instrument of another's moral passion. In contrast, Bulstrode seems to appear out of nowhere and ultimately vanish with no trace left—yet he is unforgettable, even haunting.

He is a banker at first acquaintance, a newcomer to Middlemarch, one who is selfish, and again, power-hungry, but also progressive. The old established wealth, such as that possessed by Dorothea's brother-in-law, Sir James Chettam, is unobtrusive and arguably more dangerous. Sir James wants no changes. Why should a perfectly ordered and comfortable Middlemarch be undone by new ideas, new programs? He is the staunch conservative, not romanticized, however. He has his clear interests and will fight to defend them. He is haughty, smug, self-satisfied—and headed for a decline in power as a result of the political reforms on the brink of being enacted. Celia loves him and he is good to her, provided she keep within the limits he has set. His antagonism to Dorothea is maintained throughout the novel—he had first wanted to marry her—and only somewhat attenuated, in a live-and-let-live arrangement, at the very end; for such stubborn pique we are disposed against him. He uses social custom to enforce his whims and prejudices. But his manners and background shield him from criticisms Bulstrode easily comes upon.

Sir James manipulates, pulls levers of influence, dominates, inflicts vengeance, but all the while displays impeccable manners. As a result he is seen as a proper gentleman. Refinement cloaks a mind's nature, a person's deeds. Bulstrode has no such sanctuary. He is blunt and forceful, looked up to because he is a man of means, but not for any other reason. No one in Middlemarch at that time wanted to lose its aristocrats; and one way of keeping them is to be blind to their schemes and warts, their solid capacity to be as malevolent as anyone else. Bulstrode was always there, a man to be feared and suspected. He may have done many things to warrant just such an attitude from his fellow Middlemarchers, but even before the critical drama of his life unfolds, we find him no mere greedy banker. His bluntness and candor contrast with the deceit that social prominence can cover up. His reformer's instincts are also apparent. He is a rational man, and impatient with out-moded traditions, or superstitions. He is with Lydgate in his desire to reform the medical profession. True, his progressive inclinations are with justice seen as excuses for his greed or ambition. If the old customs are ended, the old authorities weakened, his kind of agres-sive wealth has a much easier time extending itself.

But reform was needed badly, and George Eliot makes it all too clear that the kind of enlightened, regenerative conservatism Edmund Burke placed his faith in was simply not forthcoming in Middlemarch. Sir James Chettam is no political monster, anxious to turn the clock back and keep everyone firmly under his authority. He is quite simply self-contented without exception. He will lift no finger to make anyone else even remotely as well off as he is. Consequently, others have to have the nerve, the drive, the skill and cunning to move in, if not take over. Then it is, of course, that the Chettams of this world look surprised: why the uproar? And besides, look at those complaining or trying to exert their influence—their gall, their coarseness! Meanwhile, not a few people, whatever their actual needs, side with the Chettams. Perhaps they are people who have given up hope for any change in their own condition, or perhaps they find satisfaction in favoring what is established and has an aura of respectability and gentility, as against the brash, the new, the somewhat ungraceful. Perhaps, not unlike Hobbes or Edmund Burke, they prefer the authority that *is*, and dread the uncertainty if not the chaos that often enough accompanies social change.

There are rhythms to injustice that become familiar; new noises, however promising, only grate upon the ears. Nor is resignation of a highly philosophical kind to be dismissed as beyond the ken of a peasant. Caleb Garth, who abruptly turns on Bulstrode, is more than a peasant, anyway, though he has the somewhat exaggerated honor and righteousness city people in search of heroes sometimes grant peasants. They are felt to be so good, those men of the earth—so decent, so hard working, so uncorrupted, so near to being Rousseau's natural man. They are credited with seeing so much—more than the Bulstrodes, more than the Chettams, more than the Casaubons, even the Lydgates—and also with being beyond temptation: they hold everything together. However, the truth may simply be that they stand with the prevailing system often enough and block social and political changes that might well help them live better. They do so not out of virtue, nor out of malice, either. They do not wish to cut their noses to spite their faces. Resignation may indeed be the word: they feel in their bones what the new programs and leaders will bring: yet more mischief.

Against such a background of forces and counterforces, established authority and rising power, crying needs and grave doubts about anyone's reasons for meeting those needs, Bulstrode suddenly moves from a peripheral figure, one of those minor Middlemarchers who have mainly sociological interest for us, into the exact center of the novel's stage. With him comes Raffles, whose name and manner are right out of Dickens. With him, too, comes an acceleration of drama that almost takes the reader aback. After nearly five hundred pages of almost stately progression (which reflects England's remarkable nineteenth-century capacity for gradual but significant political transformation), we suddenly meet up with blackmail, night terrors, political anguish, a virtual murder, followed by the swift exposure and ruin of a prominent citizen.

All this is done, however, with a minimum of melodrama. Even more important, the author shirks other temptations. She has already told us how pious a man Bulstrode is, how devoted to evangelical religion. She might easily have exposed not only him but his beliefs—his constant outward show of faith, his larger corruptions of spirit that more than match the lies and deceptions Raffles happens to have known and threatens to reveal. A pompous banker who preaches Jesus Christ's message, then goes on to the next bit of cynical financial double-dealing, Bulstrode may not be the first hypocrite in the history of the novel, but one might have thought him irresistible to George Eliot. She has never been really cruel to any of her characters, but she is a teacher and a moralist, and Bulstrode offers her the resort to a serviceable tradition of edifying satire.

Properly restrained, yet deftly used, such satire can be enormously suggestive. The world is full of show and pretense, and we crave their unmasking. Particularly helpful is the novelist who doesn't ruin the job with scorn; then we become uncomfortable because we feel somehow cheated. Insincerity and sanctimony are not as flagrant and extraordinary as some satirists make them out to be. Anyway, we fancy ourselves sophisticated, and we want a subtle if not gentle analysis; that way a lot more ground can be covered, many more connections made. After all, Bulstrode was not Middlemarch's only liar or crook dressed up in good clothes and married well and able to intimidate people not only financially but morally. Pharisees plagued Christ; and this side of heaven they persist everywhere, certainly in churches all over that bear his name. He was betrayed by his disciple; he is betrayed every day by those who call on others to believe in him. It is an old story, and Middlemarch is no special place where a different twist to the story will be found. Or so it seems for a while, as Raffles wields his power and Bulstrode begins to crumble—though he fights back with every resource at his command.

Yet gradually the author introduces a new element in her narrative. She reveals how skilled a storyteller she can be; as mentioned, the narrative quickens, and plenty of action takes place. But more than that happens. At a certain point we begin to lose Bulstrode as the object of scorn. We even begin to sympathize with him, however obvious his crimes. Indeed, as he plots and calculates, tries everything his mind, well versed in tricks and bluff, can come up with, we almost wish him success. Raffles is a no-good, and not in any way explored psychologically, so good riddance to him is easy. But the way Bulstrode's mind is revealed to us contrasts with the level and range of analysis given every other character in the novel. The motives of others are brought to light in a leisurely fashion, and to a great extent, in order to build up a variety of individuals, each of them different in a number of respects. In the case of Bulstrode something else is done. His complexity of character, his anguish, his malevolence, all of it virtually explodes upon us, and before we know it we are strangely caught up—implicated is perhaps the word. The crucial turn in the narrative occurs in chapter 68: "For Bulstrode shrunk from a direct lie with an intensity disproportionate to the number of his more indirect misdeeds. But many of these misdeeds were like the subtle muscular movements which are not taken account of in the consciousness, though they bring about the end that we fix our mind on and desire. And it is only what we are vividly conscious of that we can vividly imagine to be seen by Omniscience."

We already know that Bulstrode is quite able to deceive people; yet the author now brings up this distinction of "a direct lie." Furthermore, words like *consciousness* and *conscious* appear. Even God becomes "Omniscience." The question of awareness gets linked to that of "a direct lie" or "more indirect misdeeds." Bulstrode may not only fool others; it is quite possible that he himself does not know exactly what his intentions are, what he is aiming at, trying to accomplish. We know for sure that this man is no vague, wandering, self-deluded failure. Nor is he a mental case. He seems all too effective and directed in manner. More than others in Middlemarch he seems to have a clear idea of what he is after. Yet, of all things, his mind's activity is called into question—almost as if he were alive today and some of our lawyers and psychiatrists, concerned about the issue of right-versus-wrong in the light of psychoanalytic determinism, were not quite sure how to regard the man. To some extent Raffles's behavior, steadily worse, makes us move closer to Bulstrode. Raffles is appeased, bought off, then reneges and makes new demands and threats. He also begins to deteriorate, break his part of the bargain, drink to excess and talk the same way. And soon he is very sick, quite possibly on his death bed. It is natural for us to feel that Bulstrode may deserve our contempt, but not the injury an alcoholic confidence man and ne'er-do-well wants to impose.

While all that is going on in *our* minds, George Eliot is moving closer and closer toward Bulstrode's private mental life. His "nervous energy" under the strain is mentioned. There is a marvelous scene in which one kind of liar confronts another. Bulstrode mobilizes his "cold, resolute bearing" and Raffles, so full of swagger, so convinced he has the upper hand, melts. Bulstrode's servants imagine Raffles "a poor relation," rather a nice moment for Bulstrode, given what he is afraid of. And by this time we are enough with Bulstrode to settle for that as a proper punishment: let Raffles properly embarrass him. That way the banker will come off his high horse and stop preaching all the time. He will have to attend his own before he finds fault with others.

But matters go from bad to worse. Raffles becomes more garrulous, hence dangerous. He also starts becoming a victim of his success. Ever greedy, he demands more from Bulstrode, then drinks away what he has secured. For "various motives" Bulstrode stiffens his defenses, squarely threatens to call Raffles's bluff, but is generous with him, noticing the man's decline and perhaps hoping against hope for more of it. None of that is especially revealing to us—only rendered forcefully and tersely. Even when the author comes up with one of her especially pointed paragraphs of a single sentence ("Who can know how much of his most inward life is made up of the thoughts he believes other men to have about him, until that fabric of opinion is threatened with ruin?"), we are still relatively detached from Bulstrode. We have simply been reminded once again that no one's life is all that private; that a society like Middlemarch's works its way into everyone's mind and heart, exacts tributes, prompts attitudes and desires, generates assumptions, imposes restrictions or inhibitions, expects and to a degree obtains a form of allegiance, a code of behavior—all of it, as the rhetorical question indicates, the more influential because submerged in life's everyday flow of feeling and action, rather than noticed and considered.

Relentlessly the author pushes on, however. She goes from those "other men" to Bulstrode. She has this particular person examine himself, wonder why Raffles has come with his threats as well as when he will leave and stay away. "Divine glory" comes to mind: can God have his purposes, unapparent to man? Bulstrode, the man of piety, had always thought God's purposes could be ascertained—proven visible, even, by a show of religious devotion. Now a more inscrutable and devious God is conjured up by the desperate man. And in such desperation he becomes a deeper, more reflective man. Rather as Adam and Eve must once have, he wonders to himself what God does see: everything? only so much? Anyway, might an apparent disaster be but the advance sign of some good news? Might the Lord visit and chastise those he has singled out for

eventual recognition of quite another kind? Is submission to a
tormentor like Raffles in truth obedience to God? Or ought one be
more self-protective, so that the good Lord sees quite clearly the
justice of one's cause and one's faith in oneself?

As Bulstrode asks himself such questions, directly or by implication, his mind moves back and forth from the things of this world
to an almost Biblical resignation before the felt presence of an
altogether different world. God's mysterious ways, and Satan's,
obsess him; and his mental activity does not disintegrate into
psychopathology or into cowering religious ingratiation, a last
ditch effort to stave off disaster through divine intervention. His
ruminations and moments of confrontation, not long and not overly
dramatic, are nevertheless worthy of Augustine's. A sinner, he is
also a sincere believer, but also a thoroughly imperfect one. A moral
hypocrite and a man capable of being mercilessly out for himself,
he can be conscientious, open to new ideas, genuinely self-critical
in his own stop-and-go journey toward repentance. He never loses
his scheming, vastly materialistic side. He can pray hard and long,
while all the time estimating what to do with his various properties.
Yet his prayers, his desperate effort to meet with God and understand his purposes, are an unquestionable part of him and, significantly, are not subjected to the author's mockery. Even the obvious
irony of his conflicting dispositions begins to wilt under the heat
of his scrupulous self-examination before God: we become, with
him, totally immersed in a supplicant's religious fervor and begin
to forget his other qualities. In his own way he asks why—not only
why Raffles has appeared thus to curse and quite possibly destroy
him, but why God tempts man with possibilities, moments of
triumph, situations just ambiguous enough to allow the worst to be
done in such a way that it seems not so bad, after all, and maybe,
all things considered, even rather virtuous.

Bulstrode is no secure, relaxed Anglican, at church on Sunday
but otherwise all taken up with his daily responsibilities. One can't
picture James Chettam in church, only standing outside on a sunny
day, quite delighted with what he has just heard and especially
glad to meet his friends and neighbors. Bulstrode gets feverish
about God and his will, and extremely curious, too. What is God
up to? How might that be found out? Bulstrode is a devout banker,
a man apprehensive not only about creditors but his own credit in
God's universe. But he does not simply call upon his nineteenth-

century capitalist mentality when he seeks after God's Grace and, eventually, his forgiveness. Though George Eliot herself abandoned evangelical Christianity for philosophical rationalism, she did not turn on those she once knew so well before she became so prominent a part of London's intellectual world. Devious people, even wicked people, she knew, can experience genuine remorse as they look beyond themselves and try to earn God's favor. The most confident and acceptable of people, high in everyone's esteem, never inclined to cheat or steal, often fastidious about involvements in the grosser, more vulgar things of life (others before them have been so involved, and handed down the results in amenities) are not necessarily driven by a hunger for God, even if they attend church regularly with a great deal of pleasure and enthusiasm.

Again one is moved to mention Augustine. Christian theologians like him, aware that Adam was a sinner, mindful of Christ's involvement with the scorned and the despised, and of Paul's self-lacerating descriptions of his earlier years, have never been embarrassed by the paradox of outcasts abruptly become believers. By the same token Kierkegaard makes plain the sin of indifference: the temptation to self-contentment and pride that virtuous burghers have as a fact of their existence.[11] And as Bulstrode struggles with himself, a number of such philosophical and theological issues become subtly absorbed into his moment of intense and prayerful introspection—a psychological crisis we would call it. He wonders how God can possibly permit him, a man of avowed faith, to be destroyed by an obvious heathen. He prays, whereas Raffles drinks and has nothing to do with any church. He prays with all his heart and soul, whereas others, his self-righteous creditors, whom he fears will soon enough be gossiping about him, go to church on Sundays, but that is that. But if he can be quite self-righteous himself, he can also feel himself to be in the very midst of a riddle that none of us can ever resolve. "He knew that he ought to say, 'Thy will be done'; and he said it often." On the other hand, he hoped against hope that "the will of God might be the death of that hated man."

This is no man throwing off a few petitions heavenward as part of a more general effort to protect his power and his capital resources. He has all the agility and shrewdness of an outsider who

---

[11]The longest analysis of that temptation—it haunted Kierkegaard and is mentioned directly or obliquely in almost every book of his—can be found in *Either/Or*.

has successfully penetrated a given society. He has all the force of
personality and cunning of a banker who knows how to be the
pitiless lender, and never a loser. Still, he sides with reformers and
has on occasion a gentle, giving nature that Dr. Lydgate comments
upon—and not only in connection with Raffles, toward whom, of
course, the banker had to be attentive: "Bulstrode seems the most
unsympathetic fellow I ever saw about some people, and yet he has
.taken no end of trouble, and spent a great deal of money, on
benevolent objects."

Raffles ultimately disintegrates and goes into what we would call
delerium tremens (perhaps even alcoholic encephalopathy) and
know how to treat, if not necessarily reverse. Doctors then knew
less to do. Often the patient was helped into coma with more
liquor; even substantial doses of opium were given. Bulstrode called
in Dr. Lydgate and the latter, ahead of his time and well read in
the latest medical advances, explains what ought to be done: no
brandy or anything else and extremely careful administration of
opium. The author has prepared the way for one of the great self-
confrontations in the history of the novel.

She is no Dostoevski; she goes about developing her characters
with more restraint, and they never will speak with the dramatic
intensity the Karamazovs possess as they reflect upon just about
everything that has to do with heaven and earth. But in her quiet
way she enables Bulstrode to look at himself and judge himself
with exceptional subtlety. More than that, as mentioned, the
reader is drawn into this self-indictment to an astonishing degree.
Before George Eliot is through with Bulstrode he has become
nothing less than an only slightly exaggerated version of everyone
else, Caleb Garth included. In so doing she denies us a scapegoat
and a romantic hero as well. What we are left with, of course, is
Middlemarch, with its many different sorts of people, some better
and some worse, but none without sins and very definite limitations
as human beings, even as none are without impressive if not redeem-
ing virtues. Interestingly enough, the one character in the novel
who has none of the latter, the one character who lends himself to
easy and unqualified categorization, is John Raffles. In a stroke
the author through him distinguishes herself from other authors
and makes her point rather clear. This outsider is not part of
Middlemarch's world, so his seeming lack of complexity, his outright
evil, itself left unexplored, is not to be taken for granted. Rather,

Raffles is outside not only the provincial life of Middlemarch but the province of *Middlemarch*. He is an outsider such as Bulstrode or Dr. Lydgate or Ladislaw is not. They have come into the community and tried in their various ways to become known. The more of themselves they reveal, the more complicated they become, the less clear-cut their involvements with others turn out to be. The author takes the trouble to delve into them, and as she does, we feel ourselves going up and down, in this direction or that direction. Is Dr. Lydgate strong or weak? Does he suffer from some fatal flaw, and if so, precisely what is its nature? Alternatively, is the well-intentioned doctor simply the victim (eventually, rather than at any particular moment) of a series of developments no one could have foreseen; a series not at all determined by anything in his personality? Ought we subscribe to the author's prelude, and her conclusion as well, and see Dorothea hopelessly entangled in the strictures and blind spots of a given time and place? Should we, on the other hand, give full vent to our occasional feeling that Dorothea needs a good shaking or, after our fashion, an extended course of psychotherapy—so that she stops thinking or saying or doing any number of things that only lead to trouble and her enfeeblement, for which we are then asked to grieve? In the case of Rosamond, are we to see her as a self-centered, shallow, but thoroughly resourceful woman who has a certain kind of emotional makeup, which Dr. Lydgate, to his own sorrow, caught glimpses of rather late in the game, or is she one of many examples of what a materialistic social system does to those who are part of it?

Those kinds of questions, to the author's great credit, never really get an answer. We are left unsatisfied, floundering even, and at a loss to figure out the author's intentions. And maybe she herself had to struggle with a conflict or two—and had the sense not to try to resolve within herself as a writer some contradictions that must have presented themselves to her as she wrote. The novelist in her may well have tried to portray particular individuals, but there is that need in all of us I have mentioned earlier on—one which philosophers, theologians, and moralists often show quite clearly: to tidy up life's hodgepodge, sort out the irritating jumble of ideas and passions and forces that go to make up a person's existence so that we can make a judgment, not only in the Calvinist fashion, but out of a less ambitious, more humdrum desire simply to feel we have got our bearings.

It is all the more ironic, therefore, that as Bulstrode becomes distinctly and with justice known as a kind of imposter—he has falsified his past, pretended and dissembled even to his wife—he concurrently begins to win us over, not as admirers, but fellow sufferers. The closer he looks at himself and the closer the author asks us to look at him, get to know him from within and at some length, the harder it gets to square what we know he has done with what we now know about his nature—as it is discovered by the man himself, in the midst of this terrible moment in his life. He has all along had a good marriage; his wife has been devoted to him, and he to her. But the depth of their feeling, the strength of the bond between them, was unknown to either until this event tested them separately and together. Might they have, anyway, realized what they meant to each other? Do we ever find out abstractly—that is, in analysis, done alone or with another's help—how we feel, or do our feelings emerge only in consequence of events, which not only bring out what is dormant but generate new possibilities for feeling? Again, such questions are never even asked until something has *happened*, brought us up short, made us stop and wonder about human nature: exactly how much real freedom do we ever have, given all that is around us and all that we have experienced?

Bulstrode was a rigid, highly controlled man. What he was free to do was exert his dominance over others. When we meet him in earlier sections of the novel he seems equally the strong one in his marriage. He has married well, and as a *nouveau arriviste* he is quickly able to take over what his wife has to offer as part of his own presentation, so to speak: the impression he strikes in others. He became a Middlemarcher of consequence, even if in the back of everyone's mind (rather than the front) there remained those twin fears that an outsider and a man of power and money can inspire. He now finds himself on the brink of exposure and humiliation; he will have to flee in ruin, though not poverty, and it is made quite clear that he isn't sure at all that his wife will want to (could bear to) leave Middlemarch, especially under such circumstances. ("To leave the place finally would, he knew, be extremely painful to his wife.") His usual characteristics never leave him. He offers Lydgate money, having refused to do so the day before. Lydgate is, of course, Raffles's physician. So we have every right to believe that Bulstrode is up to something. He is mobilizing his intelligence and his considerable resources in the service of his self-interest.

Hobbes would know his number. Locke has given him the leeway he has. Rousseau could only say, yes, this creature is what we have come to. In two sentences the author indicates how such a man springs to action: "Bulstrode's native imperiousness and strength of determination served him well. This delicate-looking man, himself nervously perturbed, found the needed stimulus in his strenuous circumstances, and through that difficult night and morning, while he had the air of an animated corpse returned to movement without warmth, holding the mastery by its chill impassibility, his mind was intensely at work thinking of what he had to guard against and what would win him security."

Yet immediately after that description a slight shift takes place. We move from the realm of those political and social philosophers to a world more congenial to theologians. Of all people, Augustine comes to mind as an intensely prayerful and yet still lustful man is evoked by an author uncannily able to suggest the mind's capacity to walk on various tightropes. Bulstrode wants to be good, wants God's forgiveness; still, he sins. He appeals to God for more than help; he acknowledges his responsibility to assist Raffles and submit himself to "the punishment divinely appointed for him rather than to wish for evil to another." All the while, though, "there pierced and spread with irresistible vividness the images of the events he desired." Abraham, prompted to sacrifice his own son, must have felt similarly torn apart. Bulstrode might not have struck Kierkegaard, had he lived to read *Middlemarch*, as a nineteenth-century equivalent of Abraham, but there is something of the high moral tension in this scene that would appeal to a philosopher who scorned the pretensions of the pious and appreciated the ironic and dramatic revelations that life is capable of offering.

Slowly the scene is revealed for all its significance. Bulstrode has it in his power to do away with Raffles. He need only go along with the prevailing medical knowledge, rather than heed Dr. Lydgate, who has entrusted him with instructions for the care of a supposed friend. The banker watches, hopes against hope the man will die— the sooner the better, a reflection of divine justice. He also is quite frightened that Raffles will not die, in which case he and Mrs. Bulstrode might as well leave Middlemarch right away and for good. However, Bulstrode's calculations are tempered by a moral and religious disposition that the author is not disposed to brush aside as mere show. It *is* show; she has made that clear, using Bulstrode as an example. But it is also something else. Bulstrode does not feel capable of putting an end to the life of his miserable tormentor. It is not a matter of an inhibition, a too strong conscience, a plaguing and impending sense of guilt or anxiety. "He was impenitent, but were not public criminals impenitent?" (So the man thinks as he contemplates a semicomatose Raffles.) Rather, the issue is an important religious one: who is one man to deny another the chance for final submission to God's will, with a consequent chance for his Grace? An unlikely question for a self-sufficient capitalist? A flimy question, not really taken seriously? A token rhetorical question thrown out by a hard-pressed gambler, a man whom Pascal could understand if not at all admire? Or did something like this come to mind: if God pays attention, hears his devoted and humble servant Mr. Bulstrode, in this most critical hour, worrying about another man's right to repent of his considerable sins—*if* he does, then who knows? He might be disposed to return a favor to the likes of a Bulstrode!

All those lines of thinking are not foreign to this cagey man. He was truly driven to think of sin, his as well as those others commit. He was also a man who knew that no rationalizations or petitions would be of avail to his own mind's vision, let alone God's unless "he scrupulously did what was prescribed." And yet, he would counter as his mind pursued its almost frenzied self-scrutiny, "human prescriptions were fallible things." And yet, once again, "intention was everything in the question of right and wrong." So it went. He tried to "keep his intention separate from his desire," a rather large if not heroic psychological task for anyone.

Saints like Paul and Augustine—and surely the pragmatic Theresa— have aimed to do no less, and acknowledged their failures. Hobbes never doubted that any of us fail all the time to do so. Locke was sure there was no real point trying. Pascal thought the effort was worthwhile, but success is elusive. Rousseau, in some of his moods at least, would agree, but say it needn't be that way: man might even in the future get back to what it was like in the distant past when intention and desire were fused and both were far removed from anything like Bulstrode's particular intentions or desires. Kierkegaard would smile at the whole enterprise, the legalistic vanity of making such distinctions and settling on them the degree of importance we do. Intellectual pride, he knew, makes for a good deal of theology, not to mention philosophy (and maybe these

days, psychology). As for Freud, he might smile impatiently for
other reasons. Desires make slaves of intentions, he was sure. Not
unlike Hobbes, he was immensely skeptical, though both men had
their escape clauses: given the right kind of government or the right
kind of Ego, the former strengthened by full-fledged and widely
accepted political authority, the latter by the power psychoanalytic
awareness brings, there is a better than slim hope that the worst in
man will be held at bay, and that is all anyone who is not fatuous
ought expect.

That delicate balance those two pessimists, Hobbes and Freud,
held up in their theoretical writings as our fated condition gets an
almost unnerving anthropomorphosis in Bulstrode. For a moment
in the novel he loses all other aspects of himself and becomes the
very essence of conflict, which George Eliot describes in this one
sentence paragraph: "Strange, piteous conflict in the soul of this
unhappy man, who had longed for years to be better than he was—
who had taken his selfish passions into discipline and clad them in
severe robes, so that he had walked with them as a devout squire,
till now that a terror had risen among them, and they could chant
no longer, but threw out their common cries for safety."

That conflict is steadily heightened by the page, and also made
as explicit as Freud could have wished; but made explicit in such
a way that the opposing psychological forces at work are acknowledged rather than banished by some formulation that makes what
is murky seem all to definite: *this* has to be, or usually is, the
outcome in such instances. It is the indefiniteness George Eliot
spoke about over five hundred pages before that persists in the
tormented man, in certain respects smarter than anyone else in the
novel, yet doomed as even Casaubon was not: "imperious will
stirred murderous impulses towards this brute life, over which will,
by itself, had no power." The author is attempting to convey
Bulstrode's state of mind as he hovers over this suddenly vulnerable antagonist. But more, she is preparing to show us how even
under the most compelling and extraordinary of *psychological*
circumstances, we are all agents of one another, members of one or
another Middlemarch, driven not only by drives and the associations they prompt but tied to people who are at our side out of
relatively impersonal (social, economic, cultural, religious, or
philosophical) imperatives.

Who is Mrs. Abel, to whom we are directed after such a striking summary of a man's torment? Not Bulstrode's wife, not a relative, and not anyone he covets or hates; not someone toward whom he bears any feeling at all. She works for him. A servant, an everyone and a nobody, she becomes of a sudden the most intimate person in the banker's life. Through her a passion of the most urgent and gripping kind will, finally, work its way into an ambiguous (more indefiniteness!) form of expression. Through her a man's conscience will be somewhat placated; his mind put somewhat at ease. But with or without her presence, a soul continues in its evasive, treacherous, earnest, candid effort to know its Creator's intentions and desires. The manner in which this most intimate and casual of collaborative undertakings gets going gives us a clue to what the author is about as she comes toward the end of her story. Bulstrode first talks to himself: he is tired, he lacks the energy to deal with this physically and psychologically demanding watch he has found himself taken up with. When Raffles wakes up he begins "to administer the opium according to Lydgate's directions." Half an hour later he pronounces himself unable to go on. Mrs. Abel must take over. He calls her, tells her what the doctor has told him, says he is leaving the room for the night but is available if anything serious develops. Mrs. Abel comments on how spent he seems. He is indeed that, but his mind is alive with worry and fear. Ought he ask the doctor to come again? Will the delirious man say something incriminating?

Bulstrode does not go to bed. He is torn by conflict. He hopes for the slow demise of Raffles—as a sign that providence has taken notice of an injustice and wants it corrected. He fears the worst: the scoundrel will recover and matters will go from bad to worse. As he sits by the firelight his mind suddenly jolts him. He rises to light a bed candle. He realizes he must go see Mrs. Abel at once. Why? He hadn't told her when to stop giving Raffles opium. He stands there in the room; he is unable to go, unable to sit down or go to bed. He takes himself upstairs, not sure in his own mind whether he will retire to his room or end up talking with Mrs. Abel and looking at his mortal enemy. A pause: the sound of a man not yet asleep and obviously in pain. He turns to his room: let the man get the opium his moans and groans entitle him to.

Minutes later Mrs. Abel arrives; she is certain the man is going all the way downhill and deserves some brandy. Bulstrode remembers

Lydgate's instructions: no spirits, only a limited amount of opium. He says nothing, is motionless. Mrs. Abel persists, even becomes annoyed. How can he deprive a fast dying man of this final solace, a touch of brandy? Well, how can he? Is he supposed to follow the letter of one doctor's (admittedly unorthodox) advice at this moment? Is he to try heroic measures, call doctors from all over? He is being importuned by Mrs. Abel, held back by his conscience, driven to comply with her request by his desire to see Raffles vanish from the earth. He says nothing, for a while; finally, he hands her the key to the wine cooler, tells her there is plenty of brandy there. Then, to bed; and early in the morning he is in fervent prayer. What kind of prayer? Hypocritical petitions to a God who is, in reality, but an excuse for his own selfish cravings? Superstitious offerings to his own guilty conscience, called divine providence—all in the hope that what is convenient and best for him will be cloaked with the imprimatur of heaven itself and made apparent? Nervous words thrown out into the vast space of the universe on the outside chance that there might be a good return? (After all, who knows—and a banker is not one to pass up any opportunity.)

The author takes Bulstrode's morning worship seriously—and again, treats him with respect. She could have plunged into a forceful critique of this suddenly hesitant and fugitive banker in his room asleep, and later with hands outstretched to the sky, while his agent, maybe his agent provocateur, sits down the hall with an open bottle of brandy, nourishing Raffles to death. One version of the Victorian death scene! Instead she dares—and at such a juncture, no less—to link up Bulstrode's mental state with everyone else's, even connecting the reflections of any century's proudly aware and self-critical agnostics or atheists with this man's supplications: "Does any one suppose that private prayer is necessarily candid—necessarily goes to the roots of action? Private prayer is inaudible speech, and speech is representative: who can represent himself just as he is, even in his own reflections? Bulstrode had not yet unravelled in his thought the confused promptings of the last four-and-twenty hours."

With that question and the renewed emphasis on the genuine struggle going on in the banker, we are ourselves thrown hopelessly into confusion, prompted by lingering suspicions, growing if un-expected sympathies, and, by now, a realization of what the author may once more be up to: no one will escape her requirement of indefiniteness. Bulstrode seems a solid character, easily grasped and as representative as can be; later on a book with the title *The Protestant Ethic and the Spirit of Capitalism* would do sociological justice to him and his kind.George Eliot had her antennae out for the type, and knew which ingredients to mix—religious piety and business acumen, both well larded with certain characteristics necessary to make things believable: sincerity, dedication, a not unattractive bluntness that enbales people to know immediately and exactly where they stand. Nevertheless, this man, carefully built up in our mind, as are all the Middlemarchers we meet, on closer inspection becomes even more complicated than he seemed, and by the end of our acquaintance with him we are at a loss to know what we think. In case we have any lingering doubts, the author says this as we contemplate the situation in Bulstrode's house: "And who could say that the death of Raffles had been hastened? Who knew what would have saved him?"

One can argue that the entire sequence has been melodramatically staged and is a flaw in the novel. Even so, the author has obviously sought for an occasion that would allow her to plumb the nature of human consciousness. Like Freud, she wanted to know how much we know about ourselves, how much we deliberately hide, how much we seem never to comprehend or deviously happen to ignore: bothersome eruptions, thoughts that won't quite go away but (it is felt) certainly should. Even more of a challenge, she was not content to do her psychological examination in a vacuum; the same vacuum, I fear, many psychiatrists build for themselves as they relentlessly track down associations, and make formulations about their meaning as if the owners of such associations have lives all their own—apart, that is, from their particular Middlemarch.

With Raffles dead, Bulstrode's psychological thinking, made so hard for us to figure out and label as characteristic of a type of person, merges with the thinking of Middlemarch's people, a real masterstroke of the author's. Gossip mounts, rumors get repeated, various people have their say. Whatever the sources and outcome of a mind's labor, there are others to consider. The intense isolation of the banker's home, with the attendant "confused promptings" we have had laid before us, gives way to a public meeting—of all things, convened "on a sanitary question which had risen into pressing importance by the occurrence of a cholera case in the town." Soon the inner tension of Bulstrode's mind gets remarkable reflection in the outer tension of a Middlemarch crowd. Bulstrode ultimately is humiliated; Raffles has, after all, made known his secrets. But before that happens a man will fight not only to save himself but bind himself close and hard to his accusers, aided by the author's interest in doing the very same thing. "Who shall be my accuser?" Bulstrode asks, and no one will ever be able to answer him. He is attacked, convincingly so. But he made his point: hypocrisy is rampant, thievery not only limited to those called thieves. We are back to Christ's admonition: "He that is without sin among you, let him first cast a stone at her."

At that meeting Dr. Lydgate also becomes implicated, in his own mind as well as in the mind of others. He, too, might be seen as a bribed one, a debt-ridden man who for a crucial second ignored a chain of events: his presence as Bulstrode's physician, after having been denied a loan by the banker; his recommendations as a doctor; and, next, a mysterious reversal, in which a thousand pounds now becomes quite available to him. Had Bulstrode intended to bribe him, reward him, make him feel obligated, implicate him in a plot—or merely show through an act of generosity his good intentions, his hope that things would work out, and Raffles live? Had he, Dr. Lydgate, overlooked the obvious? Had he failed to notice what was, in any case, not very clear? Or had he fooled himself, having been at the same time fooled by his new benefactor?

It is simply impossible to know what really went on either in Bulstrode's mind or Dr. Lydgate's when they went through their experience before and at a slight distance from John Raffles. Bulstrode was desperate. He wanted to atone for past sins. He no doubt hoped against hope that this doctor would help him—in a direction he only intermittently dared acknowledge. But he had lost any real hope of surviving the threats coming at him as a result of Raffles's loose tongue, so was preparing to defend himself with his money, to find what support he could get, from anyone available. He was quite simply clutching at any straw he could find. He was also no stranger to charity, and at this moment would certainly not harden, but rather soften. He was prayerful, mindful of Christ's redemptive spirit: sinners could be saved, provided they came upon faith—and why not go the next step, *show* one's conversion, give so one shall receive?

As for Dr. Lydgate, he was being a good doctor. True, the matter of a loan came up when he was there, attending a patient— but so what? He was also a worried, overburdened man, about to collapse of debts and his wife's determination that she would not be denied her rights as a proper lady who had married with certain expectations very much in the forefront of her mind. Under such circumstances he might have missed hints, overlooked important clues, persuaded himself to ignore what was all too obvious to Bulstrode. Or did he miss Bulstrode's hints? Did Bulstrode even give any? What *were* the banker's thoughts, the doctor's? How does one describe their motives? Which motives? Do motives assert themselves relentlessly, or appear, then disappear, or often enough cancel one another out? And to make matters more confusing, do one person's motives depend for their relative degree of strength and possibility of expression upon the presence of another's motives?

To all those questions George Eliot has no answers; only the richly suggestive fabric of her novel for us to gaze at and, more often than not, feel in awe of, rather than be made the recipients of solutions. Her much discussed "wisdom" is not abstract, but tied to the particulars of individuals to whom she has virtually given the breath of life, so strikingly themselves are they![12] She has com- pelled us to regard their moral ambiguities and complexities of character and temperament with increasing relaxation. They emerge out of the context of their lives, but they never become mere symbols for that context. One moment they are distinct types, or themselves and no one else, a bit later on they blur into the nearest available crowd. So far as the world and what it offers is con- cerned, that so-called environment (or society, or culture, or historical era) that impinges upon all of us, she has given us Middlemarch, as hard to fasten down as it is easy to locate in space and time. Middlemarch is provincial all right, but no more so than any community; in it are the refined and the coarse, the thoughtful and the narrow-minded, the sophisticated and the ignorant, the urbane and the countrified, or rude, the mostly honorable and the—well, less than honorable. If there was in the nineteenth century any community of grown-up people that didn't possess

---

[12]See Isobel Armstrong's *"Middlemarch:* A Note on George Eliot's 'Wisdom,'"* in *Critical Essays on George Eliot.*

such a mixture of people, such a mixture of those qualities and others in each of its members, then George Eliot was no doubt unaware of the place when she wrote *Middlemarch.*

As for us today, will the "counterculture" or "transcendance" or a place "where the wasteland ends" permit us at last to glimpse a community George Eliot never really expected any of us to find, this side of heaven at least? No doubt if she were alive today she would keep her customary reserve and refuse us an absolutely certain reply. She has such a habit of turning coins over, moving from one chair to another, looking out of every window she can find. She has such a habit of arguing for, then against—even when the "against" is, in turn, directed at a "for" previously held by her. She has such a habit of turning round on us, taking away what she has seemingly given for keeps, only to come forth with yet another gift, and a valuable one at that. She won't let up with her paradoxes and ambiguities, her complexities and contradictions; most of all there are ironies, so elusive and yet firmly instructive, so hard to see coming, but in retrospect inevitable or seemingly foreordained. At the very end she lets us know what it is all about, and the finale is not so different from the prelude: "Every limit is a beginning as well as an ending. Who can quit young lives after being long in company with them, and not desire to know what befell them in their after-years? For the fragment of a life, however typical, is not the sample of an even web: promises may not be kept, and an ardent outset may be followed by declension; latent powers may find their long-waited opportunity; a past error may urge a grand retrieval."

It is not exactly a definitive statement, nor one congenial to an age like ours, when determinants are deemed so precious, when the slightest tinge of mystery is felt to represent a problem to be solved, when any leeway we have, any openness to each day's flow of events and circumstances is seen as a phantom, a bit of pretense on the part of the deceived, a posture meant to buttress an illusion. *Middlemarch* gives us nothing authoritative or definitive. Indefiniteness of character becomes indefiniteness of wisdom. The word is "may," not "will." Those who have Dorothea's "soul hunger" may not be offended, but those who hunger to put the life of the mind squarely in its place may well cringe or walk away in search of more "relevant" approaches. As for a word like *maturity*—and *Middlemarch* is concerned with grown-up, serious, intelligent people—no novelist like George Eliot is going to bandy that one around, not in its present-day meaning. "Maturity" has become part of our preaching vocabulary; it is demanded of people and all too rigidly defined, rather than regarded as a many-splendored thing: present as a series of values even in those lacking a good deal of it, absent suddenly among those who have a right to take it for granted much of the time, but for all of us a state of being, a condition that has to do with age, the assumption of certain responsibilities, the experience of achievements or disappointments—and a coming closer to the end.

So it is left for one more irony to vex us, and maybe give us the solace that "indefiniteness" (the haziness of George Eliot's "every limit") is meant to provide: a century that has hovered over children and talked itself hoarse about its young people doesn't quite know what to do with the longest stretch of life that follows those two "periods." Psychological reflection and analysis of various kinds meant to give us leverage on ourselves as the grown-up human beings who do the reflecting, undertake the analysis, leave us unaccountably diminished: we are called, in our thirties or forties or fifties, mere afterthoughts to what has made us as we are. We are regarded as fixed once and for all by the past of childhood and its spillover of sorts, youth. A quest by full-grown men and women perhaps deserves better of itself than such renunciation or potentially vindictive self-arraignment. We are destined to be more than pietistic alternatives like "mature" or "immature" allow. We are also destined to be more than lucky survivors or sad victims of an ever-receding infantile conflict or complex. We are destined to stumble into "indefiniteness," and not always to bad or good effect. If that is no completely pleasing design, it provides for possibilities and fortuitous moments as well as hazards and casualties. "Every limit is a beginning as well as an ending," that important passage in the finale of *Middlemarch* starts out saying. The ultimate limit, of course, is our last breath; and speaking of that, one is left to wonder whether George Eliot, evangelical Christian become tentatively optimistic rationalist and naturalist, would claim for that particular limit the same alternatives presented us by all the other limits we come across in the course of our lives.

Index

Index

Specific references to characters are located under the work in which they appear.

Some New Directions Paperbooks

Walter Abish, *Alphabetical Africa*. NDP375.
In the Future Perfect. NDP440.
Minds Meet. NDP387.
Ilangô Adigal, *Shilappadikaram*. NDP162.
Alain, *The Gods*. NDP382.
David Antin. *Talking at the Boundaries*. NDP388.
G. Apollinaire, *Selected Writings*.† NDP310.
Djuna Barnes, *Nightwood*. NDP98.
Charles Baudelaire, *Flowers of Evil*.† NDP71,
Paris Spleen. NDP294.
Martin Bax. *The Hospital Ship*. NDP402.
Gottfried Benn, *Primal Vision*.† NDP322.
Wolfgang Borchert, *The Man Outside*. NDP319.
Jorge Luis Borges, *Labyrinths*. NDP186.
Jean-François Bory, *Once Again*. NDP256.
E. Brock, *The Blocked Heart*. NDP399.
Here. Now. Always. NDP429.
Invisibility Is The Art of Survival. NDP342.
The Portraits & The Poses. NDP360.
Buddha, *The Dhammapada*. NDP188.
Frederick Busch, *Domestic Particulars*. NDP413.
Manual Labor. NDP376.
Ernesto Cardenal, *Apocalypse & Other Poems*.
NDP441. *In Cuba*. NDP377.
Hayden Carruth, *For You*. NDP298.
From Snow and Rock, from Chaos. NDP349.
Louis-Ferdinand Céline,
Death on the Installment Plan. NDP330,
Guignol's Band. NDP278.
Journey to the End of the Night. NDP84.
Jean Cocteau, *The Holy Terrors*. NDP212.
The Infernal Machine. NDP235.
M. Cohen, *Monday Rhetoric*. NDP352.
Robert Coles. *Irony in the Mind's Life*, NDP459.
Cid Corman, *Livingdying*. NDP289.
Sun Rock Man. NDP318.
Gregory Corso, *Elegiac Feelings American*.
NDP299.
Happy Birthday of Death. NDP86.
Long Live Man. NDP127.
Robert Creeley, *Hello*. NDP451.
Edward Dahlberg, *Reader*. NDP246.
Because I Was Flesh. NDP227.
Osamu Dazai, *The Setting Sun*, NDP258.
No Longer Human. NDP357.
Coleman Dowell, *Mrs. October . . .* NDP368.
Too Much Flesh and Jabez. NDP447.
Robert Duncan, *Bending the Bow*. NDP255.
The Opening of the Field. NDP356.
Roots and Branches. NDP275.
Richard Eberhart, *Selected Poems*. NDP198.
E. F. Edinger. *Melville's Moby-Dick*. NDP460.
Russell Edson. *The Falling Sickness*. NDP389.
The Very Thing That Happens. NDP137.
Wm. Empson, *7 Types of Ambiguity*. NDP204
Some Versions of Pastoral. NDP92.
Wm. Everson, *Man-Fate*. NDP369.
The Residual Years. NDP263.
Lawrence Ferlinghetti, *Her*. NDP88.
Back Roads to Far Places. NDP312.
A Coney Island of the Mind. NDP74.
The Mexican Night. NDP300.
Open Eye, Open Heart, NDP361.
Routines. NDP187.
The Secret Meaning of Things. NDP268.
Starting from San Francisco. NDP220.
Tyrannus Nix?. NDP288.
Who Are We Now? NDP425.
F. Scott Fitzgerald, *The Crack up*. NDP54.
Robert Fitzgerald, *Spring Shade*. NDP311.
Gustave Flaubert,
The Dictionary of Accepted Ideas. NDP230.
Gandhi, *Gandhi on Non-Violence*. NDP197.
Goethe, *Faust*, Part I. NDP70.
Albert J. Guerard, *Thomas Hardy*. NDP185.
John Hawkes, *The Beetle Leg*. NDP239.
The Blood Oranges. NDP338.
The Cannibal. NDP123.
Death Sleep & The Traveler. NDP393.
The Innocent Party. NDP238.
John Hawkes Symposium. NDP446.

The Lime Twig. NDP95.
Lunar Landscapes. NDP274.
The Owl. NDP443.
Second Skin. NDP146.
Travesty. NDP430.
A. Hayes, *A Wreath of Christmas Poems*.
NDP347.
H.D., *Helen in Egypt*. NDP380
Hermetic Definition NDP343.
Trilogy. NDP362.
Robert E. Helbling, *Heinrich von Kleist*, NDP390.
Hermann Hesse, *Siddhartha*. NDP65.
C. Isherwood, *The Berlin Stories*. NDP134.
Lions and Shadows, NDP435.
Philippe Jaccottet, *Seedtime*. NDP428.
Alfred Jarry, *The Supermale*. NDP426.
Ubu Roi, NDP105.
Robinson Jeffers, *Cawdor and Meda*. NDP293.
James Joyce, *Stephen Hero*. NDP133.
James Joyce/Finnegans Wake. NDP331.
Franz Kafka, *Amerika*. NDP117.
Bob Kaufman,
Solitudes Crowded with Loneliness. NDP199.
Hugh Kenner, *Wyndham Lewis*. NDP167.
Kenyon Critics, *Gerard Manley Hopkins*.
NDP355.
P. Lai, *Great Sanskrit Plays*. NDP142.
Tommaso Landolfi,
Gogol's Wife and Other Stories. NDP155.
Lautréamont, *Maldoror*. NDP207.
Irving Layton, *Selected Poems*. NDP431.
Denise Levertov, *Footprints*. NDP344.
The Freeing of the Dust. NDP401.
The Jacob's Ladder. NDP112.
Life in the Forest. NDP461.
O Taste and See. NDP149.
The Poet in the World. NDP363.
Relearning the Alphabet. NDP290.
The Sorrow Dance. NDP222.
To Stay Alive. NDP325.
With Eyes at the Back of Our Heads.
NDP229.
Harry Levin, *James Joyce*. NDP87.
Enrique Lihn, *The Dark Room*.† NDP452.
García Lorca, *Five Plays*. NDP232.
Selected Poems.† NDP114.
Three Tragedies. NDP52.
Michael McClure, *Gorf*. NDP416.
Antechamber. NDP455.
Jaguar Skies. NDP400.
September Blackberries. NDP370.
Carson McCullers, *The Member of the
Wedding*. (Playscript) NDP153.
Thomas Merton, *Asian Journal*. NDP394.
Gandhi on Non-Violence. NDP197.
The Geography of Lograire. NDP283.
My Argument with the Gestapo. NDP403.
New Seeds of Contemplation. NDP337.
Raids on the Unspeakable. NDP213.
Selected Poems. NDP85.
The Way of Chuang Tzu. NDP276.
The Wisdom of the Desert. NDP295.
Zen and the Birds of Appetite. NDP261.
Henry Miller, *The Air-Conditioned Nightmare*.
NDP302.
Big Sur & The Oranges. NDP161.
The Books in My Life. NDP280.
The Colossus of Maroussi. NDP75.
The Cosmological Eye. NDP109.
Henry Miller on Writing. NDP151.
The Henry Miller Reader. NDP269.
The Smile at the Foot of the Ladder. NDP386.
Stand Still Like the Hummingbird. NDP236.
The Time of the Assassins. NDP115.
The Wisdom of the Heart. NDP94.
Y. Mishima, *Confessions of a Mask*. NDP253.
Death in Midsummer. NDP215.
Eugenio Montale, *New Poems*. NDP410.
Selected Poems.† NDP193.
Vladimir Nabokov, *Nikolai Gogol*. NDP78.
Laughter in the Dark. NDP470.
The Real Life of Sebastian Knight. NDP432.
P. Neruda, *The Captain's Verses*.† NDP345.
Residence on Earth.† NDP340.

New Directions in Prose & Poetry (Anthology).
    Available from #17 forward. #37, Fall 1978.
Robert Nichols, *Arrival*. NDP437.
    Garh City. NDP450.
Charles Olson, *Selected Writings*. NDP231.
Toby Olson, *The Life of Jesus*. NDP417.
George Oppen, *Collected Poems*. NDP418.
Wilfred Owen, *Collected Poems*. NDP210.
Nicanor Parra, *Emergency Poems*.† NDP333.
    Poems and Antipoems.† NDP242.
Boris Pasternak, *Safe Conduct*. NDP77.
Kenneth Patchen, *Aflame and Afun of*
    Walking Faces. NDP292.
    Because It Is. NDP83.
    But Even So. NDP265.
    Collected Poems. NDP284.
    Doubleheader. NDP211.
    Hallelujah Anyway. NDP219.
    In Quest of Candlelighters. NDP334.
    The Journal of Albion Moonlight. NDP99.
    Memoirs of a Shy Pornographer. NDP205.
    Selected Poems. NDP160.
    Sleepers Awake. NDP286.
    Wonderings. NDP320.
Octavio Paz, *Configurations*.† NDP303.
    Eagle or Sun? NDP422.
    Early Poems.† NDP354.
Plays for a New Theater. (Anth.) NDP216.
J. A. Porter, *Eelgrass*. NDP438.
Ezra Pound, *ABC of Reading*. NDP89.
    Classic Noh Theatre of Japan. NDP79.
    Confucius. NDP285.
    Confucius to Cummings. (Anth.) NDP126.
    Gaudier Brzeska. NDP372.
    Guide to Kulchur. NDP257.
    Literary Essays. NDP250.
    Love Poems of Ancient Egypt. NDP178.
    Pavannes and Divagations. NDP397.
    Pound/Joyce. NDP296.
    Selected Cantos. NDP304.
    Selected Letters 1907-1941. NDP317.
    Selected Poems. NDP66.
    Selected Prose 1909-1965. NDP396.
    The Spirit of Romance. NDP266.
    Translations.† (Enlarged Edition) NDP145.
James Purdy, *Children Is All*. NDP327.
Raymond Queneau, *The Bark Tree*. NDP314.
    The Flight of Icarus. NDP358.
    The Sunday of Life. NDP433.
Mary de Rachewiltz, *Ezra Pound:*
    Father and Teacher. NDP405.
M. Randall, *Part of the Solution*. NDP350.
John Crove Ransom, *Beating the Bushes*.
    NDP324.
Raja Rao, *Kanthapura*. NDP224.
Herbert Read, *The Green Child*. NDP208.
P. Reverdy, *Selected Poems*.† NDP346.
Kenneth Rexroth, *Assays*. NDP113.
    Beyond the Mountains. NDP384.
    Bird in the Bush. NDP80.
    Collected Longer Poems. NDP309.
    Collected Shorter Poems. NDP243.
    New Poems. NDP383.
    100 More Poems from the Chinese. NDP308.
    100 More Poems from the Japanese. NDP420.
    100 Poems from the Chinese. NDP192.
    100 Poems from the Japanese.† NDP147.
Rainer Maria Rilke, *Poems from*
    The Book of Hours. NDP408.
    Possibility of Being. NDP436.
    Where Silence Reigns. (Prose). NDP464.
Arthur Rimbaud, *Illuminations*.† NDP56.
    Season in Hell & Drunken Boat.† NDP97.
Edouard Roditi, *Delights of Turkey*. NDP445.
Selden Rodman, *Tongues of Fallen Angels*.
    NDP373.
Jerome Rothenberg, *Poems for the Game*
    of Silence. NRP406.
    Poland/1931. NDP379.
    Seneca Journal. NDP448.
Saikaku Ihara, *The Life of an Amorous*
    Woman. NDP270.

Saigyo. *Mirror for the Moon*.† NDP465.
St. John of the Cross, *Poems*.† NDP341.
Jean-Paul Sartre, *Baudelaire*. NDP233.
    Nausea. NDP82.
    The Wall (Intimacy). NDP272.
Delmore Schwartz, *Selected Poems*. NDP241.
    In Dreams Begin Responsibilities. NDP454.
Kazuko Shiraishi, *Seasons of Sacred Lust*.
    NDP453.
Stevie Smith, *Selected Poems*, NDP159.
Gary Snyder, *The Back Country*. NDP249.
    Earth House Hold. NDP267.
    Myths and Texts. NDP457.
    Regarding Wave. NDP306.
    Turtle Island. NDP381.
Gilbert Sorrentino, *Splendide-Hôtel*. NDP364.
Enid Starkie, *Rimbaud*. NDP254.
Stendhal, *Lucien Leuwen*.
    Book II: *The Telegraph*. NDP108.
Jules Supervielle, *Selected Writings*.† NDP209.
W. Sutton, *American Free Verse*. NDP351.
Nathaniel Tarn, *Lyrics...Bride of God*. NDP391.
Dylan Thomas, *Adventures in the Skin Trade*.
    NDP183.
    A Child's Christmas in Wales. NDP181.
    Collected Poems 1934-1952. NDP316.
    The Doctor and the Devils. NDP297.
    Portrait of the Artist as a Young Dog.
    NDP51.
    Quite Early One Morning. NDP90.
    Under Milk Wood. NDP73.
Martin Turnell, *Art of French Fiction*. NDP251.
    Baudelaire. NDP336.
Paul Valéry, *Selected Writings*.† NDP184.
P. Van Ostaijen, *Feasts of Fear & Agony*.
    NDP411.
Elio Vittorini, *A Vittorini Omnibus*. NDP366.
    Women of Messina. NDP365.
Vernon Watkins, *Selected Poems*. NDP221.
Nathanael West, *Miss Lonelyhearts &*
    Day of the Locust. NDP125.
J. Williams, *An Ear in Bartram's Tree*. NDP335.
Tennessee Williams, *Camino Real*, NDP301.
    Cat on a Hot Tin Roof. NDP398.
    Dragon Country. NDP287.
    Eight Mortal Ladies Possessed, NDP374.
    The Glass Menagerie. NDP218.
    Hard Candy. NDP225.
    In the Winter of Cities. NDP154.
    One Arm & Other Stories. NDP237.
    Out Cry. NDP367.
    The Roman Spring of Mrs. Stone. NDP271.
    Small Craft Warnings. NDP348.
    Sweet Bird of Youth. NDP409.
    Where I Live, NDP468.
    27 Wagons Full of Cotton. NDP217.
William Carlos Williams.
    The Autobiography. NDP223.
    The Build-up. NDP259.
    Embodiment of Knowledge. NDP434.
    The Farmers' Daughters. NDP106.
    Imaginations. NDP329.
    In the American Grain. NDP53.
    In the Money. NDP240.
    I Wanted to Write a Poem. NDP469.
    Many Loves. NDP191.
    Paterson. Complete. NDP152.
    Pictures from Brueghel. NDP118.
    The Selected Essays. NDP273.
    Selected Poems. NDP131.
    A Voyage to Pagany. NDP307.
    White Mule. NDP226.
    W. C. Williams Reader. NDP282.
Yvor Winters, *E. A. Robinson*. NDP326.
Wisdom Books: *Ancient Egyptians*, NDP467;
    Wisdom of the Desert, NDP295; *Early*
    Buddhists, NDP444; *English Mystics*, NDP466;
    Forest (Hindu), NDP414; *Jewish Mystics*,
    NDP423; *Spanish Mystics*, NDP442; *Sufi*,
    NDP424; *Zen Masters*, NDP415.

Complete descriptive catalog available free on request from
New Directions, 333 Sixth Avenue, New York 10014.   † Bilingual